MULTINATIONAL STRATEGIC PLANNING

MULTINATIONAL STRATEGIC PLANNING

Derek F. Channon with Michael Jalland

Manchester Business School

A Division of American Management Associations

Published in the United States by
AMACOM,
a division of American Management Associations,
135 West 50th Street, New York, N.Y. 10020.

ISBN 0 8144 5575 1

Library of Congress Catalog Card Number 79–51293
Printed in Great Britain

Contents

List of Tables

List of Figures

Preface

The basic purpose of this book is to describe the process and practice of strategic planning in the multinational enterprise. We have not started at the first principles of strategic planning systems but rather we assume that these are well understood by the majority of our readers. Rather we have concentrated on dealing with various areas of strategic planning as they have developed, with particular reference to international operations. Thus, we have included chapters on international treasury management, tax planning, political risk management and cross-border investments. In addition we have endeavoured to show how the process of planning in the MNC varies according to a number of important characteristics which can be identified.

Finally, the external environment in which the MNC must operate during the next quarter-century is likely to be considerably more hostile than that experienced from 1950 to the early 1970s. Already it has been seen how the considerable impact of discontinuous changes such as the oil crisis can make obsolete corporate plans based upon a steady state or a slowly changing environment. As a result planning systems, too, are responding to a world with much greater uncertainty and we have endeavoured to capture the type of changes that are taking place.

The main basis for preparing the book has been a research programme at the Manchester Business School conducted over the past few years under the sponsorship of the Centre for Business Research and the Social Science Research Council, and led by R. M. Jalland and myself. We would like to express our thanks to these sponsoring bodies for their support and encouragement. This research has led to the production of a number of MBA dissertations which form the source and inspiration for much of the content of the book, and I would like to thank the research assistants involved for their efforts.

Firstly, I would thank John Lovering and Warwick Jones who undertook the initial studies into multinational strategic planning systems and linked them to the strategy and structure of the firm. Although not cited directly, many of the examples used in Chapter 3 and elsewhere were drawn from their research notes. Next, after these initial research studies which surveyed current planning practice in some 40–50 British, American and European MNCs subsequent work focused upon a series of specific problem areas that were highlighted as a result of the initial research.

Secondly, therefore, I would like to thank Jeremy Kimber who conducted the first such specialised study into financial and tax planning in MNCs. This work has provided major contributions to Chapters 5 and 6. In these specialised studies our sample sizes were smaller than in the initial phase and were deliberately skewed to include only firms who were known or hypothesised to be in the forefront of the area of study. Thus Kimber's sample included only companies which were known to operate relatively well-developed financial and tax planning systems, although the sample was also balanced to include a deliberate mix of organisation structures and industrial strategies.

Similar studies were conducted by John Grewe and Jeremy Smith in the areas of political risk and external affairs, and I would thank them for contributing substantially to Chapters 9 and 11. Again skewed samples were chosen: for example, the planning of political risk was assessed in firms subjected to high levels of political risk with one relatively low-risk industry being used as a control. In the case of external affairs, companies with an advanced management position were identified from published reports and from external sources such as the church and other such agencies.

Tim Green's study of capital investment decision-making built upon Kimber's earlier sample and was designed to be complementary. This study was helpful in preparing Chapters 5 and 7. Jeremy Kimber also conducted a second study which focused upon how a number of major MNCs planned to handle a particular political risk, namely the attempted imposition of national planning agreements by a British Labour Government. The detailed results of this latter study are not reported here in view of their sensitivity. However, in all these more specialised studies we have endeavoured not only to focus upon the specific but also to build up our general knowledge of the planning systems and processes prevailing in the companies researched. As a result, in some cases we have talked with the same companies in both the initial general survey, and later during specific studies. This has helped to provide a cross-check on the research findings since each of the specialised studies was only expected to collect certain general data concerning the planning process in the firms studied. Each of the special studies involved in the second phase of research had a sample of between 15 and 20 companies while overall, during the research to date, general data has been collected on over 100 major MNCs from Europe, the UK and the USA, and to a much smaller extent Japan.

The task of the researchers was only made possible by the extremely generous help we have received from the companies researched and the many senior executives interviewed. We would like to express our thanks for this help and hope that the book in some small way helps to repay their kindness. Structured interviews were the standard research tool used throughout the research, although each company was extensively desk-researched before this stage. We were extremely pleased with the frankness with which details of many relatively delicate subjects were provided and in writing the book we have kept very strictly to our research code of confidentiality for individual companies. As a result, while a number of case examples from the research are used in the text they are not identifiable. Many named examples are used in the book, however, basically from published sources and a substantial number of these firms were included in one or more phases of the Manchester research.

My colleague and co-researcher during the research programme has been Mike Jalland, who not only played a major role in the work itself but has contributed significantly to the production of this book. Apart from his most useful and constructive criticism and inspiration Mike has written Chapter 11 and parts of Chapters 3, 7 and 10. I am deeply grateful for this contribution.

Finally, I would thank Mrs Sue Chapman who has laboured through another series of drafts; my publishers for their encouragement and patience; and my long-suffering wife and family who have endured the production of the book with patience and understanding. Despite all the help and guidance I have received and for which I am indebted any remaining errors or mistakes in the text are entirely mine.

Manchester DEREK F. CHANNON
September 1977

Acknowledgements

The authors and publisher wish to thank the following who have kindly given permission for the use of copyright material:
The Academy of Management *Journal* and Dr Keith Davis for a table adapted from 'The Case For and Against Business Assumption for Social Responsibilities,' Vol. 16, No. 2, 1973; George Allen & Unwin (Publishers) Ltd and Halsted Press, New York, for the extracts from *International Marketing* by S. Marjaro; Associated Business Programmes Ltd for a table from 'Business Survival and Social Change' by J. Hargreaves and J. Dauman; Business International Corporation for the diagrams from *Business International*, 1975; the tables and diagrams from *Business International, S.A. Geneva*, 1973, by J. Kitching, and a table from *Business International Money Report*, 1976; The Controller of Her Majesty's Stationery Office for a diagram from *Strategic Alternatives for the British Motor Cycle Industry*, House of Commons Paper 532/(1974/75); *Harvard Business Review* for the diagrams from 'Strategic Choices in Diversified MNCs' by C. K. Prahalad, July/Aug 1976, Copyright © 1976, 'New Financial Priorities for MNCs' by John T. Wooster and G. Richard Thoman, May/June 1974, Copyright © 1974, and 'Multinationals View Marketing Standardization' by Ralph Z. Sorenson and Ulrich E. Wiechmann, May/June 1975, Copyright © 1975, all published in *Harvard Business Review* and copyright of The President and Fellows of Harvard College; Longman Group Ltd for a table from *Taxation and Multinational Enterprise* by John F. Chown; Longman Group and Professor Raymond Vernon for a diagram from *The European Internationals* by L. Franko, based on material from 'Managing the Multinationals Enterprise' by Stopford and Wells; Pergamon Press Ltd for tables from 'Strategic Planning in a Turbulent International Environment' by K. A. Ringbakk, from 'The Identification and Assessment of Political Risk in the International Environment' by B. Lloyd, and from 'Social Pressures on Business: A Systematic Analysis for Corporate Priorities' by I. H. Wilson; Prentice-Hall

Inc., for a diagram adapted from *Manager in the International Economy*, 3rd Edn © 1976, by R. Vernon and L. Wells; The Royal Dutch Shell Group Ltd for a table and a diagram from *The Directional Policy Matrix*, Company Publication, 1975; Professor S. Prakash Sethi for a table from 'Dimensions of Corporate Social Performance: An Analytical Framework' which appeared in *California Management Review*, Spring 1975, Vol. XVII, No. 3; and the United Nations for a table from 'Material Relevant to the Formulation of a Code of Conduct'.

1 Multinational Strategy and the Role of Planning

In the short time since the 1950s the rapid growth of international direct investment resulting in the emergence of the multinational corporation (MNC) has made these organisations a crucial component in the world economy. It is not that international corporate activity itself is new, for many of today's largest corporations, both in the USA and Europe, had established themselves in overseas markets before the turn of the century. Further, new industries such as oil first developed essentially as multinational operations. Today the concern which has been voiced by the United Nations, the International Labour Office, individual nation-states and many other national and international organisations is based on the scale and methods of these enterprises, which pose dramatic potential threats to individual economies or even to economic independence. For the coming of the MNC raises the threat of a new form of economic colonialism and significantly reduces the power of individual nation states to determine their own independent economic, and hence social and other such policies.

It has been estimated[1] that by the mid 1970s more than 20 per cent of the industrial output of the free world was provided by multinational enterprises. Further, the subsidiaries and associates of these concerns have been increasing their share of the national product in many countries and in over twenty account for more than a third of manufacturing output. In the high-technology, more rapidly growing industries such as computers, chemicals, pharmaceuticals and the like, multinational strategies are paramount and such concerns also dominate the supply and distribution of many essential raw materials such as oil, zinc and aluminium.

How then has this phenomenon come about, and in such a short period? What have been the strategies adopted by the multinationals which have led to their rapid growth and do these indeed pose the threat feared by many observers? Further, how have these firms managed the complexity of increasing multinational activity?

THE MULTINATIONAL CORPORATION

Before examining these questions it is necessary to establish what we mean by the term multinational corporation. Although this has become a widely established and well used term, a precise and generally accepted definition of what constitutes a multinational enterprise is not available. Perhaps the most widely used definition is an arbitrary one, chosen as the basis of the research programme directed by Professor Raymond Vernon at the Harvard Graduate School of Business Administration, which has led to a series of major studies of multinational enterprise.

Vernon adopted the thesis, based upon empirical evidence, that a firm would be called multinational if it possessed at least six overseas manufacturing subsidiaries. By choosing such a number of overseas manufacturing plants it is possible to study a group of concerns for whom the increased complexity of managing a firm based in many different environments is potentially common. It helps to eliminate distortions which might be expected when firms are changing their basic state from a domestic orientation to a multinational.

Nevertheless, while clearly such firms have extensive overseas commitments, the number of subsidiaries criterion is arbitrary and says nothing concerning how such firms actually manage their operations. As will be seen it is quite possible for firms, which numerically qualify as multinational, to have little concept of themselves operating a carefully coordinated and integrated global strategy. Moreover it is confined to manufacturing industry and automatically neglects the growing importance of multinational service corporations in banking, insurance, retailing and the like. This definition, although it has been found useful in research, thus is of little help to companies about to embark on a multinational strategy and who require guidance on how best to approach it.

Our definition of a multinational corporation, therefore, is perhaps academically less rigorous, but hopefully more embracing and of more immediate relevance to practitioners. For us an MNC is a company which seeks to operate strategically on a global scale and our objective is basically to identify planning systems and management methods which will better enable such firms to formulate and achieve such a strategy.

WHO ARE THE MULTINATIONALS?

From the Harvard Business School research studies some indication of the origin and scale of the world's leading manufacturing based multinationals has been established.[2] While traditionally the widespread development of MNCs has largely been attributed to the expansion strategies of major US firms, the Harvard evidence indicates that roughly one third of leading multinationals are of European origin. Further, in 1970, the overseas subsidiaries of these non-US-based firms had an estimated turnover of $80 billion dollars, or about the same as the turnover of the overseas operations of US manufacturing firms. Moreover, the growth rate of the European MNCs was actually faster than that of the US concerns.

Thus, while US firms constituted the largest volume of overseas direct investment in both numbers of subsidiaries and scale of operations, companies based in other Western industrialised nations have also developed widespread overseas interests. Britain in particular has provided a strong base, UK parents accounting for 35 per cent of the number of non-US-owned overseas subsidiaries and the same percentage of the turnover of these operations. This dominance by Britain stems from the size of British manufacturing firms relative to many of their European counterparts and to the one-time spread of the British Empire. The Netherlands, whose companies accounted for some $17 billion turnover, operated only 5.5 per cent of the total number of subsidiaries found, but Dutch firms tended to be concentrated in industries such as oil, chemicals, tobacco and electrical products.

West German multinationals owned 19 per cent of the overseas subsidiaries of the non-US multinationals, and accounted for only $8 billion turnover. The relatively small scale of German overseas activity was partially attributable to the loss of Germany's colonies after the First World War and seizures for reparations after the Second World War. Following the government-inspired rationalisation of its domestic economy, many industrial sectors in France had been concentrated into a limited number of major firms and, by 1970, these concerns were rapidly expanding their international operations. In 1970, therefore, France accounted for 10 per cent of the overseas subsidiaries of non-US-based MNCs and some $7 billion turnover. With post-war growth of France and Germany, the main country to see a decline in the importance of its MNCs has been Switzerland, which by 1970 accounted for 4.3 per cent of the number of subsidiaries and 8 per cent of aggregate turnover. This apparent decline was largely due to industry structure, Swiss firms being mainly concentrated in light industries such as pharmaceuticals.

Since 1970 rapid growth in overseas direct investment has continued with European companies increasing their share relative to the US. However, this period has also seen a rapid expansion in direct overseas investment by Japanese industry. In 1969–70 the outward flow of Japanese capital for direct overseas investment amounted to $665 million dollars. By 1973–74 this had more than quadrupled to $2794 million dollars, while the total for the five-year period reached $9567 million dollars.[3] Faced with a growing dependence on overseas raw materials, expensive domestic labour costs and the need to protect export markets from nationalist protection, Japan, too, has begun to emerge as a major MNC base.

Various theories have been advanced to explain the emergence of MNCs but none of these is wholly satisfactory. The classical economic theory of comparative advantage assumes that each country will specialise in the manufacture of those goods which it produces relatively the most efficiently, while importing those which other countries produce relatively most efficiently. This theory therefore implies that the critical factors of production – land, labour and capital – are essentially immobile. However, this is patently not so. Today, for example, it seems perfectly reasonable for a US firm to raise finance by a Eurodollar loan in London, which is used to buy machinery in Germany for delivery to a plant in Taiwan, which makes components for electronic calculators. These in turn are shipped to Mexico for final assembly before ultimate sale in North America and Western Europe.

Modifications to international trade theory, such as the concept of the international product life cycle, and the addition to traditional theories of variables such as managerial competences and technology, help in gaining understanding. Nevertheless, the basic reasons for the evolution of individual firms are usually unique in at least some way and have frequently changed over time as a result of changes in personalities, leadership, internal resources, competitive position and other influences in the external environment. Indeed evidence suggests that the process of making international investment decisions is often one of only limited rationality due to imperfections in the scanning process caused by factors such as a lack of management time, imperfect information, lack of organisational effort and the personal values of key decision-makers.[4] Thus, for example, a European retailing company operated and largely owned by Jewish families refuses to invest in West Germany because of personal values; similarly a leading British chemical manufacturer has not attempted to penetrate potential Latin American markets because no executive time is available to explore possible investment opportunities; or, finally, an American agribusiness corporation refuses to consider producing in Black Africa for fear of expropriation of its assets despite firm local guarantees to the contrary.

For many companies therefore the evolution toward a multinational status is a gradual, even haphazard process. In the first instance, initial overseas activities often are the result of the development of exports via third-party agents. This in turn may lead to the appointment of exclusive sales agents in more markets as business expands. The use of agents, however, often proves ultimately unsatisfactory especially for the servicing of large markets and as a company grows it usually seeks to exploit foreign markets directly. The next logical step, therefore, is the establishment of a direct sales presence, where necessary backed up with warehousing and servicing facilities. The ultimate step in this initial stage of international development is the investment in overseas manufacturing facilities. This may be brought about by the demands of the market-place, but today is often the result of local political pressures to minimise balance of payments deficits, provide local employment and aid economic development. The smaller firm exploiting technology may often use licence agreements as an alternative to direct manufacture. However, this method can easily lead to future difficulties, for as the firm grows and develops adequate financial and other resources to exploit overseas markets directly, it may find the licences granted become a severe strategic limitation.

The development of an international strategy for most firms is, therefore, rarely carefully worked out as a logical planned progression. In different markets a firm will probably be at different stages of development. Thus in some markets a firm may operate with sales agents, in others use a licensee, while elsewhere may have established a direct sales or even a manufacturing presence. This gradual process of internationalisation of a company's strategy has been termed 'creeping incrementalism'.[5]

While it is not always possible during the early stages of the development of international operations to see clearly ahead, mistakes made at this time in such areas as exclusive licence agreements, corporate, legal and fiscal structures, financial strategy and the like, in addition to creating potential problems in marketing and manufacturing policies, can have serious future consequences. For example the Xerox Corporation, prior to the widespread acceptance of xerography, ceded its international patent rights outside North America to the Rank Organisation. Although this resulted in the formation of a highly successful joint venture, Rank Xerox, 51 per cent was owned and operations, therefore, were controlled by the Rank Organisation. In order to regain the controlling one per cent shareholding and managerial control of the operation Xerox were required to pay a high cash price and grant Rank Xerox the right to all new Xerox technological developments for the next twenty years.

Even when a significant presence in overseas markets has been established, few MNCs at present attempt to operate a global strategy. The vast majority still operate primarily as a series of almost independent subunits. A growing number of these firms, however, are now by necessity or design attempting to introduce the planning systems needed to operate their activities on a global scale.

PATTERNS OF MULTINATIONAL EVOLUTION

Despite the deficiencies in theory and the difficulties of reconciling theory with managerial practice it is still possible to identify some generalisations about the routes adopted by firms in their pursuit of a multinational strategy. It is important to realise, however, that there are many routes, not merely a few, although some are more common than others. It is not, therefore, our intent to advocate simplistic or universalist solutions for the process of multinational strategic planning. An examination of the strategies of many multinationals clearly reveals the need for variation in planning systems, in organisation structure, in information and control systems, and in the roles expected of and decision-making powers granted to various levels in the organisation hierarchy. Nevertheless, some general patterns can be seen.

The overseas direct investment by many US firms commenced before the turn of the twentieth century, usually going first to Canada and Europe and especially to the United Kingdom. The firms engaged in these activities tended to be the producers of consumer products such as food and electrical appliances or engaged in industries where product differentiation was possible, as in sewing machines. Such early international multinationals thus included firms like Heinz, Hoover, and Singer.

Direct investment in Canada and Europe expanded rapidly during the 1920s but slowed down in the depression and during the Second World War. Investment in Latin America, Asia and the British white Commonwealth increased steadily but at a slower pace than to the developed economies of Western Europe. Firms commencing operations in these markets were the great raw material and agricultural product concerns such as Standard Oil of New Jersey (Exxon) or the United Fruit Company (United Brands).

In the period since the 1950s the rate of new subsidiary formation by US firms has grown rapidly. Although the number of new operations based in Latin America and in the developing countries grew especially fast, the location of overseas assets and the volume of trade conducted by US firms abroad remained heavily concentrated in the developed economies. The volume of investment overall, however, has expanded dramatically in the post-war period, rising from $11,788 million dollars in book value of total investments in 1950, to $78,090 million dollars in 1970. Thus while this growth included the continued expansion of the early international pioneers of American industry, it represented also a marked shift in policy on the part of nearly all the leading US corporations to expand in overseas markets.

In particular the post-war period brought a dramatic increase in US direct investment in Western Europe where the net book value of investments rose from $1733 million dollars in 1950 representing 14.7 per cent of US direct overseas investment to $24,471 million dollars in 1970 or 31.3 per cent.[6] Taking manufacturing investment alone, the relative importance of Western European operations for US firms is even greater, with over 42 per cent of total manufacturing investment being located there.

The increased emphasis of US companies on speciality products, based upon technology or marketing skills, is to an extent shown up by the relative decline in the importance of overseas investment in mining, smelting and agricultural industries. This has been compensated for by a corresponding growth in the significance of manufacturing investments from 32.5 per cent of total in 1950 to 41.3 per cent in 1970.

This period, which witnessed a nearly seven-fold expansion in US overseas investment, was especially favourable to such growth. The US firms, faced with relatively slow growth in their domestic economy and institutional constraints on growth by acquisition, saw themselves with significant advantages over their overseas competitors. Firstly, they often had the advantage of scale and superior technology. Secondly, they had superior marketing skills developed in a strongly competitive domestic market-place, unlike the Europeans, for whom cartels were much more common and who did not have the skills needed to operate in the newly created large market of the EEC. Finally, the Americans possessed an ability to organise and manage large-scale corporations, in a way almost unknown outside the United States.

The host countries to which this new investment was directed were, moreover, keen to attract the emerging US multinationals, to provide jobs, technology, management and capital which were lacking in their own economies. Further, the potential of the multinational enterprise was still unknown. The strategy of the new arrivals was essentially simple. Most new subsidiaries were formed to supply a local market rather than import, and each subsidiary operated independently of the others and was principally identified with the needs of the local market. Management decision-making, although heavily centralised with regard to investment, tended to be delegated wherever possible to local management, who were principally concerned with the operations of the subsidiary.

Then, in the late 1960s, the first truly multinational enterprises began to emerge, which attempted to build an integrated global strategy where national boundaries were no longer the relevant building block. While companies operating in industries such as oil were forced to coordinate centrally global movements of raw materials and finished products, local managers were still required to exercise considerable autonomy due to difficulties in communication and the like. Gradually, however, this autonomy has been eroded and more of the key strategic decisions determined centrally. Thus, as economies of scale have increased, new refineries are built not merely to service a local market, but to meet the needs of a geographic region. A computer company such as IBM begins not only to build a model range of computers to service world markets but to specialise its production by machine or component and tranship finished products from one country to another; an agricultural products manufacturer such as Massey-Ferguson specialises its production to such an extent that one plant in England may produce the engine, to be fitted to a German chassis and a Canadian gearbox, and assembled in France for sale in Turkey.

This recognition of the opportunities and advantages of coordinating international operations which has gradually become recognised has resulted in changes in the systems of management of the multinational concerns. The overseas subsidiaries have, therefore, come to act less and less like local national concerns in many industries and it is this phenomenon which has led to much of the concern expressed by governments and other agencies. For at the same time as the multinational enterprises have been learning how to optimise their activities on a global scale, so governments have been endeavouring to take an increasingly active role in the management of their national economies.

In general it is the US firms which have advanced most rapidly in the development of global strategies, although even amongst US firms it is still the minority which is endeavouring to operate fully integrated strategies. Most European multinationals are much less coordinated. In part this is due to their different pattern of evolution. Amongst the European concerns two main routes can be discerned.

The first of these, typified by the British multinationals, traces its roots back in the days of the British Empire when Britain dominated world trade and was the world's leading industrial power. With the spread of Empire, British domestic firms enjoyed an established source of raw materials for their production and protected overseas markets in the territories under British rule. Unlike the US firms, the majority of British overseas investment was in low-technology, commodity-like industries where initial operations had largely been concerned with the development of raw material sources to service the domestic production units. Thus, excluding oil, 34 per cent of British overseas direct investment was in the food, drink and tobacco industries, while other large interests were held in paper and mining and extraction.

By 1950, 23 of the largest 81 British manufacturing concerns were already multinationals.[7] Unlike the US companies, much of British overseas investment occurred prior to 1946 and was predominantly located in former Empire territories, especially the 'White Commonwealth' of Australia, Canada, South Africa and New Zealand. The only significant exception to this policy was the extensive British investment in the English-speaking United States market. By 1970, 58 per cent of the largest British manufacturing concerns were multinationals, but unlike the US counterparts the British firms had rarely explicitly endeavoured to establish an overseas strategy. For many the achievement of multinational status was largely accidental and resulted primarily from changes in domestic policies.

The influx of US direct investment after the Second World War came first to Britain, and this new competitive pressure, coupled with legal restrictions against cartels at home and the decolonisation of the Empire overseas, meant that the 1960s saw a marked increase in the competitive climate faced by British industry. The response of the major firms to this change was to rationalise their activities and diversify, usually by acquisition. During the 1960s, therefore, there was a marked increase in industrial concentration in Britain as a result of domestic merger activity. A corollary of this domestic activity was that it often brought together firms each of which operated a few overseas subsidiaries but which in combination created a new enterprise with a substantial international commitment.

The first priority of these newly formed or consolidated firms, however, was to rationalise their domestic management structures. Initially the widespread strategy of acquisition led to the creation of unstable holding company systems of management. These quickly proved unsatisfactory, as financial performance continued to decline and led ultimately, toward the end of the 1960s and early 1970s, to widespread adoption of a multidivisional form of organisation – the system already used by the emerging US multinationals.

With this new organisational pattern the largest British firms have begun to develop coordinated strategies, firstly toward their domestic operations, but latterly embracing overseas activities. These foreign subsidiaries, which had been long accustomed to enjoying virtual independence from their British parents, have begun to be integrated and coordinated as, like their American counterparts, the British firms move to establish global strategies.

The introduction of these new strategies has in turn sharply changed the pattern of capital asset deployment. Since 1970 the rate of British overseas direct investment has increased sharply. Hindered by a falling currency and rigorous exchange controls, much of this new investment has taken the form of acquisitions, in particular in Western Europe and North America, financed by local borrowings or by access to the Eurocurrency markets based in London.

In contrast to the early colonial tradition of British overseas investment, which was also partially mirrored by French and Dutch experience, the non-colonial developed nations of Western Europe have pursued a policy somewhat more akin to the US firms. Like the British firms, many major German enterprises were diversified geographically well before the First World War. While some of this overseas subsidiary activity was located in the German colonies, the much more limited nature of this colonial empire meant that the strategies pursued were more centred on expansion elsewhere in Europe. After the war these operations were largely confiscated but they were again largely reformed between the wars only to be confiscated for a second time in 1945.

The principal direction of investment nevertheless remained

inter-European which, until 1945, included Eastern Europe. In large part therefore European foreign investment has been attributed to classical economic reasons of tariff barriers, patent protection and transportation economies.[8] Thus in dyestuffs, steel and electrical goods foreign investment resulted from the introduction of high tariffs and restrictive patent laws.

Relatively little direct investment was made by German firms either in raw material source developing countries, or in the high-wage-cost US economy. By the late 1960s, however, German industry was beginning to increase its penetration in the USA. By 1971 German firms accounted for 7 per cent of all European direct investment in the USA, although the dominant investors remained Britain, the Netherlands and Switzerland who between them held 81 per cent of foreign direct investments.[9]

THE CHANGING NATURE OF MULTINATIONAL PLANNING METHODS

The Emergence of Environmental Turbulence[10]

The environment for multinational business from 1950 to the mid-1970s was one rich in opportunities and the third quarter-century saw the growth of MNCs as a potent force in the world economy. Suddenly, from a world of great opportunity MNCs are realising that fundamental changes have appeared in the environment which make the past quarter-century appear full of hostility and uncertainty. While the most dramatic impact has arisen as a result of the oil crisis, other discontinuities have also emerged which are transforming the business scene, overturning many of the established attitudes of managers, and significantly changing what were considered desirable strategies. These fundamental shifts have also resulted in the serious modification of strategic planning and control systems.

A summary of the major environmental changes for MNCs is shown in Table 1.1. The period following the Second World War was characterised by general stability and only gradual change in global political terms. There was an established political order

Table 1.1 Changes in the Multinational Corporate Environment

Parameters	*Third quarter-century (1950–early 1970s)*	*Fourth quarter-century (late 1970s–)*
Geopolitics	1. General political stability	1. Breakdown of old alliances, nationalism, new conflicts
	2. Ideologically based Cold War	2. Resource-based 'economic war'
	3. US dominance in international political economy	3. Erosion of US pre-eminence and superiority
	4. North–South gap	4. Food, population, Fourth World problems Interdependence with shifting locus of power
Resources	5. Ready availability of low-cost energy	5. Uncertain availability but high cost
	6. Ready access to raw materials	6. Resource nationalism and cartels
	7. MDC-controlled exploration, exploitation	7. LDC and resource-rich controlled production
Economics	8. Reconstruction in Europe and Japan	8. Preventing Malthusian prophesies of doom
	9. Economic growth objectives	9. Socio-ecological balances
	10. Closing international gaps	10. Problematique: multivariant, interactive, global
	11. 'Limits to Growth' unknown	11. Conserving resources
	12. GATT: promising free international trade	12. Bilateralism, regionalism, and barter
	13. IMS: offering monetary stability	13. Breakdown of Bretton Woods system
Institutional Framework	14. International communications and transportation	14. Improved communications and transportation
	15. International banking and financial markets	15. More prudent and controlled developments
	16. Eurodollars, Eurobonds, Eurocurrencies	16. Currency cocktails, shifting currency strength
	17. EEC, EFTA, LAFTA, COMECON, ANCOM	17. OPEC, IBA-type political-economic organization

Table 1.1 Changes in the Multinational Corporate Environment – *Continued*

Parameters	*Third quarter-century (1950–early 1970s)*	*Fourth quarter-century (late 1970s–)*
Foreign Investments	18. Long tradition of portfolio investments	18. Foreign dominance or influence resisted
	19. Open host environments welcoming direct investment as means to close gaps	19. Restrictive host environments scrutinising existing and new foreign investments
	20. Home country tolerance for export of capital, technology, and management	20. Home country concern with export of jobs and loss of national economic welfare
	21. Emphasis on short-term benefits, discounting long-term costs	21. Perception that costs exceed benefits and that MNC is a threat to sovereignty
	22. Direct investments a means to national ends	22. Important gaps are closed and direct investments have served primary purpose
	23. Minor government involvement or interference	23. Extensive government involvement in national planning and management of economic affairs

Source: K. A. Ringbakk, op. cit.

and an economic gap between the developed countries and the less developed, resulting in market-oriented investments being made in the former while investments aimed at developing and exploiting natural resources were made in the latter. Partially as a result of these investment patterns natural resources were both readily available and cheap. The international economic environment was also favourable to overseas investment. There was high economic growth in Western Europe and Japan creating many opportunities. Investment funds were readily available from local borrowing and exchange rate stability was assured under the Bretton Woods Agreement. In addition, free trade was being progressively encouraged by the General Agreement on Tariffs and Trade, concurrent with the formation of major new free trade areas such as LAFTA, the EEC and EFTA. Most importantly, MNCs were actively encouraged politically by many countries who perceived them as large potential investors helping to create jobs, add new technologies and provide a stimulus to the development of domestic economies.

By contrast the fourth quarter-century offers the prospect that many of these positive forces will be reversed. In geopolitics, stability has been replaced by new conflicts, a breakdown in traditional alliances and the emergence of new centres of power such as the Arab world. Resources are no longer readily available but have become the weapons of a new resource based economic conflict. Moreover, resource nationalism has been intensifying with governments intervening to break established contractural arrangements so as to maximise their own benefit from resource exploitation. This is usually at the expense of the MNCs who were primarily responsible for providing the necessary initial investments in discovery.

The economic order of the third quarter-century has given way to widespread currency fluctuation, high rates of inflation, the growth of barter deals, and the emergence of economic protectionism. Resource allocation has become much more political and the relationships between MNCs and both their home and host governments has been significantly changed. Attitudes toward direct foreign investments and international production have begun to reverse and be replaced by restrictions, suspicions and new constraints and regulations. In their home environments MNCs have come under criticism for exporting technology and thus reducing domestic job opportunities, exploiting low labour costs overseas, contributing to an unfavourable balance of payments by exporting less and importing more and by investing overseas rather than at home.

THE MODIFICATION OF MANAGEMENT ATTITUDES AND EXPECTATIONS

As a result of the changes that have occurred in the environment, managers have quite suddenly been forced to modify the attitudes and expectations developed during the third quarter-century. Again, as seen in Table 1.2, the change has often been a near reversal of their former thinking. These changes in attitude have brought about significant modifications to existing

Table 1.2 Changes in Managerial Expectations and Attitudes

	Third quarter-century (1950–early1970s)	*Fourth quarter-century (late 1970s–)*
1.	High growth potential and growth is good	Real growth overall low or negative
2.	Increasing levels of discretionary income	Reduced discretionary income focus on necessities
3.	Resources and raw materials readily available, recycling unnecessary	Resources scarce and finite, recycling increasingly important
4.	Finance available from borrowing	High debt possibly dangerous
5.	Economic stability and low to modest inflation	Widespread exchange rate fluctuation, high inflation
6.	Past is a guide to the future and change is modest	Past is no guide to the future, change is discontinuous
7.	Government sets the rules but does not intervene	Government changes the rules and increasingly intervenes
8.	Growth is important and all elements must grow	Growth can be bad and selectivity is essential
9.	Earnings per share are the key to share prices	Equities severely depressed and no hedge against inflation
10.	Cash flow secondary to EPS	Cash flow and liquidity critical to survival

Table 1.3 Changes in Planning and MICS Systems

	Third quarter-century (1950s–early 1970s)	*Fourth quarter-century (late 1970s–)*
1.	Annual plans for around five years ahead, prepared annually	Annual plans with shorter horizons, modified quarterly
2.	Single-point estimates based on a single set of assumptions	Multiple scenarios of possible outcomes with built-in decision points
3.	Little evaluation of risk or alternative courses of action	Extensive sensitivity analysis coupled with contingency plans

Table 1.3 Changes in Planning and MICS Systems

	Third quarter-century (1950s–early 1970s)	*Fourth quarter-century (late 1970s–)*
4.	New investment planning only, including diversification	Corporate portfolio analysis with selective investment and divestment
5.	Little evaluation of competitive strategies	Detailed competitive analysis
6.	Little evaluation of political and social environment	Development of socio political reaction models
7.	Little account of inflation and currency fluctuation in capital investments	Focus on cash flow, exchange risk
8.	Capital investments evaluated pre-tax	Tax planning for capital investment and operations
9.	Plans based on monetary measures and monetary volume	Plans take account of exchange risks and physical unit measures
10.	Periodic reporting usually monthly decentralised cash management	Faster feedback some financial monitoring weekly, some cash daily and control centralised
11.	Simple measures with few variables	Composite, comprehensive measures, concentration on critical factors like cash and exchange risk
12.	Performance appraisal over time	Comparison of actual or adjusted standards; focus on activities with built-in action trigger points
13.	Focus on measurement of historic results	Focus on future actions
14.	Broad, across the board controls	Provide close, detailed controls from the centre when possible
15.	Planning assumptions and responses modified annually to environmental changes	Fast responses to short term environmental changes
16.	Plan for maximum EPS growth	Plan for balanced cash flow
17.	Planning essentially a manual process	Widespread adoption of modular 'what if'-type corporate models

strategies. The maximum pursuit of earnings per share, higher sales levels, greater financial gearing, all-round growth and increased diversification both by product and geography have given way to a new concentration on cash flow, the development and maintenance of a viable basic business, a concentration on improved efficiency, internal finance generation and a selectivity of businesses for growth, maintenance and divestment. In order to manage such new strategies widespread changes have been made to existing planning and control devices which are outlined in Table 1.3.

In particular, the rapid rate of change in the environment has led many companies to develop a range of plans with shorter time-horizons, at least for quantitative projections and with much greater qualitative supporting argument from line management rather than the forward extrapolation of existing financial positions. Further, rather than relying on a single corporate plan, top managements are increasingly adopting a series of alternative future scenarios. These may contain built-in trigger points which activate predetermined contingency plans.

The plans themselves are reviewed much more frequently. Instead of being up-dated annually, the widespread adoption of corporate models capable of responding to 'what if' questions allows plans to be up-dated quarterly and in a few extreme cases, weekly. In a recent survey of 346 US firms, 73 per cent were already using or developing a corporate planning model.[11] At Ralston Purina Company for example, a one per cent change in the price of a prime commodity triggers a change in the company's cost models and the whole corporate plan may change accordingly. Similarly at Dow Chemical 140 separate cost inputs – constantly revised – are fed into a corporate model while such factors as major raw materials costs and prices by country and region are monitored weekly.[12]

Traditionally capital investment planning centred upon economic evaluations using techniques such as discounted cash flow to measure pre-tax rates of return. Usually there was little evaluation of risk or alternatives while each capital request was considered on its merits and irrespective of any corporate view on the business unit the investment formed part of. Today while DCF techniques are still used, payback is also used automatically as high interest and inflation rates make long time-horizon projects increasingly difficult to assess, cash flow and exchange exposure considerations are carefully taken into account, international tax, financial sources and remittance possibilities are included in the financial evaluation, for major projects a full risk sensitivity appraisal is conducted, and irrespective of projected returns resources are allocated according to a corporate strategic view of each business within the total portfolio.

Two relatively new areas for planning are in competitive analysis and socio-political trend analysis. Traditionally competitive analysis tended to be relatively simple since competitors were readily identifiable and their strengths and weaknesses could be assessed. Today this is increasingly untrue as substitution competition increases and many industries are faced with new competitors brought about by geographic market interpenetration by other multinationals or by new industry entrants which have diversified by acquisition. Similarly, there is a need to identify if possible changes in the socio-political climate both for the corporation as a whole and for individual businesses or investment decisions in order to avoid legal and political actions and societal pressures which may threaten.

In the same way, management information and control systems are being modified to respond faster and in a more meaningful way to external change. Not only is more environmental information required and processed, control systems have become much more detailed, more future- and action-oriented and increasingly centralised as technology provides the mechanisms for improved communication and data processing.

THE SCOPE OF THE BOOK

The different environments from which multinational firms have developed, therefore, has significantly influenced the strategies they have adopted. Nevertheless, with the gradual adoption of an integrated global strategy by more firms these differences in strategy and management style are diminishing. However, just as the MNCs are learning how to adapt to planning on a global scale, the environment in which they operate is itself changing rapidly. From a benevolent international scene rich in opportunities during the third quarter-century, the MNCs are finding increased hostility to their operations both at home and overseas and a world where uncertainties are much greater and change discontinuous. In order to respond to these changes and endeavour to prepare for future events the MNCs have never needed planning more. Unfortunately the accuracy of historical systems has proven inadequate for the task and as a result there is currently a phase of dynamic evolution in multinational strategic planning. This book attempts to describe these trends in planning systems, dealing both with the mechanisms adopted for integrating operations on a global scale and with the new systems and techniques necessary to cope with a rapidly changing environment.

In the following chapters we first identify the organisational forms normally experienced by firms evolving as a multinational. As an international strategy develops so organisation tends to evolve in response to changing management needs. The formal organisation adopted at various stages of strategy development in large part determines the types of strategic planning system used which are also modified to suit the specific needs of particular businesses. The main strategic planning variants are discussed in detail in Chapter 3. In addition we are not merely concerned with the formal content of planning, but also with the process, including its timing and the specific roles performed by different hierarchical levels of management. The chapter thus describes planning systems under alternative organisational forms and in addition deals with the content of plans at the business unit level. In Chapter 4 a number of advanced portfolio planning techniques are discussed which are increasingly becoming adopted by multibusiness multimarket firms. The potential advantages of strategic portfolio planning systems must, however, be treated with caution since there are many pitfalls for the reckless user. The chapter, therefore, points out a number of the more serious problems which can occur with this type of planning technique.

The role of treasury management is especially important in the multinational enterprise and this is dealt with in detail in Chapter 5. Again financial management tends to change according to the companies stage of international development and the ways in which major areas of treasury management are dealt with are identified and discussed. The following chapter deals with the related topic of tax planning, a topic area of vital importance to the multinational planner and one which tends to be relatively neglected.

Capital investment planning is discussed in detail in Chapter 7 with particular attention being paid to the problem of plant location, and the use of licensing and joint venture entry strategies. In Chapter 8 the specialised investment area of cross-border mergers and acquisitions is examined in detail with indications given as to reasons for success and failure, tax treatments and practical methods of identifying and implementing suitable acquisition strategies.

Political risk is an area of increasing concern for many MNCs. Chapter 9 examines the problem of political risk and the methods of measuring it suggested and used in practice. It concludes with a review of methods of reducing political risk exposure. Chapter 10 discusses multinational marketing management. It describes where global marketing approaches are appropriate and when it is more useful to adapt to meet local needs and conditions. The chapter also deals with international product strategy, pricing, channel management and communications policies. The book concludes with a review of external affairs management. The growing importance of societal pressures both within individual countries and as a result of the intervention of supranational bodies such as the United Nations and the like has forced the MNC to plan carefully its response to these new factors. The role of external affairs management is therefore reviewed and the problems faced and some of the techniques used are discussed in some detail.

Our overall objective has been to concentrate on a number of the major topic areas in strategic planning for the MNC. We have described what we believe to be the forefront of theoretical concepts but in particular we have endeavoured to report the best of current actual practice. We have relied heavily on the use of actual examples drawn from current ongoing research at the Manchester Business School and elsewhere. In this way we believe that the book will not only provide a description of actual practice but will serve as a prescriptive guide to practitioners in many of the areas of multinational strategic planning.

2 Organising for International Operations

For the management of the multinational enterprise the choice of organisation structure to adopt which is best suited to implement the firm's chosen strategy is a key decision. This choice also largely determines the form of the planning, information and control systems to be used. In reality organisation structure tends to evolve, with events placing strain upon an existing structure, leading to the development of informal processes and communication networks to enable managers to carry out their work. These are tolerated until they become so serious that a major rationalisation of the formal structure is undertaken which tends to legitimise the trends that have emerged informally.

As firms evolve from entrepreneurial beginnings they tend, firstly, to increase in size in their originally narrow area of chosen product market operations. At this stage some specialisation of the management task becomes necessary and leads to the adoption of a functional form of organisation, which subdivides the firm into a series of specialist functions, such as production, sales, research and development and finance. So long as the firm remains relatively undiversified this basic form of organisation, although becoming more complex, remains adequate.

However, many firms find that they are unable to maintain their objectives for expansion, or capitalise on new opportunities, without adding to their original operations new activities which extend the firm into new products and markets. Often these events occur simultaneously and the firm rapidly comes to adopt diversification moves which significantly complicate the administrative tasks of management. This is especially true at senior levels where the previous involvement in short-range operating problems becomes an overwhelming burden with a wider range of products and markets to serve. As a result, therefore, a further structural adaptation is made which transforms the corporation into having some form of divisional organisation, where the central office and its staff become divorced from day-to-day operations and rely on managing these through other managers. The key operating responsibilities then tend to fall to the chief executives of the operating divisions, which are usually so designed as to be quasi-autonomous, measurable profit-centres. These individuals are general managers, responsible for coordinating a multi-functional team of line specialists needed to manage the affairs of the division.

For a growing number of firms, not only does expansion via diversification of product line and geographic coverage take place within the domestic market, but also internationally. The new managerial demands experienced in dealing with cross-border geographic expansion thus adds a further dimension to be taken into account in the design of an organisation structure for the MNC. Thus the MNC, in choosing its organisation, must achieve a satisfactory blend between functional activities, products and product groups and countries or geographic areas. There is no one optimal organisation form which should be adopted by the MNC. Rather the structure should be consistent with the strategy in so far as this is possible. Moreover, since strategy itself tends to change over time so might organisation structure expect to undergo modifications.

Further, the most strategically appropriate structure will often not be adopted due to the intervention of variables such as national political requirements, internal political power alignments, personal values and legal, fiscal and cultural constraints. Indeed there are a number of conflicting forces operating in the MNC which tend to pull in the opposite directions of centralisation and decentralisation as illustrated in Figure 2.1. The specific conditions of the business or businesses within the MNC tend to result in different balances between these forces yielding a particular series of organisational transitions which appear to represent a widely used evolutionary path in multinational structural development. This chapter identifies each of the main multinational organisation forms and illustrates them in practice by descriptions of actual organisations which approximate to them. In addition, a number of the modified organisation forms which have emerged are examined. These may well be more common in future as factors such as political intervention make 'pure' organisation structures, relying on total ownership for their implementation, increasingly difficult to achieve.

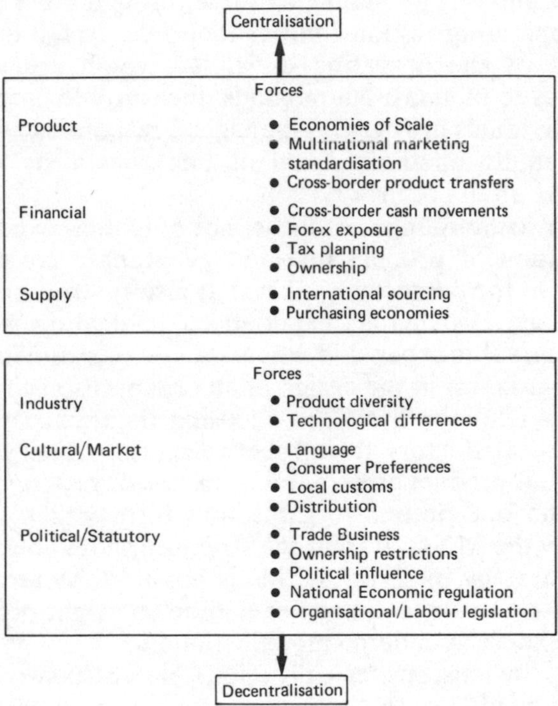

Fig. 2.1 Forces for Centralisation and Decentralisation

THE PATTERN OF MULTINATIONAL STRUCTURE EVOLUTION

Export Sales Organisations

For most small firms international activities begin with export sales to other countries. Such firms, if not diversified domestically, will normally be organised along functional lines and export sales will be an adjunct of domestic operations as shown in Figure 2.2. Export sales will usually be made via overseas agents and such firms tend to have little detailed knowledge of overseas markets, no direct customer contact and no local representation.

Non-domestic markets are usually served by periodic visits by senior management and an export manager where appointed. Surprisingly this form of organisation can be remarkably successful in specific narrow niche situations. Company A for example, which specialises in the production of a narrow niche industrial consumable product with worldwide sales of some $50m, has no well-established export organisation other than documentation. Overseas markets are serviced by agents who maintain contact with the company via periodic visits from the chief executive and the sales director. Company A is, however, a world leader in its particular product, and has successfully withstood several onslaughts from larger organisations on its market.

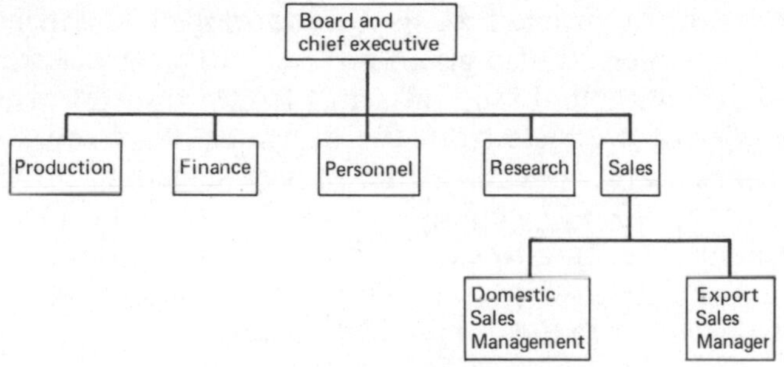

Fig. 2.2 Undiversified Small Exporting Organisation

Domestic growth normally leads to diversification of the company's product line, and when the administrative strains created become significant enough this leads to the adoption of a product divisional form. Where, however, the company is still relatively small it is not economically viable to have a specialist exporting operation for each product division. Exports, therefore, tend to be centralised through a small specialist export department as shown in Figure 2.3.

As exports become of greater significance the staff of the export department will tend to increase, leading probably to some specialisation on an area or product line basis. It is also possible to convert the export operation into a profit centre in the same way as the product divisions, as is done in Company B, a small but diversified industrial products supplier with annual sales of $40m, some $7m of which are exported. This

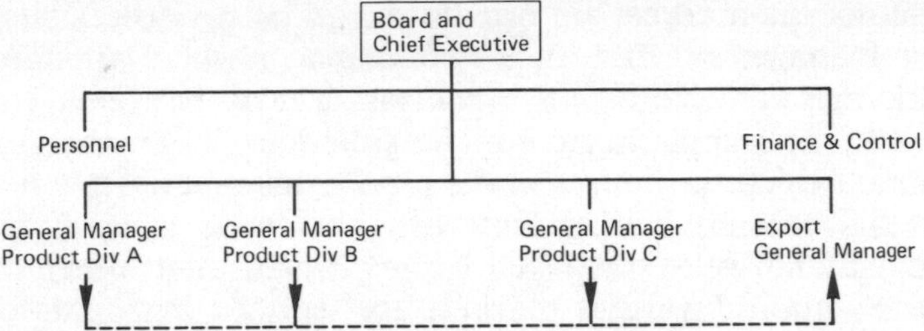

Fig. 2.3 Diversified Concern with Centralised Export Structure

company has centralised the exports of its line divisions and has increased its specialist export marketing force to six people with responsibilities being divided on an area basis for developing countries and a product basis for developed countries. The export department is also given responsibility for licensing and is profit-accountable, based on arm's-length transfer prices, for export sales of products from the divisions. As a result of this specialisation and concentration, export sales had grown at a rate of over 40 per cent in recent years, and the export department is seeking to extend its activities by developing its skills as an import-export trading house, supplying overseas factored products to the domestic divisions.

The International Division Structure

Conditions favouring this structure:

1. There is limited product diversity.
2. There are few local environmental influences of sufficient importance to lead to product modification or to different marketing strategies.
3. Overseas sales are small by comparison with domestic and export sales.
4. Geographic diversity is limited.
5. There are limited economies of scale in manufacturing or from close manufacturing coordination.
6. There are few executives with international experience.

For the larger firm, however, as overseas sales, distribution and manufacturing activities are added the need for coordination between such activities and domestic divisions becomes much greater. Moreover, there is a growing need for the skilled preparation and evaluation of overseas investment opportunities. These become increasingly complex, requiring strategic decisions to be made regarding the choice between such opportunities as licence agreements, joint ventures, acquisitions and green-field developments. As a result, therefore, it is common for all the overseas activities of the firm to be consolidated into an international division structure as shown in Figure 2.4. Below the level of the international division itself the structure can in turn be subdivided firstly either by product or by geography. Primary subdivision by function is rare and in situations where close specialist coordination is required on a global scale a global functional structure is probably more useful (see next section). In most cases the emergence of an international division results from a consolidation and increased role being assigned to the export department.

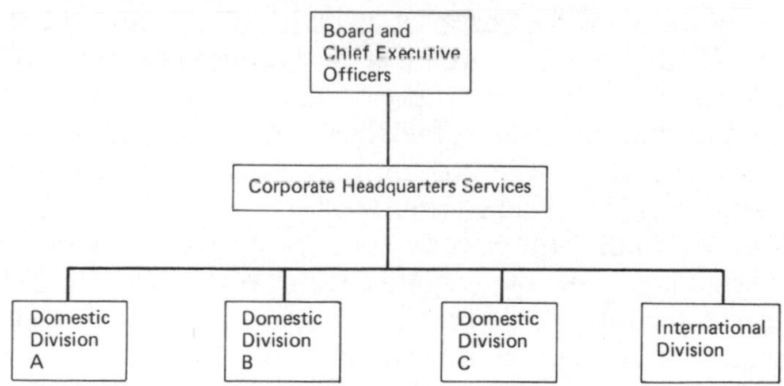

Fig. 2.4 International Division Structure

Nabisco operates a typical international division structure. An international division handles almost all the company's business outside the USA. Within the division operations are organised into a series of four regions covering Latin America, Europe, Oceania and Japan with most divisional and some regional executives located at the corporate headquarters. The division is led by a president who is also a corporate vice-president and reports direct to the parent company president. The division has its own corporate staff including a director of finance, a vice-president for planning and development, a personnel director, a director of operations and a director of distribution. All the national country operating subsidiaries, except one in Puerto Rico, are organised like the domestic operating divisions, each with its own president responsible for a variety of line and staff executives.[1]

The international division structure offers several advantages for multinational operations. Firstly it provides a central focus for overseas activities and ensures cohesion between the different countries and regions. Secondly, the presence of an international division leads to the development of a cadre of managers with a specific international orientation. Thirdly, the international division brings an international perspective to all product areas of the corporation. In addition, it often ensures that the necessary resources are available for the international development of smaller domestic product divisions which might otherwise be unable to fully exploit their overseas opportunities.

There are, however, a number of disadvantages with international division structures which tend to make them unstable as long-term solutions for corporations with high levels of overseas activity. Firstly, there is often a lack of communication between the international division and the domestic product divisions. This occurs because the domestic divisions usually receive no credit for overseas sales and are remote from overseas market needs since direct market contact is only through the international division. Secondly, there may actually be rivalry between the two components of the organisation, with the international executives feeling the domestic divisions are naive concerning overseas operations, while the product divisions regard the international division as weak on product knowledge. Thirdly, the orientation of top management is still largely toward domestic activities, resulting in a lack of trust in overseas subsidiaries, low levels of local autonomy and the excessive use of expatriate managers in overseas positions.

The Global Functional Structure

An alternative to the international division structure which does occur on occasion in firms where product market diversity is strictly limited, is the global functional organisation shown in Figure 2.5. In this form of organisation, global operations are organised primarily on a functional basis with marketing and production being the key functions. An example of such a system was the move by John Deere and Co., the US farm equipment manufacturer, from an area-based organisation to a global functional form in the early 1960s.

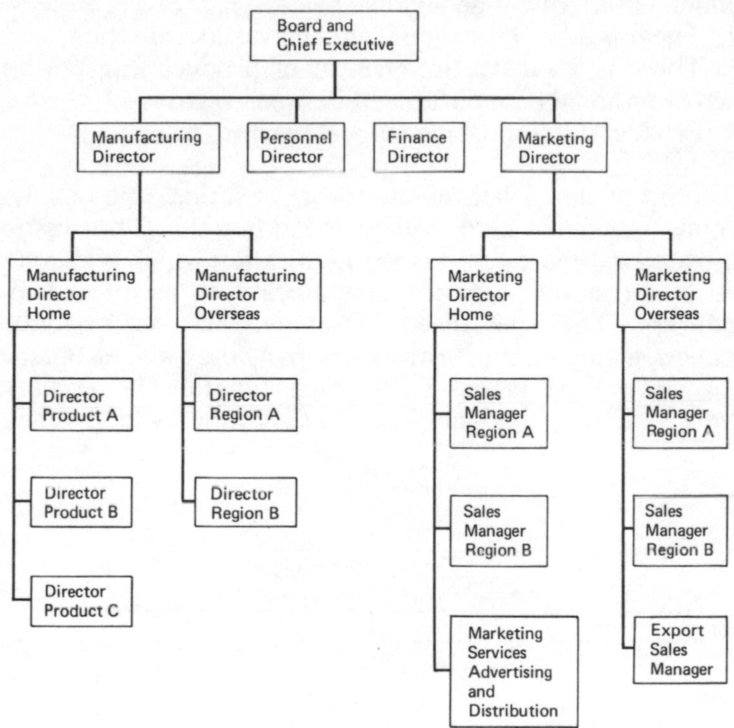

Fig. 2.5 Global Functional Structure

Integrated manufacturing and marketing functions were established. Each manufacturing plant and sales branch was given its own balance sheet and intracompany transactions made on a buy-and-sell relationship. Overseas sales units were able to buy from whatever source they chose, although cost differences were the prime determinant. Plants were responsible for centrally assigned product lines, both in the USA and overseas. Overseas marketing units sold those product lines suited to their area, regardless of plant location. All other headquarters functions were combined and integrated.[2]

The Functional Process Structure

Conditions favouring this structure:

1. There is an integrated production process each step of which is carried out on a global basis.
2. There is a need for significant central coordination.
3. There is a substantial element of product transportation across national boundaries and between regions.
4. Product differentiation in local markets is low.

A variant of the global functional organisation, and one which is found somewhat more widely, is the functional process form illustrated in Figure 2.6. It is an organisation which is commonly used by extractive industry companies such as oil and metal producers. The specialised functions such as exploration, production and refining in an oil company may well be organised on a centralised global basis, each function being in turn subdivided on a regional basis. Marketing, which tends to

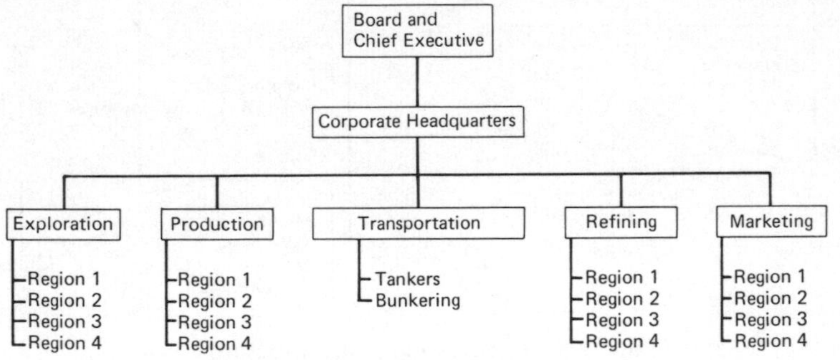

Fig. 2.6 Functional Process Structure

come at the end of a chain of such integrated processing steps, may also be subdivided by region, but in some cases a product subdivision is preferable, where a variety of end-products are manufactured at the end of the process chain. For example in oil processing the end-products are very different, ranging from gasoline to petrochemicals, and so may require quite different marketing and, in the case of chemicals, different manufacturing treatments.

This type of structure tends to be used when there is an integrated production process each step of which can be carried out on a global basis and which, therefore, requires significant central coordination. Further, there is usually a substantial element of transportation across national boundaries, and even between regions, since raw materials tend to be found in locations remote from their principal markets, resulting in significant imbalances on a regional scale.

Alcan represents an example of a company that has actually moved from a global functional organisation to a functional process form. During the seller's market of the 1950s, the Canadian-based aluminium concern produced good profit performance by selling some 80 per cent of the metal it produced to independent fabricators. Overcapacity during the 1960s forced the company to integrate forward, and by the early 1970s the company processed 60 per cent of its substantially enlarged production in its own fabricating plants. However, the company maintained its traditional functional organisation structure until the end of the 1960s.

Finally outside consultants were used to produce a functional process organisation, creating separate divisions for smelting, raw materials, fabricating and sales, each with an executive vice-president in charge. In addition seven regions were created to coordinate the activities of all the subsidiaries in a particular geographic area. Within each region, the local smelter would provide metal to all regional fabricators at a price decided at the group central office, and any inter-regional sales had first to be coordinated and agreed between the regions concerned and, on occasion, central office.[3]

The Worldwide Product Division Structure

Conditions favouring this structure:

1. The individual divisions are largely autonomous.
2. There is a significant need to integrate research, production and marketing activities within the divisions.
3. There is a limited need for local product market knowledge and product modification.
4. The divisions make little use of common marketing tools, channels or promotion.

5. There are significant economies of scale in production which require geographic coordination to achieve.
6. There is a significant technical service required with the product.

The worldwide product divisional structure tends to be adopted by a number of multimarket companies as their overseas activities expand. Such a structure is shown in Figure 2.7. In particular the structure is found extensively in industrial products companies where there is little attempt to tailor products to local tasks and where the divisions themselves are largely independent of one another. Under this structure each division is responsible for production and marketing of its product range on a global basis although most such organisations tend within the product divisions to emphasise the domestic market and treat international operations as separate.

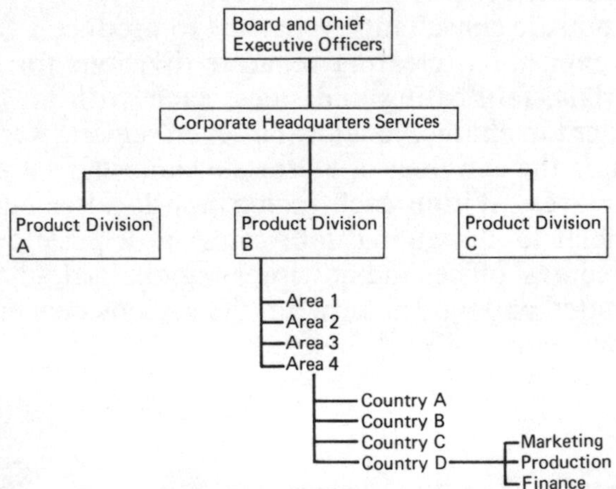

Fig. 2.7 Worldwide Product Division Structure

The major advantage of the worldwide product structure is that it ensures a single line of communication for product information and technology. Further, this structure hopefully leads to the development of an international orientation amongst domestically influenced divisional executives. The disadvantages are also manifold. Firstly, with no central international focus there may well be a lack of communication and coordination between the product divisions. This can lead to significant inefficiencies in operation as each division may duplicate facilities in particular countries. In other cases divisions might not be able to justify the addition of particular functions such as local market research on their own which, in combination with other divisions, might well be viable. Secondly, not all the product divisions may be interested in developing their overseas potential. Unless top management actively encourages international development, therefore, divisional executives with a domestic orientation may continue to pursue the home market at the expense of overseas. Finally, it is unusual for all the product divisions of a corporation to be of the same size. As a result smaller units may lack the resources to pursue an active international strategy.

An example of the worldwide product division structure is RCA. After operating with an international division organisation for many years, the computer and electronics concern began to move toward a worldwide product division system in 1967. This transition was completed by 1970, with the company being divided into 17 'major operating units' each responsible for worldwide activities and profitability. The chairman of the board, who is also the chief executive officer, has reporting to him four staff group vice-presidents covering public affairs, industrial relations, legal affairs and corporate development, and the president of the company. Reporting to the president are central vice-presidents for manufacturing services and materials, research and engineering, marketing, finance and international operations. The 17 operating divisions also report to the president through four executive vice-presidents.

Each of the staff groups have global functional responsibility. In addition the vice-president for international operations, with a small staff, is responsible for providing informal liaison and coordination among the operating units around the world. There are two aspects to this, internal and external. In the first the department smoothes relationships and coordinates the divisions' activities. Externally, the international vice-president represents the corporation in relationships with major suppliers and customers, governments and financial institutions.[4]

The Use of Local Umbrella Companies

RCA also illustrates a difficulty which occurs in the worldwide product division structure. The presence of a significant number of divisional operations in a particular country can lead to legal and fiscal difficulties, and leave the MNC poorly represented in negotiations with local governments. This has led to the relatively widespread formation of umbrella companies which legally coordinate the individual interests of product divisions under one local corporation, as shown in Figure 2.8. In the RCA case all activities in the UK, for instance, are placed under a local holding company, although the operating divisions act independently, and for management purposes report directly to their respective US division heads, while the holding company chairman would normally be vice-president for international.

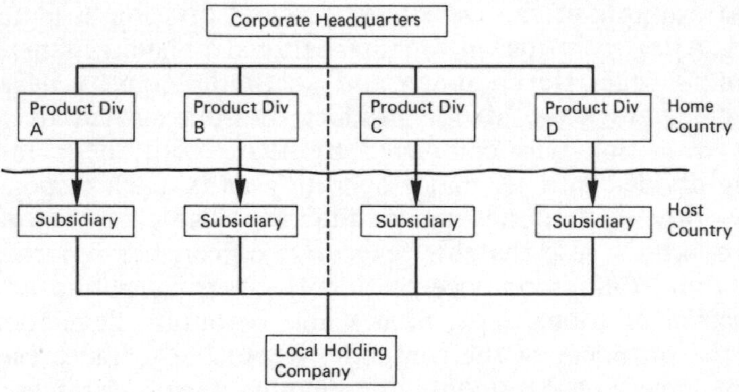

Fig. 2.8 Local Umbrella Company Structure

The creation of local holding companies does tend usually to add more than a purely legal form, however. Often it intensifies the product/geographic coordination needs and tends to lead to the further development of an area coordination organisation as described in the next section. In general a number of advantages and some disadvantages are associated with the adoption of an umbrella company including the following:[5]

Advantages

1. It presents a unified corporate face to government and the local market.
2. It provides a communication channel for details regarding existing and future operations necessary for divisional coordination.

3. It helps resolve local interdivisional differences.
4. It provides an overall corporate perspective on local opportunities.
5. It provides channels of communication with the parent.
6. It reduces duplication of effort when each division attempts to learn about a country.
7. Tax advantages are often available by writing off losses in one division against profits in another.
8. Consistent personnel policies can be introduced which also aid union negotiations and facilitate interdivisional transfers.
9. The consolidation of divisional funds tends to permit more local borrowing.
10. The subsidiary improves the ease of parent company control and provides a basis for centralised international money management.

Disadvantages

1. The establishment of a legal and administrative umbrella can result in lower morale amongst local divisional subsidiaries, accustomed to high levels of independence.
2. The emphasis on the parent company rather than local subsidiaries can heighten nationalist feelings.
3. In some countries, such as Germany, there are serious legal and fiscal disadvantages.
4. The presence of an overall national subsidiary can lead to conflict between the geographic and product organisations and a striving for increased local control by the national company management.

Area-Based Organisation Structures

The local umbrella subsidiary can be seen as a form of geographic organisation structure. In fact there are several variants of this form which are often confused with one another but which tend to be used in very different strategic circumstances.

Area-Functional Structure

Conditions favouring this structure:

1. Low level of product diversification;
2. High levels of regional product differentiation;
3. Economies of scale in production on a regional basis;
4. Low levels of interregional trading.

The first such form is the area-functional divisional organisation of the kind which tends to be used by firms with narrow product lines and is illustrated in Figure 2.9. Such firms tend to organise their global interests on a highly integrated basis in any region of the world and to link individual national manufacturing and marketing activities within a region into integrated, interdependent operations. In some cases regional product design is undertaken, while pricing, distribution, promotion and production within a region tend to be centralised and determined at the regional division headquarters.

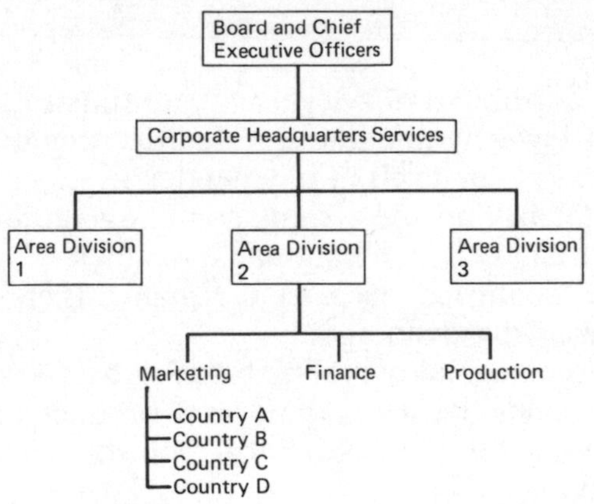

Fig. 2.9 Area-functional Organisation Structure

Ford Motor Company has moved from an international division to an area division structure. In 1967, the company established its first regional headquarters with the formation of Ford of Europe, a UK-based company charged with integrating together Ford's various automobile manufacturing and marketing operations throughout Europe. Prior to this time Ford had had two main manufacturing plants in the UK and West Germany, each of which operated essentially independently of the other, producing separate model ranges. Moreover, these model ranges tended to reflect the specific characteristics of their respective home markets and catered less for the needs of other European markets where Ford did not have a manufacturing presence.

The new organisation was therefore expected to move towards the introduction of a single European range of cars and trucks, with manufacturing being specialised in particular locations, so offering economies of scale. Moreover, new investment could be strategically located to reduce political risk, as well as to permit the economic manufacture of specialist components, such as automatic transmissions, previously not viable, without the economies of scale of integrated model design. Other advantages expected were an increased sales presence in countries other than Germany and the UK, protection against local component suppliers' strikes; improved purchasing power; economies of scale in marketing, promotion, distribution and spare parts stocks; and the reduced duplication of expensive services such as model design studies and test equipment.

Area Product Divisional Structure

Conditions favouring this structure:

1. Very large MNC activities involving a network of product and geographic interests and no home market dominance;
2. Need to provide extreme coordination on an area basis between local national activities;
3. Product flow between national subsidiaries high within regions but relatively low between regions.

The second, increasingly widely used, regional structure is the area-product divisional organisation which is illustrated in Figure 2.10. This type of organisation is an extension of the local umbrella company principle and is widely used by diversified companies as a means of coordinating and controlling operations for a variety of product areas within a geographic region. Such regional holding companies may also offer significant fiscal and financial advantages which are discussed more fully in Chapter 6.

This type of organisation represents the most complex matrix form of organisation which tends to be widely used, requiring multi-level product and geographic coordination and integration

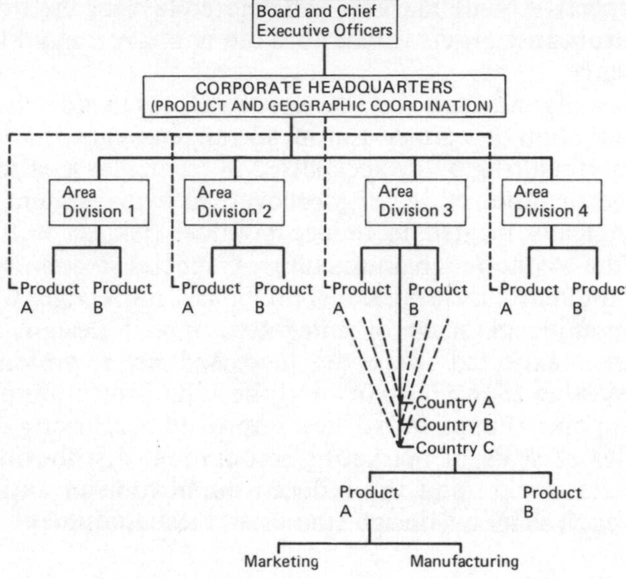

Fig. 2.10 Area-product Organisation Structure

and usually involves multiple executive reporting relationships. The area division becomes in many respects a regional headquarters and is often seen as a localised extension of the corporate headquarters. The use of this form of organisation tends to be concentrated in very large MNCs which have an extensive network of overseas product and geographic interests. As overseas operations become an increasingly important element in the overall activities of the enterprise, there is a felt need that they must be closely supervised in order to prevent any serious losses of control. A regional headquarters, therefore, performs this type of role as well as reducing local frictions and ensuring co-ordinated activity. Moreover, it is still possible to use expatriate managers to fill key positions in regional offices, to ensure that close linkages with the headquarters culture are maintained.

Such structures have tended to be introduced first in particular areas. Thus many US companies have initially established a European or Latin American headquarters, before extending the principle on a global scale, the ultimate move being the treatment of North America as one such area. Regional headquarters operations tend to be located in favourable tax environments such as Panama or Switzerland, although in the former case such a location for a holding company may not actually result in a physical presence, as is explained in Chapter 6. Nevertheless, many companies have regarded central location, good transportation and communication facilities, and proximity to business information, governments and supranational agencies to be key factors in selecting a suitable site. As a result other major centres in Europe include Brussels, and to a lesser extent, London and Paris.

An example of such a matrix organisation is offered by Corning Glass, which has sales of over $1 billion with over 30 per cent of these generated outside the USA. The company operates 42 production plants, and has over 50 per cent of its work force and offices in 23 countries outside the USA. The company had had an area-based organisation since 1965, with three area managers for non-US operations being responsible for profitability in their respective areas. Then in 1972, in response to a growing degree of product line diversity, Corning introduced business managers into its international structure. The chief responsibility of these men, of whom there are four, is to take a long-term strategic view of Corning businesses worldwide, regardless of geographic boundaries.

To assist the business managers, Corning introduced seven 'world boards', each responsible for coordinating strategy for a closely related group of products. These groups in the main correspond with the seven US product divisions, into which home country operations are divided. Previously, the area managers were responsible for liaison with the US divisions, but now the business managers perform this role and also have contact, within the world boards, with executives of foreign affiliates within the area managers' domain. One effect of this has been the development of a certain amount of 'creative tension'.[7]

This type of tension is common to product geographic matrix structures, and tends to emerge from the often differing viewpoints posed by adopting a product versus a regional perspective. The case of Corning illustrates perhaps the more common, and often higher, degree of tension, which emerges when the need for global product coordination is introduced into an area-based organisation. Although still present, this tension is not usually as great amongst product-based organisations, when an area-based coordination structure is overlaid on the existing product structure.

The Mother–Daughter Structure

Characteristics of this structure:

1. Overseas subsidiaries often old-established and designed to service individual national markets;
2. Little management contact with the central office except personalised board level exchanges;
3. Parent company domestic organisation often a holding company structure;
4. System primarily found amongst European MNCs.

One major reason for the lower degree of tension in product-based organisations is that there has not usually been an extended history of local autonomy, which has been developed under an established local umbrella company. The clear establishment of local custom and precedent is not, therefore, seen as being removed by the introduction of a regional headquarters system. By contrast the introduction of area or global product coordination systems onto geographic structures is often a cause of significant tension. This is especially true in mother–daughter structures as illustrated in Figure 2.11.

This form of organisation is still widespread amongst European MNCs, which in many cases first established their overseas affiliates in earlier periods of development, when geographic distance tended to equate with difficulty of communication. As a result, such local offspring were expected to stand on their own feet and contact with head office tended to be limited to occasional visits by top management. Further, such subsidiaries were often formed with a particular competitive advantage which enabled them to survive without recourse to central resources. Many such subsidiaries were formed in colonial territories administered by the parent company's home country, where they enjoyed strong tariff protection. The relations between the parent and its subsidiaries were therefore essentially those of a holding company with high local autonomy remaining, except in areas of large-scale capital investment and provided a suitable annual dividend was usually produced for the parent. The parent itself was also rarely structured in a cohesive manner, many operating in their home markets with a mixed holding company-functional structure.

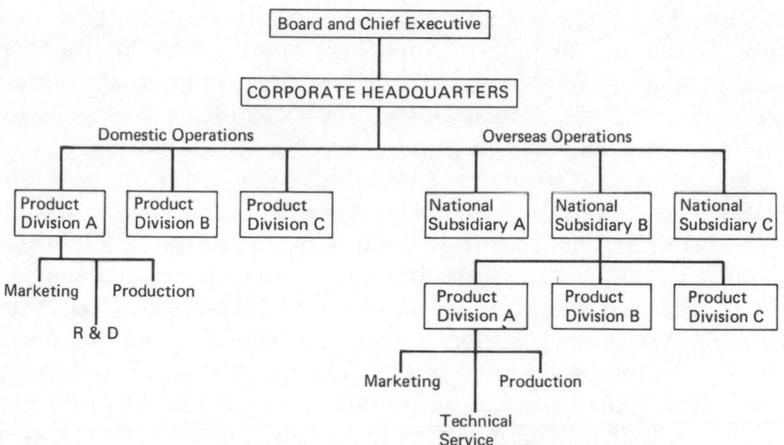

Fig. 2.11 Mother–Daughter International Structure

Increased competition, the loss of tariff protection and the growing homogeneity of international markets have pushed mother–daughter structures towards closer coordination, along the lines of the divisional structures discussed previously. In companies such as Philips and Unilever, where local subsidiaries had enjoyed a high level of autonomy, product coordination has been introduced despite significant resistance from entrenched local subsidiary managements.

This was especially true in the case of Philips, where during the Second World War, the parent company was completely cut off from its principal overseas subsidiaries during the Nazi occupation. The company had, moreover, taken substantial precautions in preparing for the war, and had placed its overseas interests, in North America and the British Empire, in two specific trusts which theoretically reduced the possibility of parent company control. Many of the company's research and management staff were also evacuated to overseas subsidiaries.

As a result, by the end of the war when the overseas staff returned to Holland, the subsidiaries had developed many products unknown to the parent and were operating completely independently. The task of re-establishing central coordination has, therefore, proved difficult and the national subsidiaries have often resisted and resented moves by the central product divisions to plan on a global basis when this has meant a loss of activities under their control.[8]

Some European companies have actually allowed their local subsidiaries to continue to pursue an autonomous line, adding new product market areas which are not found in the parent corporation. Reed International, for example, a British-based multinational engaged in paper, packaging and building products, operates a structure composed of a series of domestic product divisions and overseas geographic divisions. These overseas activities were traditionally managed using a mother–daughter structure. In Australia and South Africa, however, all Reed International subsidiaries have been consolidated under local umbrella corporations, shares in which have been sold locally. These concerns, while in the main staying within the product market scope of the parent, have also moved into new activities, such as wine-growing in Australia, which are unknown elsewhere in the group.

Many European companies have, however, begun to adopt a regional grouping approach like their US counterparts, especially in those technology- and process-based industries, where economies of scale from wider geographic groupings are possible. As a result many such firms have structures similar to the Corning model, with a series of domestic product divisions and a number of overseas area divisions. The liaison problems between overseas area and local product divisions usually remain unresolved, however, and few European firms have as yet adopted business-unit-based management structures.

Mixed Structures

The major structural forms which can be identified in MNCs and outlined above are seldom found in a completely pure form. Rather corporations are constantly changing, as is the environment in which they operate, and as a result it is common to find companies operating with mixed or hybrid structures.

One such fairly common hybrid is the combination of an international division structure coupled with worldwide product divisions. This structure tends to get round some of the disadvantages noted for each and in particular it provides a partial solution to the problems of different divisional sizes and of very disparate activities. For example, many US pharmaceutical companies which have entered the market for toiletries and cosmetics by acquisition have found subsequently that despite much commonality in the channels of distribution, other factors such as pricing, new product development and promotion are distinctively different. As a result, several pharmaceutical firms have moved their overseas consumer products from an international division to the domestic consumer division, so creating a worldwide product division. Other such hybrids include Uniroyal, which handles most products through its international division, while chemicals and plastics are organised as worldwide product divisions; all products except refractory materials, prosthetic devices and certain consumer products in Pfizer are handled by an international division; and American Can, whose international division handles some 90 per cent of overseas business, has separate worldwide divisions for chemicals and fashion products.[9]

In addition to this type of hybrid structure a further form is found associated with highly diversified and conglomerate corporations and where different international structures are found most appropriate for different business areas. Thus for example IT&T has different organisational forms for its telecommunications, electric appliance, hotels and insurance divisions according to the particular needs of the specific businesses.

While it will be more common that a highly diversified conglomerate will utilise such mixed structures to manage very disparate businesses, relatively few MNCs have all their businesses at a similar stage of product and geographic development. Thus some variation on the relatively pure organisation forms discussed is to be expected. However, it is important to examine the characteristics of each major business and determine what structure is most appropriate for it rather than trying to apply a universalist solution. As a result it is probable that mixed structures will become increasingly common as product market diversification continues and the corporate headquarters role will become one of managing an investment portfolio of businesses with only limited relationships between one another.

THE IMPACT OF LEGAL STRUCTURES

Home Country Mergers

One further reason why much less central control exists amongst European MNCs is the manner in which many have been created. A significant number of the largest European MNCs are in fact the result of local industrial rationalisations, often government-inspired, which have led to a strategy of industrial concentration in a bid to fend off increased competition, especially from expanding US-based MNCs. Further, in some European countries it has been a tradition for cross-shareholdings to exist between firms and for firms to combine in new joint ventures. Such complications make clearly defined structural organisations difficult to achieve.

In 1972, for example, the merger was completed between Pechiney and Ugine Kuhlmann, both of which had extensive interests in aluminium and in France operated a joint sales company. Ugine Kuhlmann, however, itself only created in 1966, was also significantly diversified into chemicals via Kuhlmann and steel products via Ugine. The result of the merger with Pechiney therefore created a highly diversified enterprise but there were severe difficulties in the introduction of a suitable organisation structure. Although, in the main a product divisional system was adopted, this is complicated by the fact that the aluminium business is in the hands of three executives at divisional chairman level, one of whom is the product chairman while the other two are responsible for geographic regions. A further problem is created by the continued existence of a large number of subsidiaries and associates with varying degrees of ownership and cross-holdings, some of which are also publicly quoted stocks. One 70 per cent owned investment company, for example, owns one-third of Pechiney's principal copper converter, and 40 per cent of the group trading subsidiary in the USA, which in turn holds 70 per cent of Howset, a US aluminium company.[10]

Transnational Mergers

The structural problems created by mergers are compounded when these are transnational. A number of major MNCs have been created as a result of transnational mergers, the most long-lasting of which are the Royal Dutch Shell Group and Unilever. These companies, created during the 1920s, have both adopted a twin holding company approach with identical board structures operating the main management companies, as is illustrated by the Shell structure shown in Figure 2.12.

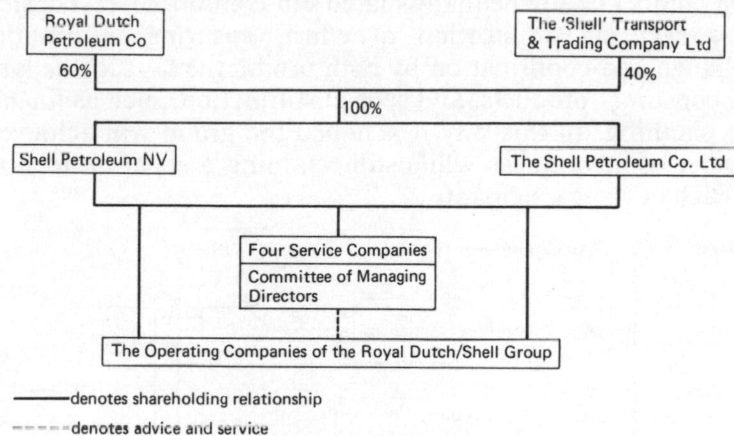

Fig. 2.12 Royal Dutch Shell Group Structure

These organisations, both formed as near equal mergers of partners in Britain and Holland, initially continued to act in nationalistic ways with relatively little true integration taking place. It has taken many years for both concerns to integrate to the point where each acts as a cohesive unified group. This slow process of integration has still to take place amongst the other major post-war transnational mergers, such as Agfa Gevaert or Dunlop Pirelli. Initially, in such creations it is difficult to change the habits of the participants to ensure that they identify with the combined enterprise rather than the component element with which they are familiar. Moreover, unlike in an acquisition such firms do not exhibit a clear dominance of authority by one element over another. Rather there may be carefully constructed legal safeguards to ensure key positions pass back and forth between the participants, so tending to sustain separation rather than unification.

In the case of Dunlop-Pirelli, for example, the structure of which is shown in Figure 2.13, a twin holding company approach was adopted whereby management responsibilities remained with the individual parent companies, with both partners being represented on the boards of all group companies. At the top of the structure is a central governing committee consisting of eight members, divided equally between Dunlop and Pirelli. This committee meets monthly and its chairmanship alternates between the parties. Beneath the central committee are a number of other equally shared sub-committees responsible for preventing duplication of effort, ensuring information exchange and coordination by both product area, such as tyres and consumer products, and specialist function, such as finance and planning. In this way it is hoped the group will achieve a number of advantages while still retaining a separate identity for each of the participants.

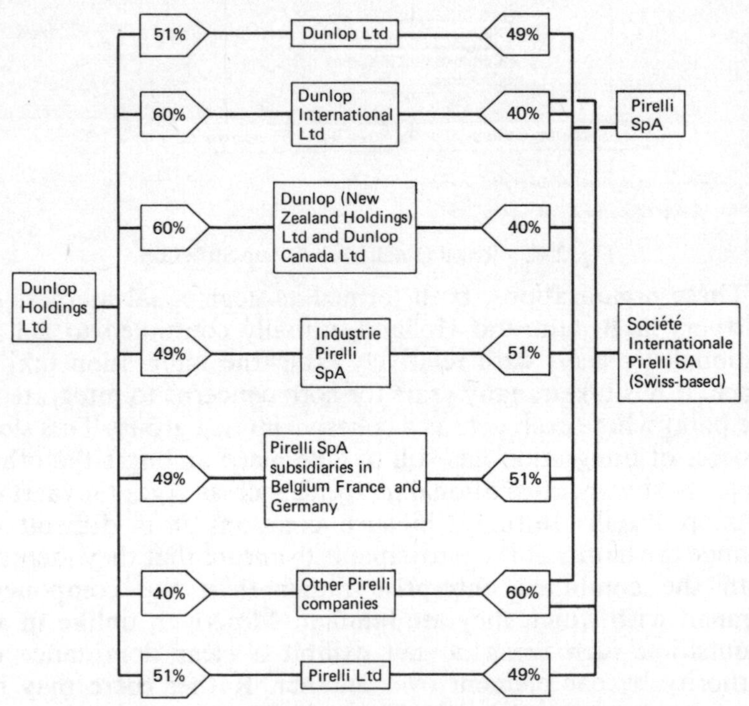

Fig. 2.13 Dunlop-Pirelli Holding Company Structure

THE JAPANESE APPROACH

The evolutionary trend in organisation design described has

mainly been based on the development of US corporations, although with some significant differences European concerns broadly develop in a similar way. The cross-shareholdings widely found in some European countries, however, coupled with an increasing tendency for shared ownership and local joint ventures will make the US model more difficult to implement. The Japanese organisational system may therefore become a model, which with cultural adaptation may be more common. This is illustrated in Figure 2.14 which shows the web-like structure of a family of enterprises around the axis of a central trading company linked to a major bank.

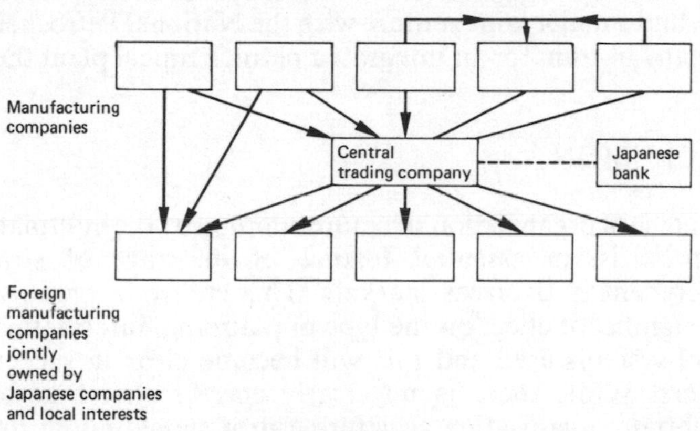

Fig. 2.14 Schema of Zaibatsu Structure including International Linkages
Source: adapted from R. Vernon and L. Wells, *The Manager in the International Economy* (Prentice-Hall (third edition) 1976) p. 32.

In the major Zaibatsu – Mitsui, Mitsubishi and Sumitomo – several leadership companies, usually consisting of a central trading company and a major bank, established a pattern for a larger number of other firms, many of which bear the family name. Today, however, although cross-shareholdings exist to a limited extent the central concerns do not have voting control over the satellite corporations. The central trading company acts as an intelligence centre, collecting information from around the world on market trends and identifying new growth opportunities. The bank acts as a source of finance for the group. Having identified new potential markets, where these do not clearly fit within the area of one of the group manufacturing satellites, a number of these may combine to create a new enterprise. For example, Mitsui Oil Exploration was formed in 1969 by 17 Mitsui Group companies; Mitsui Knowledge Industry Co., a 'think tank', was organised in 1970 by 19 Mitsui companies; and Nippon Atomic Industry Group Co. by 20 Mitsui group backers.

The Japanese have extended this system overseas and therefore are quite ready to form joint ventures in response to local government pressure, with Mitsui being perhaps the most active of the Zaibatsu. Amongst over 200 overseas operations concluded are a major copper and cobalt mining project by Mitsui Group companies and a number of local partners in Zaire, and a major joint venture with the National Petrochemical Company in Iran, for an integrated petrochemical plant there.[11]

CONCLUSION

The choice of organisation structure adopted by the multinational enterprise is an essential feature of its stage of strategic development in overseas markets. This choice of organisation has a significant effect on the type of planning, information and control systems used and this will become clear in succeeding chapters. While there is no clearly correct choice as to the appropriate organisation structure a firm should adopt for any particular point in its strategic development, some clear patterns do emerge.

Although the nomenclature is slightly different these patterns are illustrated in Figure 2.15, which traces the organisational evolution of the major multinational firms in the USA and Continental Europe. UK-based multinationals tend more toward the continental pattern than the American pattern.[12] The global structures category refers to the worldwide product, area and matrix structures discussed above. In Europe there has been a much greater tendency for mother–daughter structures to be adopted for overseas subsidiaries, coupled usually with a functional form of organisation at home. Reorganisation, when it has come, has tended to coincide with an ultimate realisation of a need to change the domestic organisation. As a consequence, most European firms have not experienced the international division stage, passed through by nearly 90 per cent of the 170

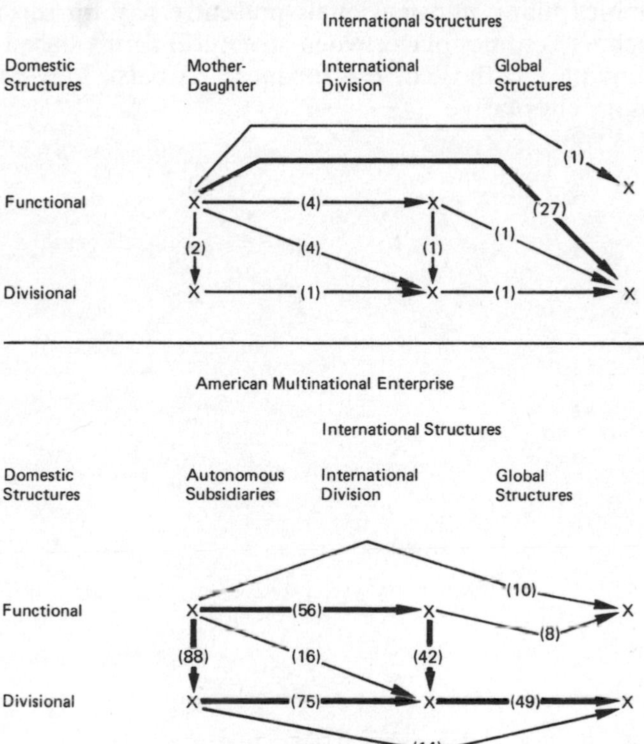

Fig. 2.15 International Organisational Evolution of Multinational Enterprise

Source: L. Franko, *The European Multinationals,* op. cit., p. 203.

American multinationals observed, which had usually found and adopted a divisional structure for their domestic operations somewhat earlier.[13]

While this pattern of organisational development is useful and will provide a major determinant in the choice of internal planning systems, the constraints on this pattern must be remembered. Firstly, major domestic, and especially, transnational mergers can play a dramatic role in shaping organisation structure which may make it difficult for some companies to adopt a specific structure in its pure form. Secondly, the growing trend to transnational joint ventures is causing many of the principles of clear lines of responsibility and central control to be sacrificed. In future, the advise-and-consent philosophies many multinationals presently pay lip service to may become commonplace, when structural forms based upon such principles as those of the Japanese Zaibatsu may become a necessary alternative.

3 Multinational Strategic Planning Systems

THE PROCESS OF MULTINATIONAL STRATEGIC PLANNING

Multinational strategic planning differs significantly from planning purely for domestic operations. There are differences in distance, culture and language which must be taken into account; markets are no longer essentially homogeneous but fragmented and diverse; the collection of market data is often difficult and the data itself suspect in accuracy; the environment in which business operates is also likely to differ from country to country, while the ability to manage political factors becomes much more important; and business is conducted in a variety of currencies which are themselves subject to varying values rather than in a single currency. Consistent planning assumptions are thus more difficult to establish as a result of differences in culture and business tradition, not only between domestic and foreign operations but also between foreign operations themselves.

There are also important differences in measurement and control systems. Implicit in the concept of planning is a rational, comprehensive future-oriented approach to decision-making based upon standardised procedures and methods of analysis. To aid the headquarters operation of the MNC in the crucial resource allocation process it is therefore useful to have similar, if not identical, approaches to planning throughout its operations in order to permit comparability and evaluation. However, differences in accounting convention from country to country, in attitudes to work measurement, different government requirements for disclosure and information – all impose constraints on the adoption of standardised measures and control systems.

There is no one way of planning in MNCs but rather there is

usually the need to ensure that adequate steps are taken to achieve strategy integration between business and geography and, in particular, to deal with the legal and fiscal complications of operating across national boundaries. In practice there are a number of factors which have an important influence on the type of planning system adopted. These include the degree and type of product diversity a company is engaged in; the amount and direction of cross-border product flow; the economics of the production process; and, to a somewhat lesser extent, the key characteristics of marketing and research and development policies. The planning process appropriate to a particular multinational also varies in relation to the decision-making powers appropriate at both different levels of the hierarchy, notably at local subsidiary, area and product divisions, and corporate headquarters, and the balance between the needs of product and geographic adaptation and integration.

The strategic decision-making powers in a multinational can actually be depicted as a form of continuum as in Figure 3.1.[1] At the early stages of multinational development overseas operations are small relative to the total and undiversified both by product and geography. There is therefore a low need for adaptation or a diversity of managerial approaches to cope with varying local conditions and a limited degree of interdependence between the overseas activities themselves. Such companies tend to be managed with an export or international division structure where planning systems are largely determined by the characteristics of existing domestic operations.

As overseas interests expand, the desire for managerial diversity to cope with different operating environments may increase simultaneously. When this is coupled with a low level of interdependence between overseas operations, the locus of relative power tends to reside in the geographic component of the organisation. Businesses in culture-bound consumer markets, such as food, tend to operate in this manner. As the need for interdependence increases, pure area-based structures move toward area-product matrix systems and the use of additional integrating devices such as area-product committees and the like. Where the benefits of worldwide or area integration are greater than the need to adapt to local conditions a product-dominated matrix tends to occur. Such businesses include high-capital-intensity, technology-based industries, such as chemicals,

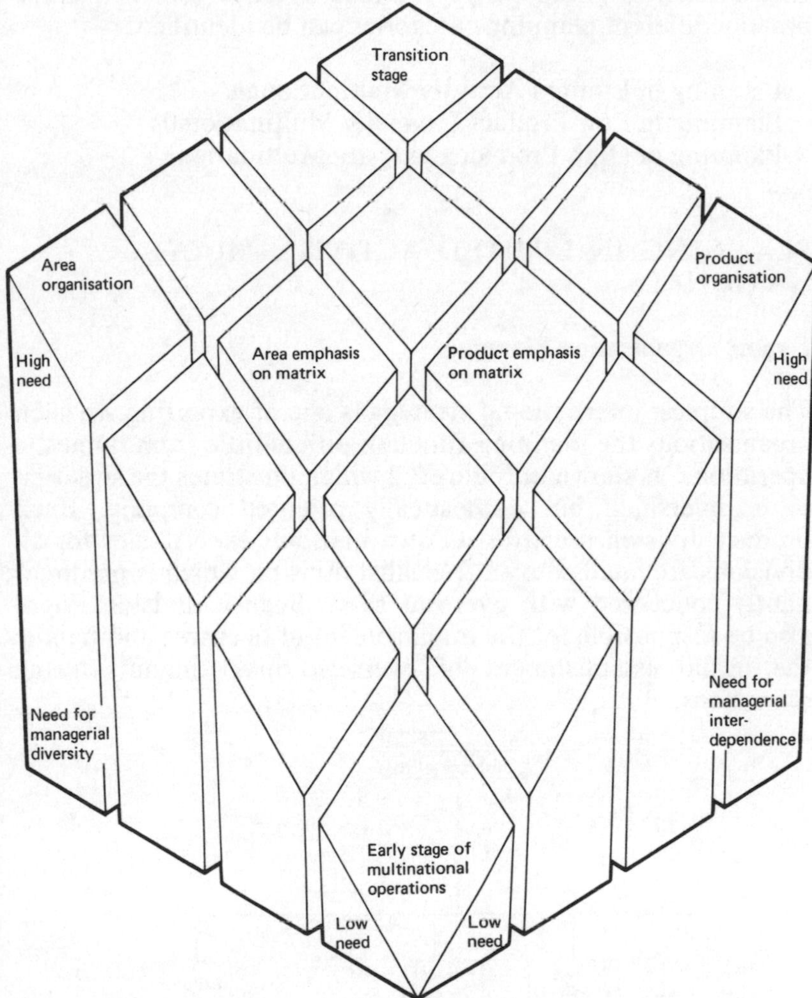

Fig. 3.1 Effect of Managerial Diversity and Interdependence on Relative Power in Decision-making in MNCs

Source: C. K. Prahalad, op. cit., p. 75.

and marketing-intensive firms with products that do not need to be culturally adapted.

The process of corporate planning in MNCs can therefore be examined in the context of relevant strategic and organisational characteristics. Although a continuum tends to exist, three broadly different planning categories can be identified:

Planning in Limited Activity Multinationals
Planning in Low Product Diversity Multinationals
Planning in High Product Diversity Multinationals

PLANNING IN LIMITED ACTIVITY MULTINATIONALS

Export Organisation Planning

The simplest international strategy is one of exporting. In such organisations the planning function differs little from domestic operations, as shown in Figure 3.2 which illustrates the situation in a diversified but domestically oriented company. Each product division prepares its own plan but export sales for all divisions are handled by a specialist division which is predominantly concerned with overseas sales. Such a division might also be responsible for the management of licensees and handle the initial establishment of overseas direct manufacturing operations.

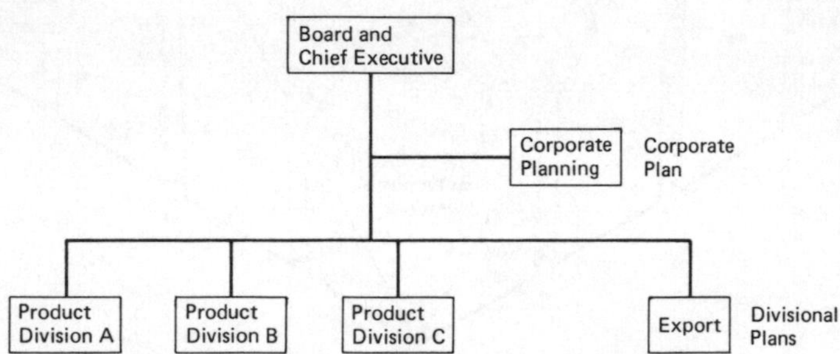

Fig. 3.2 Export Organisation Planning

At this stage of international development there are no overseas manufacturing plants to coordinate, although dependencies can exist between domestic operations and these may need to be integrated. While it is possible that such firms may be large and highly diversified it is more common for export organisations to be small or medium in size and/or relatively undiversified.

As a result such a company may have no need for a specialist planning function. Planning itself tends to be primarily budget-oriented. Each division normally prepares an annual budget and indicates its strategy by major function for the coming year or possibly somewhat longer. Strategy is mainly determined by the development of the capital budget which serves to commit the resources of the organisation on the basis of expected rates of return. Export sales activities are allocated priorities according to overall corporate objectives, but it is not unusual for exports to be treated as secondary to domestic requirements.

The principal planning activities are thus largely of an accounting nature. As a result planning is often contained within the controller's function. At the corporate level the principal planning task is the financial consolidation of divisional plans and possibly some qualitative conceptualisation of where the organisation should move for the future – this being largely determined by the Chief Executive Officer (CEO) and the board. The CEO in effect is also the company's chief planner, while planning itself is basically geared to short-term operational activities for which budgeting provides the formal mechanism for implementation.[2]

International Division Planning

The international division structure may be found associated with narrowly or highly diversified companies. The primary emphasis of such firms, however, tends to be domestic. The international division is responsible for both the management of overseas operations and the integration of the international activities of domestic divisions. The division thus contains most of the international expertise within the company.

Planning systems in international division structures tend to reflect the degree of product diversity more than any other factor, but where such companies are of a significant size a specialist planning department is usual. The degree of sophistication in planning varies substantially, however, but the dominant orientation is to the domestic operations.

At one extreme, the (American) General Electric Company, one of the most sophisticated planning companies, until very recently had significantly neglected international operations. Overseas operations were organised into an international division in turn subdivided into five divisions, Europe, Latin America, Far East, Middle East and International Sales. The first four of these were designated strategic business units (SBUs), while the fifth was a pooled export operation used by domestic product divisions. An SBU, as defined by General Electric, is a discrete unit which has an identifiable independent business mission, an identified set of competitors, is a fully-fledged competitor in an external market, is capable of integrated strategic planning and is multi-functional in operation. Such a business unit may be multi-product, multi-geographic market or some combination of both. We will frequently refer to business units in subsequent chapters and the General Electric definition of a discrete, multi-function independent unit coincides closely with our meaning.

Planning in General Electric is very well developed and in essence consists of strategic plans being produced at the level of the SBU which are then consolidated and coordinated centrally. The key control function in this system is via the resource allocation process, where corporate management allocates resources on the basis of the relative expected future of each of the SBUs.

Despite the sophistication of the General Electric planning system, elements of which are dealt with in greater detail in subsequent chapters, the system remains heavily oriented to domestic operations. International activities have been very secondary to growth within the USA, and as a result the company was very late in moving overseas with its traditional electrical engineering products. In 1974, after restructuring its European organisation, planning was tied much more closely to the US SBUs. This has led to an increase in interdependence in some areas and the first real development of an integrated global strategy largely in General Electric's newer areas of technology, such as medical systems and silicones and in service ventures.[3]

By comparison with the sophisticated planning of General Electric, some international division firms operate little differently to the simple export organisation described earlier. At this stage of international development in overseas operations therefore, when there is little interdependence and plants are normally present to serve the needs of local markets, the individual overseas subsidiary company may often enjoy a reasonably high level of autonomy over its operations, subject to the supervision of International division management.

PLANNING IN LOW-PRODUCT-DIVERSITY MULTINATIONALS

Manufacturing technology is a key determinant of both organisation structure and planning systems. This is readily observable in low-diversity companies when multinational activities are largely managed with area-based organisations. International integration in such firms is at the functional level and manufacturing technology largely determines the relative importance of such area and functional integration. In an oil company, therefore, where there is a considerable movement of product between geographic regions as well as within such regions there is a need for corporate level functional coordination. By contrast, in a business such as the production of industrial gases there is little movement of product across national boundaries and the need for integration of cross-border operations at the corporate level is minimal. As a result local subsidiary autonomy is usually high. Automobile production lies somewhere between these two extremes, with product design and manufacture tending to focus on a geographic region, such as Western Europe, but with limited amounts of product flow between regions. As a result, coordination takes place largely at the regional level with strong functional feedback to the centre. These differences are reflected in the planning systems adopted by such firms. In particular they result in different roles being performed in the planning process at the national company, regional and corporate levels of the organisation and on differing degrees of autonomy being granted to each. By and large the greater the degree of cross-border product flow the more coordination takes place at corporate headquarters and the corresponding reduction in autonomy at, first, the national company and, secondly, the regional level.

Planning in High Interregional Product Flow Businesses

In Company C, for example, a major European oil company, planning is established largely on a global scale utilising functional and regional inputs to head office which are coordinated centrally by a large corporate planning and economics staff unit. National company subsidiaries of Company C are predominantly concerned with products marketing, although the chief executive of such a company can possibly be partially responsible for manufacturing facilities located within his territory. Such manufacturing sites are also partially responsible to a central office manufacturing function.

The local subsidiary units prepare annual detailed market plans, subject to a series of central constraints sent out from the corporate headquarters covering factors such as product availability sourcing and certain transfer prices (such as the price of crude oil). These local units plans are returned to the centre via regional coordinators, who are located in the central office but with their own staff.

The regional coordinators are active in the preparation of local subsidiary plans and in their consolidation to a regional basis. The consolidated regional plans are also subdivided into the specific functional areas of oil production, refining, shipping and supply, engineering and marketing.

Oil is allocated from the central office on a global basis, bearing in mind the political necessities of oil production. At the same time the central office functional staff group establishes pricing limits, determines refining locations and arranges bulk transportation. In addition the corporate planning staff prepares its own long-term forecasts of the oil industry environment up to seven years ahead, which are fed into an overall group plan. This latter plan, which runs for five years, is concerned primarily with the allocation of oil and capital between the various functions. Finally, since the gestation period for major projects is so long the central planning staff also prepares a developmental facilities plan to examine major investment projects, capacity and technical requirements for up to fifteen years ahead.

The local subsidiaries, on whose boards the regional coordinators sit, can initiate capital expenditure requests for their specific areas, but any decision on these is established centrally in response to expected global requirements. The role of the local subsidiary, thus, is largely one of predicting expected future refined product demand, while corporate headquarters takes most of the major product allocation, pricing, transportation and capital expenditure decisions. This high degree of central coordination and control is considered necessary to ensure a balance in product flows on a global, rather than a regional, basis. A further problem is caused by the different time-horizons of the specific functions. Exploration, for example, can be heavily capital-consuming but does not produce returns for a considerable time; tanker purchases on the other hand can take several years from ordering to actual delivery; while marketing expenditure on gasoline stations might be much more near-term. Further, political considerations are constantly changing the environment in which the company operates.[4]

Planning in Highly Localised Manufacturing Businesses

In Company C, the planning system reflects a high degree of central decision-making which affects many elements of day-to-day operations. The local subsidiary plans, therefore, receive as given such factors as raw material prices, sourcing and product availability. Even at the regional level planning is very closely linked to corporate headquarters. Further, the nature of the business requires the development of long-range contingency plans at the centre, with no real inputs from the national companies. Integration also takes place at the centre, and while there is a degree of product integration between the multiple derivatives possible from refinery operations, the predominant area for planning integration lies between the various specialised functions.

By contrast to this high degree of central office involvement, BOC International, one of the leading world industrial gases companies, permits a high level of autonomy to its local national operating subsidiaries producing industrial gases. The international gases business is grouped into four geographic areas, UK/Europe, the Americas, Asia/Pacific and Southern Africa, each of which is made up of one or more national company subsidiaries. Almost all tactical and strategic decision-making, however, is done at the national company level except for major changes in capital structure, senior personnel appointments and decisions as to what business areas to be in. Corporate-level planning is therefore essentially concerned with resource allocation across the geographic and product portfolio of businesses. Meanwhile, at the local or regional level, BOC International's subsidiaries plan their own marketing, raw materials, exporting, market research, product design and specification, advertising, pricing and distribution. BOC International has diversified its interests, however, in recent years, and while these other activities are mainly organised in a similar way to gases, its Medi Shield division operates differently, with greater central control and coordination based on nationally oriented sales operations and internationally oriented manufacturing units.[5]

In its core business, therefore, BOC International illustrates the opposite extreme to Company C. The economics of producing industrial gases are such that production is located close to the consumers. As a result even transportation within national frontiers is relatively limited, while between countries it is very uncommon. As a result there is no way that the central headquarters has the necessary information to plan operations at the local level, nor is it able to intervene significantly except in the area of choosing how to balance its geographic portfolio of assets. Even here, however, the initiation of new capital projects resides at local level. The planning task in the business of Company A and BOC International thus reflect the cost structure of manufacture in particular. Other costs may have a similar effect in other types of business, for example, standardised brand marketing in some consumer products. However, manufacturing and logistics costs are almost always key determinants of the activities to be planned at each level in the organisation.

PLANNING IN HIGH-PRODUCT-DIVERSITY MULTINATIONALS

High-product-diversity multinationals tend to be organised as worldwide product divisional or area product matrix structures. Planning in such firms entails not only the development of plans covering functions, product markets and geographic areas but the means of integrating them, as illustrated in Figure 3.3. The precise nature of the planning task tends to be a function of the relative balance between interdependence and the need for adaptability to local conditions or managerial diversity.

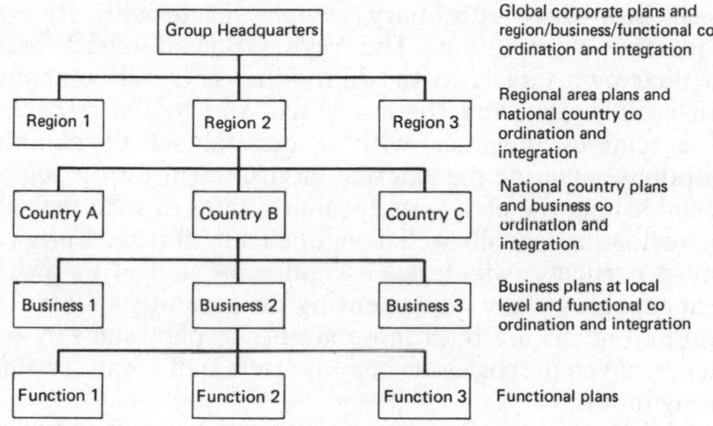

Fig. 3.3 Plan Activities in a Diversified Multinational

Planning in Multinationals with High Local Adaptation Needs

Planning in companies where high levels of managerial diversity are desirable tends to lead to more local operating control and limited strategic autonomy. In such firms, products must be adapted to local needs if they are to be successful and multi-country interdependencies tend to be low. Such businesses are typified by convenience food products where it is often necessary to institute product adaptation to cater for local tastes but where relative capital intensity is low, so permitting plant proliferation rather than a search for economies of scale from concentrated production.

Consider for example the planning system in Company D, a large US convenience food manufacturer. The system consists essentially of a five-year plan, the first year of which represents the operating budget. The planning cycle commences, some six months before the end of the current operating year, with the generation of a series of corporate objectives by the President and Executive Committee of the Board. These detailed expectations for the corporation as a whole cover return on investment, profit growth and the maximum permissible negative cash flow for the coming planning period.

The overall objectives are subdivided amongst the domestic product divisions and the overseas operations, which are grouped into three subsidiary regions each with its own headquarters organisation. The regional head offices break down their own targets to the individual national companies within each region, and these are sent out to the respective chief executives, together with a general set of planning assumptions, covering the external environment for the region, and establishing the plan assumption on rates of inflation. Not all the regions are equally well developed, and it is the European region in particular which has a significant staff of its own at present capable of fully implementing the planning system. The remaining regions are both more simple to plan and rely to a greater extent on the corporate headquarters staff for professional planning inputs.

The chief executive of each national subsidiary, upon receipt of the objectives from regional headquarters, then issues his own goals for the unit to local product division managers, together with the environmental assumptions and economic indicators, refined by the addition of specific local inputs. In addition he outlines the expected plan format and timetable for the planning process. The product executives flesh out the environmental information still further to build up a product-by-product picture. This allows each product to be planned individually according to how external conditions might specifically affect it.

The divisional executives, having completed their reviews, then pass this to the product managers ultimately responsible for the marketing of specific products. They, in turn, using information supplied upward from the sales force via sales managers, together with the environmental assumptions, prepare demand and price forecasts for the next five years. These initial forecasts are passed to the production and buying functions, who build up cost estimates and identify any production capacity constraints. Demand, price and cost estimates are then combined to produce profit projections, together with estimates of capital needs for any new capacity, working capital requirements and, hence, cash flow projections. In addition to these numerical forecasts the product managers also list their own objectives for each specific product, highlighting strengths, weaknesses, risks and opportunities and their short-term tactics to be used during the coming year. An explanation of performance variances from the previous plan of more than 10 per cent, whether positive or negative, is also provided. The numerical forecasts are also tested for sensitivity to changes in the environmental variables by means of a computer model. This model is also used for iterations outside the planning cycle to test the effect of competitive actions, raw material price changes and the like. Gaps identified between the expected performance and the objectives set from above lead to a search for new product opportunities or other means of improving performance, although product introduction planning does not itself form part of the annual planning cycle.

Some three months after the first inputs into the system come from corporate headquarters, the first draft of the plan is discussed between the product managers and their divisional executives. If the projections seem acceptable they are ready for upward transmission; if not, they are sent back and reworked at product manager level. When acceptable the divisional plans are vetted by the national chief executive and, after he has approved them, consolidated into an overall plan for the subsidiary.

At this point a 'flying squad' from the regional headquarters arrives in the local subsidiary to vet the plans again. This group, composed of a staff executive team drawn from a range of functions, goes through the plan with extreme care, making recommendations for amendments which would better fit the regional objectives. Although officially without executive authority the amendments proposed by the flying squad are usually incorporated.

Once completed the plans are presented by the chief executives of each of the local national subsidiaries at the regional headquarters. There they are again carefully scrutinised with members of the corporate headquarters planning staff in attendance. The local national plans are ultimately consolidated into an area plan, and presented at corporate headquarters with other area and domestic division plans before consolidation into the overall plan. In all the planning process lasts some six months from the President's original letter outlining corporate objectives.[6]

At the corporate level the key planning task is the balancing of resources between the portfolio of domestic product and overseas area divisions. This involves assessing the relative futures of each area in the face of economic, political and social factors linked to the range of products manufactured and/or sold in each area. This portfolio management is conducted essentially by central control over resource allocation. In strategic terms, therefore, local subsidiary companies enjoy little autonomy over *changes* in basic strategy but they are strongly involved in developing the strategies for existing product lines. Major capital commitments and significant new product introductions are all approved at the corporate headquarters, although it is unusual for a new product to be introduced against the advice of the local subsidiaries. In addition, some formulation changes are also often permitted to cater for variations in local taste.

The level of autonomy in Company D has, in fact, been reduced in recent times. This has occurred as the corporate headquarters have reorganised to gain greater understanding and control over international operations, many of which had been long established. The introduction of an intermediate regional headquarters was an important link in this process, since it provided corporate management with a second source of environmental information. Further, although not permitted high levels of capital expenditure discretion, the regional headquarters has a substantial influence on ultimate spending decisions with the corporate office usually deferring to the area management. One reason for this is that the area headquarters are usually managed at top level by US expatriates who are familiar with the political requirements of the corporation. As a result most regional headquarters organisations are largely seen as surrogates for the corporate headquarters, although in practice their close proximity to operations tends in time to lead regional offices to adopt a localised perspective. In effect, therefore, many such offices do become intermediaries in the process of planning negotiation between corporate and local management groups.

Planning in Companies with High Interdependency Needs

While food companies are diversified in terms of the breadth of their product range, they usually operate through the same distribution channels to similar consumers, and use like marketing techniques. Product-line management systems operate at the local subsidiary level and at the corporate level there is a need for integration across the product dimension.

Diversified high-technology companies such as chemical companies, however, sell their products often to a variety of end-use customers, sometimes via different channels, have a higher research requirement both to innovate and to service their product lines, which themselves tend to have a low need for local adaptation. Most importantly, there are usually substantial economies of scale in manufacture which make it desirable to concentrate production as much as possible. As a result such firms tend to plan around a product approach. These firms may also have a worldwide product division organisation or more commonly a product-oriented matrix structure incorporating intermediate regional headquarters.

The system in Company E, for example, a worldwide US chemical producer, is built around a series of area-based local headquarters, which report direct to the corporate central office. After an initial series of corporate objectives are laid down from the centre to each of the regional boards, planning is largely done by a series of product managers, each responsible for specific product lines throughout the entire region. These overall corporate objectives include a rate of profit growth, sales growth targets, market share objectives, expected levels of employee productivity, rates of return on existing and new capital, targets for new product introduction rates and social objectives covering quality of life and safety.

National-level general managers are involved to only a limited degree in the planning process, in that they essentially coordinate selling and statutory accounting activities within a particular country. They also meet annually at the early stages of the planning cycle to provide inputs for the establishment of basic assumptions on such factors as the economic climate and inflation for the product managers.

The product managers are responsible for all functions impinging on their products, including both line and staff activities. They are charged with analysing markets, evaluating competitive activity, product development requirements, pricing decisions and product acceptability. They prepare five-year sales forecasts by product and by country, which are then assigned as targets for the sales force in each national subsidiary. In addition they allocate production from specific plants to their ultimate selling points which are often outside the country of origin, although mainly within the region. Since economies of scale are usually significant, plant sizes are such that products are manufactured on a scale to service the needs of several countries. Moreover, individual product plants usually form an integral component of an overall multi-product manufacturing complex.

Coordination between regional operations is a headquarters responsibility. This is achieved both during the annual planning cycle and on an ongoing basis. During the planning cycle for example, a mutual exchange of information takes place covering sales, profits and expected expenses between domestic business division managers, functional management and area managers around the world. On an ongoing basis coordination occurs through a series of Business Unit Boards into which products are organised. Each of these is led by a business manager responsible for the profitability of the business on a global basis. Other members of the Business Board are representatives from the key functional areas of marketing, production, research, technical service and the treasury function. Product managers around the world report regularly on plan progress to their respective business board, while individual functional managers also have a line relationship to overall group functional directors.

In addition to coordination at the level of the individual business unit, overall corporate progress against plan is monitored by an executive committee composed of the chairman, president, vice-presidents and other functional heads. This group provides cross-communications between businesses, functions and areas, and influences and approves long- and short-range corporate objectives. The committee meets at least monthly to review sales and profit progress for each business against plan. Similarly, progress in each regional area is monitored against both profit plans and expected expense levels.

The product managers in Company E are not, however, responsible for the preparation of capital expenditure requests. Although the planning system may identify the need for capacity increases or new expenditure, the investigation of all capital projects is the responsibility of a series of business development managers who also establish policies for new product introductions. New capital spending plans can therefore be initiated at regional levels, after which they are first discussed by a capital expenditure committee before being rejected or passed on the area board for upward approval or dismissal. Ultimate decisions on all except modest operational expenditure requires US headquarters approval, although if capital requests are strongly recommended by the area board they tend usually to be accepted at the corporate level. Capital plans are submitted to the appropriate business board where they are again evaluated against a set of corporate level financial criteria, together with a consideration of any appropriate alternative considerations to the proposed expenditure. It is also the task of the executive committee to decide upon the allocation of corporate resources across the business units.

Planning in Company E is entirely a line operation. A corporate planning department exists at corporate headquarters but it is not responsible for planning line operations. The planning unit develops, administers and communicates the planning format, with each business, function and area being responsible for plan preparation. The consolidated effort is then submitted to the executive committee for evaluation and, if approved, submitted to the board of directors for ultimate consideration.[7]

The different balance between local adaptation needs and interdependence needs in Company D and Company E is reflected in the planning tasks assigned to the local subsidiary companies in each case. In Company D the local subsidiary is significantly involved in decisions dealing with all aspects of existing operations, including future cost and pricing plans, product formulation, and capital and capacity planning. In Company E these tasks are mainly conducted at the regional or even headquarters level with the local subsidiaries being mainly charged with market and demand planning.

Planning in Mother–Daughter Structures

The importance of product interdependence was apparent in Company E's planning system. There were no significant efforts made to tailor products for local markets and the regional headquarters had assumed much of the operating decision-making found at local subsidiary level described in Company D. While this pattern is generalisable amongst US multinationals, European companies have much less standardised planning systems, and local overseas subsidiaries often enjoy substantially greater autonomy with only formal, often personal, reporting relationships with corporate headquarters. Objectives are rarely formally stated and when they are they tend to be qualitative rather than quantitative. In part this can be attributed to a shorter period during which formal planning has been in operation in European firms. This informal attitude to strategic planning is common amongst companies operating with a mother–daughter organisation structure. However, the high technology European multinationals, or those where overseas operations are predominant, tend to be much more like their US counterparts.

Overall, therefore, the chosen strategic planning system for any MNC should reflect the particular needs of individual businesses with the nature and direction of product flow and manufacturing economies of scale being especially important. For multi-business organisations, the locus of decision-making, and hence plan content, varies according to the balance derived between cross-border operational interdependence and adaptability to local needs. While the degree of operational intervention at the corporate level varies, therefore, there remains an overall need to manage a portfolio of businesses with the primary dimension for decision-making alternating between area and product.

PITFALLS IN MULTINATIONAL STRATEGIC PLANNING

In the early part of the chapter we have concentrated on the differences between the planning systems in companies with different strategies. In particular we have described in some detail the planning process and the expected roles of different parts of the organisation in the preparation of strategic plans. Despite the now widespread occurrence of strategic planning in major corporations, however, many companies do not feel that they are achieving the best results possible from their planning systems. One recent international survey covering 460 firms drawn from the USA, Japan, Canada, the UK, Italy and Australia has attempted to highlight the major pitfalls to strategic planning. These are set out below in Table 3.1.

Table 3.1 The Ten Most Important Planning Pitfalls[8]

1. Top management's assumption that it can delegate the planning function to a planner.
2. Top management becomes so engrossed in current problems that it spends insufficient time on long-range planning, and the process becomes discredited among other managers and staff.
3. Failure to develop company goals suitable as a basis for formulating long-range plans.
4. Failure to create a climate in the company which is congenial and not resistant to planning.
5. Failure of top management to review with departmental and divisional heads the long-range plans which have been developed.
6. Failure to assume the necessary involvement in the planning process of a major line personnel.
7. Assuming that corporate comprehensive planning is something separate from the entire management process.
8. Failure to make sure that top management and the major line officers really understand the nature of long-range planning and what it will accomplish for them and the company.
9. Failing to locate the corporate planner at a high enough level in the managerial hierarchy.
10. Failure to use plans as standards for measuring managerial performance.

This list, drawn from 50 identified pitfalls, seems almost simplistic but it serves to clearly demonstrate the importance of planning as a behavioural and political process within the organisation. The understanding of this is vital for successful planning. There must therefore be a full commitment to a direct involvement in the process by the top management of the corporation, and great care must be taken to ensure full participation by line executives. Planning must not be treated as merely a staff exercise, nor can it be left to professional planners. For planning to be of value the whole organisation must be committed and educated to what is expected of them and how it should be done.

THE CONTENT OF BUSINESS UNIT PLANS

Most planning systems require the development of plans for each business over a period of three to five years. Often the first year of such a plan serves as the operating budget for the following year. However, because of the much greater levels of uncertainty inherent over the past few years, multiple estimates are becoming increasingly common for major quantitative factors according to alternative environmental assumptions. Additionally the high degree of inaccuracy experienced with forward quantitative estimates has led to the extension of qualitative argument in planning statements.

Typically plans for each business might include the following:

Business Unit Information Base
Key Assumptions and Business Unit Objectives
Budgets and Forward Estimates
Functional Plans
Action Plans
Resource Requirements

Business Unit Information Base

The plan for any business should be made against the background of qualitative and quantitative information which permits the business to be positioned relative to others in the corporate portfolio. Such information does not need to be collected each time a plan is prepared but merely updated. It is, however, a vital ingredient in the early development of the planning of any business. An abbreviated list of the key data collected on each business in one portfolio planning system is shown below:

Basic Business Data

1. Type of business, e.g. consumer durable, capital goods, distribution.
2. Age of product type, e.g. pre-1950; 1950–60; 1960–70; after 1970.
3. Life-cycle stage – introductory, growth, maturity, decline (may vary from region to region and country to country).
4. Date company entered business and category of entry, e.g. pioneer, early follower, late follower.

5. Patent protection category, e.g. product protected, process protected, unprotected.
6. Degree of product standardisation, e.g. high, moderate, customised.
7. Frequency of product changes, e.g. annual, seasonal, periodic, over one year, irregular.
8. Rate of technical change, e.g. major change in products and process within past six years, moderate change, little change.
9. Rate of new product development, e.g. less than one year, one to two years, two to five years, more than five years.

Customer Data

1. Customer type and percentage, e.g. households, manufacturers, government.
2. Number of customers; e.g. many, moderate, few (or use number code).
3. Number of immediate customers, e.g. less than 50, 50–1000, over 1000.
4. Customer concentration – (number of accounts accounting for 50 per cent of sales) e.g. high, medium, low.
5. Concentration trend over past five years; e.g. decreased, stable, increased.
6. Concentration relative to competitors; e.g. higher, about the same, less.
7. Purchase frequency; e.g. weekly or less, monthly, annually.
8. Purchase amount; e.g. less than $5, $5–100, $100–1000, $1000–10,000, over $10,000.
9. Purchase importance (purchase as per cent of annual spending); e.g. less than one per cent, 1–5 per cent, 5–25 per cent, over 25 per cent.
10. Importance of ancillary services; e.g. not important, some importance, vital.
11. Distribution of international sales; e.g. volume by region, by country.

Distribution Channel Data

1. Percentage of sales made to each of: end-users, owned distributors, wholesalers, retailers.
2. Percentage gross margin by wholesalers and/or retailers.

3. Relative vertical integration compared to leading competitors; e.g.
(*a*) forward; less, same, more
(*b*) backward; less, same, more.

Company Relationships Data

1. Percentage of total purchases of materials, etc., from within same company by location.
2. Percentage of total sales to other parts of same company by location.
3. Percentage of shared plant and equipment, etc., with other parts of same company.
4. Percentage of sales to same customers of other parts of the company.
5. Percentage of sales using same sales force, advertising and marketing programmes.

Capacity or Supply Limitations, Pricing Restrictions Data

1. Has there been any recent constraints on output due to scarcity of materials, scarcity of energy, scarcity of personnel, plant capacity?
2. Has the business been subjected to government price controls?
3. If yes, did this affect profitability?
4. Percentage capacity utilisation.

Supply Conditions Data

1. Percentage of total purchases from three largest suppliers.
2. What percentage of their total sales does the business's purchases represent?
3. Availability of alternative supply sources; e.g. easy, difficult, none.
4. Are any suppliers integrated forward?
5. Are any likely to be so?

Production Process Data

1. What sort of production process unit? large batch, small batch, continuous process.
2. What are economies of scale? high, medium, low.
3. Company's plant size relative to that of three largest

competitors, e.g. more than 2 ×, 1–2 ×, same, $\frac{1}{2}$–1 ×, less than $\frac{1}{2}$ ×.

4. Cost of transportation relative to product cost, e.g. over 10 per cent, 5–10 per cent, less than 5 per cent.

Industry Data

1. Industry concentration ratio (percentage of sales accounted for by four biggest operators).
2. Industry value-added per employee.
3. Exports as percentage of industry sales.
4. Imports as percentage of industry sales.
5. Growth rate in monetary terms over past ten years.
6. Growth rate in physical volume over past ten years.
7. Instability of volume sales over past ten years; e.g. no fluctuation, minor fluctuations, major fluctuations.

Market Data

1. Size of served market; e.g. sales value in money and volume.
2. Geographic coverage of served markets; e.g. all USA, Regional USA, EEC, UK, European Region, Middle East.
3. Number of competitors; e.g. five or less, five to ten, 10–20, 20–50, over 50.
4. Any new competitors taking over 5 per cent of market in past five years?
5. Any competitors with over 5 per cent of market leaving in past five years?
6. Market share of this business.
7. Market share of each of three largest competitors.
8. Index of prices over past five years (middle year = 100 per cent).
9. Index of basic materials costs over past five years (middle year = 100 per cent).
10. Index of average hourly wage rates over past five years (middle year = 100 per cent).

Comparison with Competitors

1. Relative product quality, e.g. percentage of sales superior, equivalent, inferior to leading competitors.
2. Relative selling prices (average level of selling prices relative to average prices of leading competitors); e.g. over

10 per cent higher, 0–10 per cent higher, same, 0–10 per cent lower, over 10 per cent lower.
3. Relative wage rates (average hourly wage rate relative to leading competitors); e.g. over 10 per cent higher, 0–10 per cent higher, same, 0–10 per cent lower, over 10 per cent lower.
4. New products innovation (percentage of total sales from new products introduced in past five years) for (*a*) this business, (*b*) leading competitors.
5. This business served market relative to competitors:

(*a*) Type of customer	less	same	more
(*b*) Number of customers	less	same	more
(*c*) Size of customers	less	same	more

Similarly the business's position relative to its major competitors is measured by a number of quantifiable ratios some of which will be easily obtainable while others may be guesstimated. These ratios include the following:

6. Relative sales force expenditure (total volume and as percentage of sales).
7. Relative advertising expenditure (total volume and as percentage of sales).
8. Relative promotional expenditure (total volume and as percentage of sales).
9. Relative technical service expenditure (total volume and as percentage of sales).
10. Relative capital intensity (total fixed assets and as percentage of sales).
11. Relative inventory cover (stocks as percentage of sales).
12. Relative sales per employee.
13. Relative fixed assets per employee.
14. Relative sales margins.
15. Relative return on investment.

The basic data included in the establishment of a business unit profile is useful for different purposes amongst the groups involved in plan preparation. At the business unit level, which may be based in the national company, region or worldwide product division, for example, the data provides the basis for the generation of operating strategy for the future. From the information, key factors for success and many of the relative strengths and weaknesses of the business can be identified. As a result, opportunities for future strategy can be observed and action plans for implementation developed, together with some indication of their relative importance. At the corporate headquarters the data serves two principal purposes. Firstly, it provides the basis for evaluating the position of the business unit relative to others within the corporation, and secondly it is the essential data needed to question the viability of proposed business unit plans at strategic review sessions.

The items listed above are not exhaustive and other factors may be considered especially important in particular businesses. Most of the data is relatively easy to collect but there may well be some difficulties in obtaining the financial information concerning other multinational and/or multimarket competitors where the business unit breakdown is not generally available. In reality surprisingly good guesstimates of this type of information can be obtained if resources are committed to developing it. Sources of such information are widespread but include the analysis of subsidiary operating returns often legally required in some countries, detailed review of trade journals, competitors' own company magazines, sales reports, statistical analysis and others. When this data is systematically collected it is possible to build up a detailed picture of a competitor's operations and, at the business unit level, identify relative strengths and weaknesses and possible reactions to changes in strategy. For multi-business competitors it is possible to build up the portfolio position for each one in order to assess the relative priority or importance attached to each particular business unit. One such system of detailed competitive analysis is shown in Figure 3.4.

Key Assumptions and Business Unit Objectives

In many MNCs local national companies play a major role in the development of planning assumptions as they affect the expected performance of the individual business unit. Alternatively such assumptions are established at the regional headquarters level from inputs by staff units, national operations and external consultants and forecasting agencies. In the main

Fig. 3.4 Summary of Competitor Analysis* Planning

Conceive/Design	*Produce*	*Market*	*Finance*	*Manage*
Technical resources	*Physical resources*	*Sales force*	*Long-term*	*Key people*
Concepts	Capacity	Skills	Debt/equity ratio	Objectives and
Patents and copyrights	Plant	Size	Cost of debt	priorities
Technological sophistication	Size	Type		Values
Technical integration	Location	Location	*Short-term*	Reward systems
	Age		Line of credit	
Human resources	Equipment	*Distribution network*	Type of debt	*Decision making*
Key people and skills	Automation		Cost of debt	Location
Use of external technical groups	Maintenance	*Research*		Type
	Flexibility	Skills	*Liquidity*	Speed
Funding	Processes	Type		
Total	Uniqueness		*Cash flow*	*Planning*
Percentage of sales	Flexibility	*Service and sales policies*	Days of receivables	Type
Consistency over time	Degree of integration		Inventory turnover	Emphasis
Internally generated	*Human resources*	*Advertising*	Accounting practices	Time span
Government-supplied	Key people and skills	Skills		
	Workforce	Type	*Human resources*	*Staffing*
	Skills mix		Key people and skills	Longevity and
	Unions		Turnover	turnover
	Turnover	*Human resources*		Experience
		Key people and skills	*Systems*	Replacement
		Turnover	Budgeting	policies
		Funding	Forecasting	
		Total	Controlling	*Organisation*
		Consistency over time		Centralisation
		Percentage of sales		Functions
		Reward systems		Use of staff

* If *multi-industry*, examine portfolio of businesses (size, priorities, importance to company) and resources provided by parent company. If *foreign*, examine national priorities of home country; degree of government ownership; supports and incentives; home market environment.

such assumptions reflect external economic and market conditions to be expected over the coming planning period. In addition, both external and internal assumptions may be listed as elements of the specialised functional plans of the business unit. Major economic and environmental assumptions, however, usually include factors such as:

Forecast growth rate in served market size
Forecast percentage changes in inflation rate by country
Forecast percentage changes in currency rates fixed by major reporting currency
Forecast percentage change in selling prices
Expected percentage change in raw material costs
Forecast percentage change in labour rates
Any anticipated changes in tax rates
Any anticipated changes in government financial incentives, legislative changes, trade restrictions, price control and the like.

Overall objectives for the business unit are mainly set in measurable financial terms. The establishment of objectives is normally a result of negotiation between the business unit management and corporate headquarters. This negotiation forms an integral component of the political and behavioural aspects of the planning process. The initial formal trigger which marks the start of the annual planning process is usually the issue of a series of overall corporate expectations on the part of top management – in many US multinationals this takes the form of the annual President's Letter to top business unit managers. Under traditional planning systems the general pattern of objectives might cover the following for the business unit as a whole over the forward planning period of around five years:

Return on sales
Return on assets employed
Changes in fixed capital
Changes in working capital
Cash flow
Level of self-financing
Market share.

Other specific objectives may be added according to the business and the position it is allocated in the corporate portfolio. Thus not all businesses will be expected to grow, but rather there will be distinctively different potential expectations for different businesses. This point is dealt with at length in the following chapter. Similarly, non-quantified objectives are becoming increasingly common, dealing with factors such as social responsibility, employee satisfaction and the like. The important consideration which must be met, however, is that the objectives eventually agreed should be consistent within themselves and with the functional strategies underlying them. In addition, the widespread move to multiple scenario planning should be borne in mind in the formation of objectives, with the expected performance changing according to alternative futures predicted.

Budgets and Forward Estimates

Frequently the first year of the strategic plan will also serve as the annual budget for the business unit. In some companies, however, the budgetary process is treated as a separate exercise. In practice this first year of the plan is by far the most accurate in quantitative terms. There are many reasons for this but clearly it is the time-period about which management can be most certain. Beyond the first year there is a strong tendency for plans to consist largely of extrapolation of the existing position. This phenomenon is modified in the case of multiple-scenario approaches which force managers to modify their forward views in the light of alternative future perspectives.

Budgets and forward forecasts are built up from the business unit functional plans and serve as part of the interfunctional integration process. Firstly, a sales volume forecast is normally generated, which in turn forms the basis of the production plan. These two in combination provide the basis for the generation of financial plans. The precise nature of the items to be budgeted varies somewhat according to the particular business but an example of the more common pieces of quantitative data (other than financial) collected are given in Table 3.2.

Functional Plans

Each of the main functional elements of the business unit

Table 3.2 Summary of Business Unit Quantitative Budgets and Forecasts

(1) Marketing	Overall served market volume (physical and monetary) Expected share Expected sales volume (physical and monetary) Sales by product line Selling prices Marketing manpower and expenses Measurements of productivity
(2) Production	Volume of output required Expected yields Capacity required Expected plant utilisation Additions to production facilities Materials, fuel and manpower required Production costs per product line Measurements of productivity
(3) Distribution	Volumes to be shipped by alternative methods Distribution facilities required Manpower required Distribution costs Measurement of productivity
(4) Research and Development	Planned improvements in production efficiency Planned improvements in process and quality Planned product development R & D costs Measurements of productivity
(5) Manpower	Overall manpower requirements Overall productivity measurements Management requirements

contributes to the overall plan and develops operating plans covering the particular function. These are often specific down to the targets for the individual salesman or plant supervisor. The functional plans and the assumptions which underline them are integrated together by the business unit management team usually composed of the functional department heads and the unit general manager. The type of content contained in such functional plans is illustrated below:

Marketing Plan

(*a*) *Objectives*

Objectives for the future five years in terms of: served market share, sales volume, selling prices and margins, marketing manpower productivity, new product introduction schedules.

(*b*) *Assumptions*

These usually consist of those listed under the business unit plan overall but may include additional assumptions such as new product availability, new market segment development, changes in regulations covering health, safety, new territorial markets etc.

(*c*) *Strategy and Action Plans*

These set out strategy for the coming five years for each of main activities such as organisation, distribution channels, product range, product mix, pricing policy and terms of payment, product rationalisation, regional coverage.

Where policy changes are made these are stated as action plans identifying who, what, where, when and why.

(*d*) *Resources*

This part of the plan sets out the resources needed in order to complete the action programmes and identifies the expected payoffs from plan achievement. Areas covered would include; advertising and promotion expenditures, market research costs, product development costs, etc.

Production Plan

(*a*) *Objectives*

Objectives for the future five years in terms of output volume, plant efficiency, capacity utilisation, maintenance efficiency, engineering development, labour productivity, inventory level ratios, value engineering.

(*b*) *Assumptions*

Additional assumptions might include estimates of technical

progress, assumptions about competitive processes, technology licensing arrangements, etc.

(*c*) *Strategy and Action Plans*

Strategies developed for the production function might cover activities such as; cost reductions, improved plant efficiency, closure of surplus capacity, improved labour efficiency, new plant introductions, etc.

Action plans would assign responsibility for particular programmes on a who, what, where, when and why basis.

(*d*) *Resources*

Areas covered would be capital plant expenditure, engineering, expenses, process development costs, value engineering costs and the like.[9]

Action Plans

The action plans developed as part of the business unit plan form one of the key elements of the planning process. They specify the actual tasks individuals are expected to perform in order to implement the strategy chosen to meet the unit objectives. Moreover, the action plans form the basis of agreed instructions and for measuring the performance of individuals. They also provide a series of controls which can be monitored in order to assess the progress of the plan and to pinpoint where further action needs to be taken to correct deficiencies in progress. Action plans should include the following key elements:

1. A reference to the objective they are intended to achieve and the strategy chosen;
2. A list of the specific action steps to be followed;
3. Statements of which person is responsible for each particular step;
4. A timetable, which also shows the time demand;
5. Who is responsible for the immediate overseeing of the activities;
6. A statement of the financial impact.[10]

Resources

The resources section of the plan summarises the resources

required to achieve plan objectives and highlights any additional requirements identified in the functional areas into five main categories, namely:

1. Land, buildings and equipment, etc., as fixed assets
2. Working capital requirements
3. Personnel needs
4. Finance needs
5. Miscellaneous

Fixed asset requirements are identified as part of the production plans in particular. Usually each significant project for capital investment is listed with a brief note giving its purpose, estimated cost and timing. Capital equipment projects are usually listed as either replacement, additional or new. Detailed capital proposals do not usually form part of the planning process but occur on an ongoing basis within the guidelines established by the planning system. The capital investment process is discussed further in Chapter 7.

Expansion usually leads to an increased level of working capital. This, too, is normally specified as part of the detailed financial appraisal for particular capital projects. In addition, changes in customer servicing levels and credit control can also lead to significant changes in the working capital needs of existing operations. Finally working capital needs can be significantly influenced by exchange rate fluctuations and inflation.

Personnel resources need to be stated in terms of requirements in numbers, categories and costs. In addition planned organisational changes should be taken into account to allow for succession, executive training and new appointments. The requirements for finance are identified from cash flow projections which reveal the resources available from internal operations and the gap which may need to be filled from external funding sources. Miscellaneous resource requirements may include the purchase of licences, external consultancy and the like.

Many of the specialised techniques now used for multinational planning are considered elsewhere in this book in some detail. The next chapter deals with portfolio planning systems while later chapters deal with aspects of financial and tax planning, capital budgeting and techniques for evaluating political risk and societal pressures. Two topics are usefully considered briefly here, however, together with examples of their use.

The Use of Contingency Planning

The need for flexibility and rapid response to environmental change has led to the widespread adoption of contingency plans. These are usually drawn up for immediate implementation once certain automatic triggering mechanisms, such as a decline in sales or a particular increase in costs, operate. While in the main they can be used for dealing with ongoing change, contingency plans can also be prepared to deal with discontinuous change such as the kidnapping of a key overseas executive, the bombing of a plant, the nationalisation of a company and the like. The relative hostility of the environment in recent years has almost certainly led to an overreaction which may well be tempered with time. However, at present it is very noticeable that most contingency plans are triggered by negative events. There has been a desire to reduce risk by cutting back both in investment and labour, and to concentrate on such factors as cash flow.

Royal Packaging Industries Van Leer BV, a major multinational packaging material concern, was led to adopt a global system of contingency planning following the oil crisis when it experienced wild fluctuations in the demand for its products. The system introduced gives each of the group's 70 worldwide operating plants detailed instructions and recommendations for dealing with sudden changes in demand. These include measures to be taken to avoid over-staffing during recession and the progressive steps to be taken when redundancy becomes inevitable. To anticipate contingencies, the group has also established an 'early warning system' for gathering details of the plans and prospects for major customers and even for ultimate users. *Force majeure* events such as major strikes, energy or raw material shortages, floods, fire and civil disturbances have also been planned for.

To cope with demand fluctuations the company in effect prepares seven budgets. First a budget is established for normal trading conditions. The remaining six budgets are intended for when business is better or worse than anticipated. These cover variations of 10 per cent, 20 per cent and 30 per cent above or below the expected norm.

When a subsidiary's operations are falling below normal, marketing and sales activities are accelerated to stimulate new opportunities. Products previously considered insufficiently profitable are introduced or actively promoted to maintain plant utilisation and employment. Overstaffing is met firstly by cutbacks in overtime, accelerated training programmes, changes in planned shutdowns and the introduction of short time. Ultimately when redundancies become necessary plans specify who should be laid off temporarily and permanently and what the company intends to do for them. Even under adverse conditions, however, maximum attention is paid to cash flow in contingency plans. Working capital is cut by higher credit controls while the headquarters determines cutbacks in investment programmes.[11]

Van Leer illustrates the relative simplicity of developing contingency plans and demonstrates the value of producing these during stable times rather than when actually faced with an emergency situation. Computer models are more sophisticated in evaluating the effect of external change and providing trigger points or allowing plans to be rolled over more frequently. Such models, although more complex than the Van Leer system, need not be overcomplicated. Although companies can usually trace some effect on operations to hundreds of factors, most actually concentrate their attention on the eight or ten variables most crucial to their industry, such as inflation rate, salary rate increases, consumer spending on non-durables and the like.[12]

The Use of Scenario Planning

Scenario planning tends to be more complex and much less precise. Scenarios attempt to establish possible consistent future environments against which the particular characteristics of the requirements for the individual firm must be matched. In reality the variables that need to be predicted in order to build up such a view of the future can be assessed with varying degrees of confidence. Six classes of variable can actually be identified thus:

1. Relatively stable (e.g. the number of persons entering the labour force).

2. Slowly (exponentially) changing (e.g. productivity).
3. Constrained (e.g. Kuwaiti short-term absorptive capacity for money).
4. Critical but uncertain (e.g. GNP growth rates, energy pricing).
5. Accidental but significant (e.g. key personalities, legislation, regime changes).
6. Incalculable (e.g. complex variables such as social values, inflation).

Many factors for a future scenario can thus be predicted with reasonable accuracy from trend evaluations and the like. For the more uncertain factors other techniques such as delphi and cross-impact analysis can be used or ultimately reasonable values might be guesstimated and later checked for sensitivity.

The key features of scenario planning are set out in Table 3.3. Normally no more than a few true alternative future scenarios should be built up to avoid overcomplication and it is important not to confuse truly different scenarios of the likely future with the marginal change budgets adopted by Van Leer which tend to relate to the near future. The range of scenarios is built up to coincide with the length of future particularly useful for the individual firm. Xerox Corporation for example has pushed its long-range planning parameters out past 1990 and has five alternative futures under review.[13]

Table 3.3 Features of Scenario Planning

Scenario Planning endeavours:
- To cope with the possibility of many different futures
- To provide scope for considering less likely possibilities, threats and opportunities
- Thus to provide greater scope for imagination and flair in perceiving major discontinuities

Scenarios should thus:
- Illuminate relevant uncertainties
- Broadly scan likely futures
- Be internally consistent
- Be dynamic and evolutionary
- Be comprehensive, simple, adaptable and usable

The leading international oil companies too have been forced to develop scenarios for looking far ahead to plan for the changing pattern of energy supply and demand and the increasing complexity and longer lead times of investment decisions. Figure 3.5 illustrates how changing social conditions led to the development of three such base case scenarios in the Royal Dutch Shell Group.

The approach of the General Electric Company has led to the development of four basic scenarios. First, the company identified nine separate views of its future business environment dealing with probable developments in international defence, social, political, legal, economic, technological, manpower and financial environments. In each case a 'brief' historical review of the previous decade is produced, major forces for change analysed and potential discontinuities and events predicted, together with some idea of their expected probability and likely impact on General Electric. Finally the policy implications of these forecasts are raised.

The separate forecasts in these segments are then integrated using cross-impact techniques. From the hundreds of specific trends and events identified, the 75 or so with the highest combined weighting and importance are selected and the impact of each on the remainder assessed. From this cross-impact analysis, domino chains with one event triggering another are constructed in order to generate four final internally consistent scenarios of the medium-term future.[14] Against the backdrop of the possible future scenarios the implications for the company can be assessed and contingency plans laid for strategic changes to be made according to which scenario actually begins to take place.

CONCLUSION

This chapter has reviewed briefly the complex process of multinational strategic planning. By the use of actual examples the process was described as it changed in line with certain key characteristics of the basic business and the organisation structure of the corporation. The most important pitfalls to successful planning were identified and observed to be largely concerned with the behavioural and political aspects of the planning process rather than its technical content. In addition

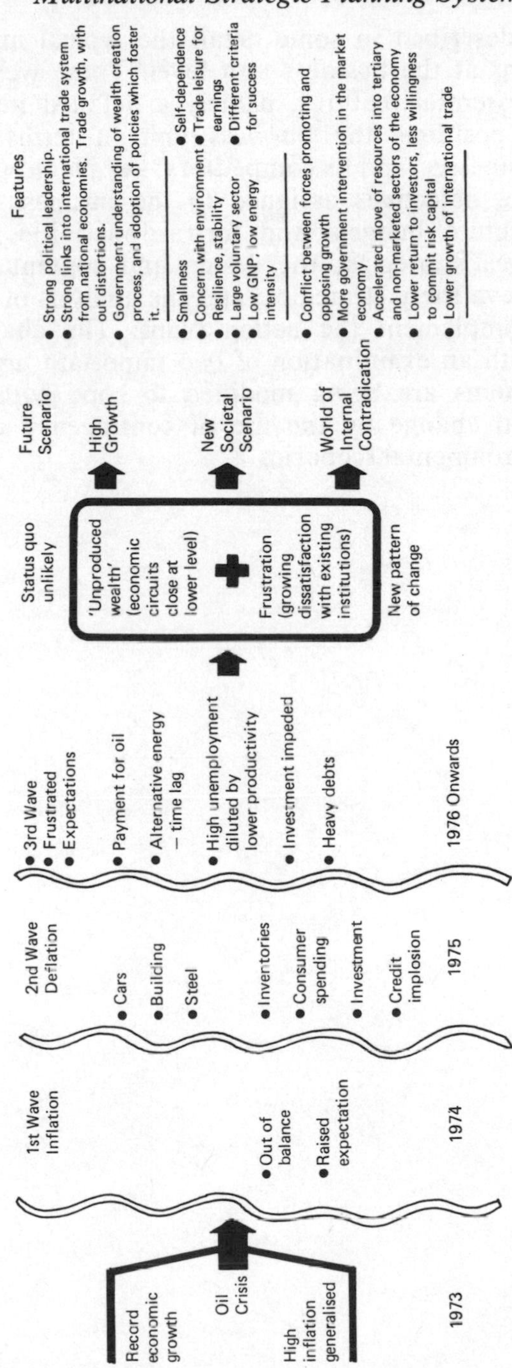

Fig. 3.5 The Development of Base Case Scenarios

Source: Royal Dutch Shell Group

the chapter described in some detail the typical make-up of strategic plans at the business unit level. These were seen to include six essential features, namely a detailed information base which positions the business unit in terms of other corporate businesses, and its competitors; key planning assumptions and the objectives assigned to the business unit; the content of future budgets and forward activities; detailed functional area strategies; the design and content of action plans to achieve these strategies; and the analysis of resources required to implement the action plans. The chapter then concluded with an examination of two important areas where planning systems are being modified to cope with external environmental change by the use of contingency plans and multiple environmental scenarios.

4 Strategic Portfolio Planning Systems

By definition multinational corporations operate in a number of countries. Moreover most MNCs also operate in a variety of different product market areas. As a result the key task for top management is the successful operation of a portfolio of businesses spread across a number of geographic markets. In recent years, therefore, there has been a rapid growth in the development of strategic portfolio planning systems designed to aid strategic decision-making in the multibusiness firms. While these systems are becoming increasingly widely used they are not without their problems and many of these are associated with international operations. This chapter therefore outlines the major portfolio planning approaches and also points out a number of the pitfalls which should be avoided if the best use is to be made of them in multinational strategic planning.

KEY DETERMINANTS OF BUSINESS STRATEGY

The Experience Curve Effect

The most widely known of the portfolio planning systems is probably that developed by the Boston Consulting Group (BCG). This organisation identified the fact that, just as the learning curve effect led to a reduction in the direct labour input required to manufacture a product, so too there was usually a relationship between the total cost of manufacturing and distributing a product and cumulative production volume. In such situations, each time the accumulated experience of manufacturing a particular product doubles, so the total cost in real terms tends to decline by a characteristic percentage, usually between 20 and 30 per cent. Using this principle an *experience curve* can be developed for any particular market. In addition, it is also possible to often subdivide particular industries or overall markets into sub-markets or definable segments. Such different segments may exhibit varying experience curves as illustrated in Figure 4.1 which demonstrates how the Japanese motor cycle industry was segmented by engine capacity and shows the variation in the experience curve effect for the different segments.

In order to develop an experience curve the deflated cost or price per unit of a product is plotted on the vertical axis against the total units produced over time on the horizontal axis. The plots are made on a log log scale which has the effect of showing a percentage change as a constant distance along either axis. A straight line on log log paper thus means that a given percentage change in one factor leads to a corresponding percentage change in the other, with the nature of the relationship between the factors being determined from the slope of the line which can be read off from the graph.

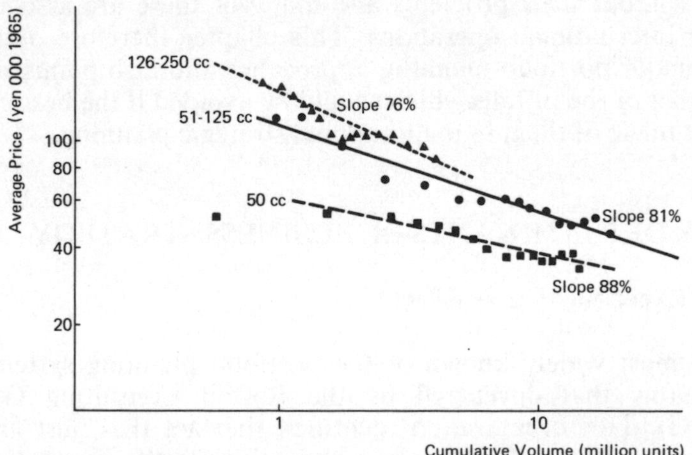

Fig. 4.1 Japanese Motorcycle Industry: Price Experience Curves (1959–74)

Source: Boston Consulting Group, *Strategic Alternatives for the British Motor Cycle Industry* (HMSO, 1975).

In practice the experience curve relationship generally holds not only between unit cost and accumulated production volume but also for unit prices. This is important since in developing experience curves it is often more difficult to obtain details of actual unit costs, especially historically, than it is to obtain similar figures for prices. It is common, therefore, for price experience curves to be developed as a surrogate for cost curves since price data is usually available. This is especially true when the method is used for conducting an analysis of competitive positions.

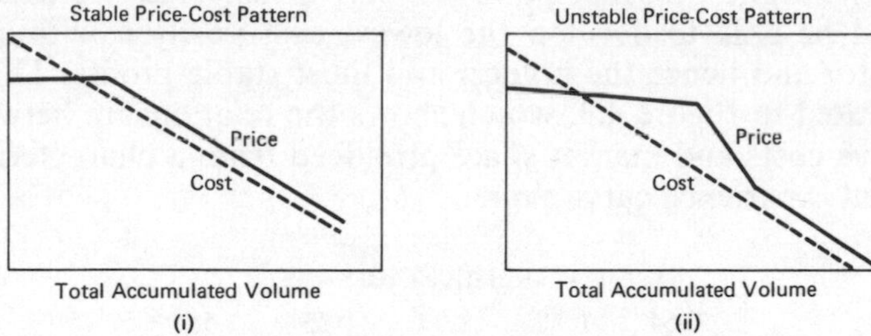

Fig. 4.2 Price-Cost Experience Curve Effects

In the classical situation the price experience curve parallels the cost experience curve after allowing for inflation as illustrated in Figure 4.2 (i). Products following this pattern tend to be found in competitive, high-growth, technological industries such as integrated circuits. When prices do not decline as fast as costs in the early years a knee effect occurs as shown in Figure 4.2 (ii). The explanation of this phenomenon is usually that the initial industry leader seeks to stabilise prices, which actually occurs in the early years of the product life-cycle (although in reality a slow real price decline occurs due to inflation). As a result of this strategy the industry leader achieves an increasing margin, so much so that new competitors are attracted to enter the market and also to grow faster. From an early high-cost position therefore, higher growth allows the new entries to reduce costs more rapidly than the industry leader and so to erode the leader's original cost advantage. Finally, a shakeout occurs in the industry when any producer decides it would be appropriate to reduce prices faster than the decline in industry costs. Actual breaks then tend to occur in the experience curves, as illustrated by a number of chemical products around the end of the 1950s. At the end of the shakeout overall prices will have been significantly reduced and a number of competitors often withdraw. A new phase of stability then tends to ensue along the lines of the classical pattern.

Strategic Implications of Experience Curves

From the experience curve effect BCG conclude that, irrespective of relative changes in the economic environment, the competitor with the highest market share or relative *competitive dominance* should be able to develop the lowest cost position within an industry and hence the highest and most stable profits. This is illustrated in Figure 4.3, which shows the relationship between relative costs and market share produced from a characteristic normal experience curve slope.

Relative Cost	0.64	0.80	1.00	1.25	1.55
Relative Share to largest competitor in specific segment	4.0	2.0	1.0	0.5	0.25

Fig. 4.3 Normal Relative Cost/Share Relationship
Source: Boston Consulting Group

The most successful competitive strategy is therefore to achieve and hold a dominant market position either through pricing tactics or by so segmenting the market into discrete sectors which can be dominated and defended. If market dominance cannot be obtained then it is argued that an orderly withdrawal may represent the optimal strategy.

Strategic Segmentation

For most businesses it is not possible for any one firm to obtain full market dominance on a global scale. It is often possible, however, to subdivide a market into a series of defendable strategic market segments in which a company can obtain a sustainable economic advantage if it concentrates on servicing the segment needs.

In order to identify strategic segments it is important to understand the underlying cost structure for a product. Such key cost factors often include:

Overhead Make-up	*Measure*
Selling costs	By number of models, number of countries
Advertising cost	By number of models, number of countries
Distribution cost	By number of countries
Production cost	By volume/model
Raw material cost	By total volume

The experience effects will normally be different for different areas of cost. This type of analysis for a business therefore seeks to identify which are the main cost elements and how these behave. Further, some assessment of competitor's positions is also important in order to assess opportunities for segmentation and relative strengths and weaknesses. From this analysis it is usually possible to identify the most appropriate dimensions for segmentation and to estimate the value of '*barriers*' between such segments. Barriers represent the level of investment required to go from one segment to another and include such factors as tariffs, brand names, patents, transport costs, privileged customer relations and the like.

The Importance of Market Dominance

Strategic market segments once identified should be dominated and each then becomes a relative decision unit which is discrete and separable from other such segments. In particular the time to accumulate a dominant market position is during the growth phase of a market, since at this time it is possible to increase share by obtaining a disproportionate share of the market growth. The alternative of taking market share from competitors in the mature phase of a market tends to be much more difficult and substantially more expensive.

Once a dominant position has been obtained, however, prices should be reduced in line with experience to deter competitors adding capacity and gaining share. The securing and holding of a dominant position is then expected to ultimately yield the best profits. During the build-up period, however, the capital commitment required may be heavy and it is therefore necessary to allow for the capital requirements needed and if possible to develop a balance between cash positive products and businesses and those that require cash. The achievement of this balance is the art of portfolio management. The relative competitive strength of a business is thus seen as a determinant of its ability to generate cash while the overall rate of growth of a particular business will also affect its cash generation capabilities, with high-growth businesses requiring cash injections in order to build or maintain market share.

STRATEGIC PORTFOLIO PLANNING APPROACHES

The Growth Share Matrix

The interplay of these two variables gives rise to the familiar growth-share matrix on which the portfolio of businesses operated by any company can be positioned as shown in Figure 4.4 (i). *Star businesses* in the upper-left quadrant have high

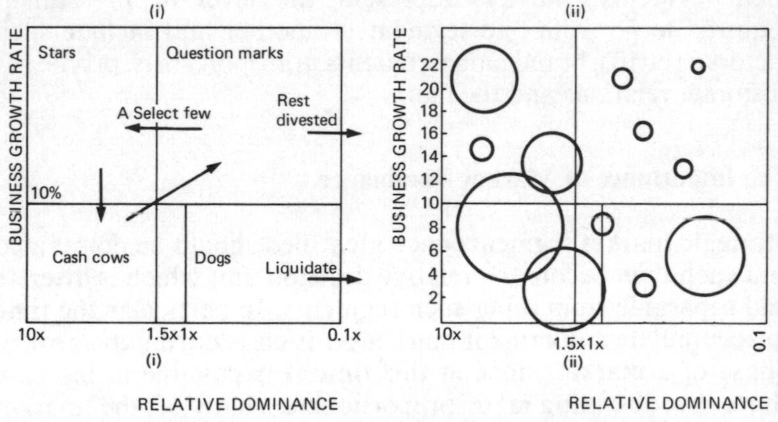

Fig. 4.4 Growth-Share Matrix and the Corporate Portfolio

growth and high share. Such businesses require significant new cash injections to maintain their position, but, as a result of their high relative dominance, they should also generate large amounts of cash. Overall therefore, such businesses tend to be in rough equilibrium in terms of cash flow and should be maintained and consolidated as a first priority for investment. As such businesses ultimately mature they become low-growth, high-share operations or *cash cows*, where the opportunities for reinvestment are not sufficient to absorb the cash generated; hence such businesses are the principal source of new investment funds.

High-growth, low-share businesses are *question marks*. Such businesses have high cash needs because of their growth rate, but poor cash generation prospects because of their low share. Usually a corporation can only adequately support a few such businesses and management decisions must be taken to either divest or harvest question mark businesses which are not selected for investment.

The final category of low-growth low-share businesses are *dogs*. Their relatively low growth means that the cost of gaining share may well be prohibitive while their low share means costs are high relative to competitors. Many such businesses tend to become cash traps, perpetually absorbing cash resources unless strong action is taken to disinvest.

The task of management is therefore to achieve a balance in the portfolio of businesses undertaken by the firm, taking cash generated by cash cows and the elimination of dogs and some question marks and placing it to support the stars and selected fledgling growth businesses with adequate financial support.

The growth share matrix is in practice quantified by carefully subdividing a company into its component businesses or segments, each of which is distinctively separable from the others as shown in Figure 4.4 (ii). For each of these businesses the deflated market rate of growth is established together with the company's relative competitive position or dominance and this is plotted on the matrix, the relative size in assets or turnover of each business being proportional to the area of the circle used to outline its position.

The relative competitive position of a business is plotted on a logarithmic scale to allow for the experience curve effect which suggests that the rate of cash generation or return on investment differences between competitors is related to the ratio of their relative competitive positions. In practice the four quadrants of the matrix are outlined at the 10 per cent real money or volume growth point and at the 1.5 times relative dominance position. These points have been largely determined empirically, although on occasion for low-growth businesses adequate cash generation can be observed at the one times relative dominance level.[2] In addition to thc overall portfolio each individual business can be examined to identify the relative strength of each competitor and the overall portfolios of competitors can be similarly derived in order to assess their relative strengths and weaknesses. Based upon an analysis of the portfolio therefore, different strategies can be derived for each business dependent upon its matrix position, the needs and desires of the company and the relative potential strengths of reaction by competitors.

A further useful aid to improving the dynamics of business assessments is obtained by the development of forward projection portfolios which plot the position of the various businesses under alternative future assumptions. Similarly frontier curves[3] as shown in Figure 4.5 can be developed to investigate the relevant business unit v. industry growth-rate dynamics, while cash requirements are illustrated from a market growth v. net reinvestment matrix in which the net cash flows of each business can be demonstrated by the relative areas of a circle. Cash generators typically have a ratio of free cash flow to reinvestment of less than one, while question mark businesses may require reinvestment funds up to 10 times cash flow generated. Star and dog businesses tend to have ratios between 0.7 times and two times.

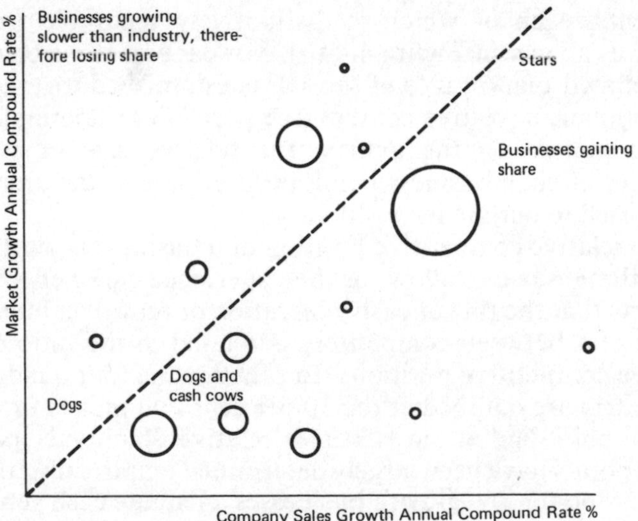

Fig. 4.5 Industry–Corporation Frontier Curve

The Early GE Planning System and its Derivatives

The portfolio approach developed by BCG has become increasingly widely adopted during the past decade and has resulted in the emergence of many imitators. These owe much to the development work at the General Electric Company. Under President Fred J. Borch, General Electric subdivided its

Basic strategy varies with different assessments of industry attractiveness and company strengths . . . .

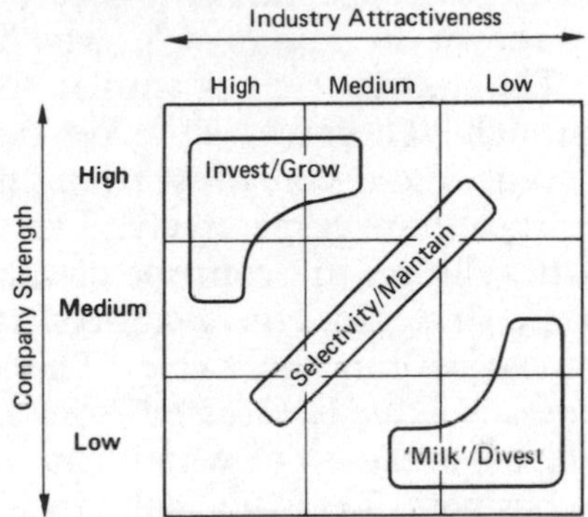

. . . . and different basic strategies imply differing objectives and elements of strategy . . . .

Basic Strategic Intention	Invest/Grow	Selectivity/Maintain	'Milk'/Divest
Primary Objective	Build market position for long-term profit	High short-term profits, medium cash flow	Maximize cash generation
Elements of Strategy			
Investment	Maximum digestible	Selective/high return segments	Minimum/dispose opportunistically
Risk	Accept/contain	Limit	Avoid
Share	Build/diversify markets	Target growth/protect position	Forego share for profit
Pricing	Lead, exploit cost/value elasticity	Stabilize for maximum contribution	Lag, even at expense of volume
Products	Lead, diversify	Differentiate – • Specialization • End-users • Performance	Prune
Costs	Utilize scale, not thrift	Aggressive reduction of variable, economize on fixed	'Variabilize' by ruthless cutting, consolidation
Marketing	Build creativity, coverage	Cut creativity, keep coverage	Cut
Management	Entrepreneurs	Sceptical, balanced	Disciplined - strong cost control

Fig. 4.6 McKinsey Portfolio Planning System

activities in a new way into *strategic business units* (SBUs). The SBUs could also be positioned on a two-dimensional three by three matrix similar to the BCG model, but where the dimensions measured *company strength* and *industry attractiveness*. These two dimensions were actually multifactor variables which were not necessarily quantified.[4]

The GE work has provided the basic model for derivatives developed by a number of other leading consultancy companies such as McKinsey and Arthur D. Little. These two actually make use of a two-dimensional matrix where the dimensions are multifactor as shown in Figure 4.6, which illustrates a McKinsey matrix. The matrix itself is similar to that used by BCG but turned through 90 degrees, while key factors included in industry attractiveness and company strength are industry growth rate and market share respectively. The three by three matrix also builds heavily on the concept of the product life-cycle with three basic strategies emerging, consistent with the position of a business within the cycle. The dimension of industry attractiveness is actually assessed from a compendium of variables, the precise make-up of which can vary according to the nature of the business. These normally include:

Industry demand characteristics
Trends in distribution channels
Buying decision motivation
Changes in product and process development
Analysis of and trends in key industry cost factors of production and marketing
Trends in investment
Industry competitive structure behaviour and profitability

Similarly, company strength is also an amalgam of a number of variables including:

Product strengths and weaknesses
Market share
Relative market price
Marketing expense level
Rate of new product introduction
Raw material position

Productivity
Capacity utilisation
Relative cost and financial performance

Clearly this system as advocated incorporates both quantifiable and qualitative variables. In this sense then there is a potential for cross-impact relationships to be taken into account. In reality however, this is not really practicable, further there is no specific weighting system for the variables on which data is collected (although some are considered essential and are always collected, while others may not be if not readily available). As a result the positioning of a business within the matrix is much less precise than with the Boston approach where both the main variables are quantifiable.

The Shell Directional Policy Matrix

One fairly simple method of overcoming the problem of the strategic positioning of a business is the Directional Policy Matrix (DPM) developed by the Royal Dutch Shell Group.[5] This system similarly makes use of a three by three matrix as illustrated in Figure 4.7, with the two key dimensions representing an organisation's *competitive capability* and the *prospects for sector profitability* instead of company strength and industry attractiveness. Similarly the two dimensions are also multifactor variables.

The Shell system was developed over the past few years, partially as a result of the weakened validity and credibility of financial forecasts caused by worldwide inflation and the oil crisis. In addition it was felt that traditional planning methods did not provide systematic explanations as to why one business had better prospects than another. Further, such methods did not provide adequate insight into the underlying dynamics of a balance between the businesses in which the company operated.

In the DPM system there are four main criteria by which the profitability prospects of a business may be assessed – *market growth rate, market quality, industry feedstock position* and *environmental aspects*. These criteria are adapted to the specific

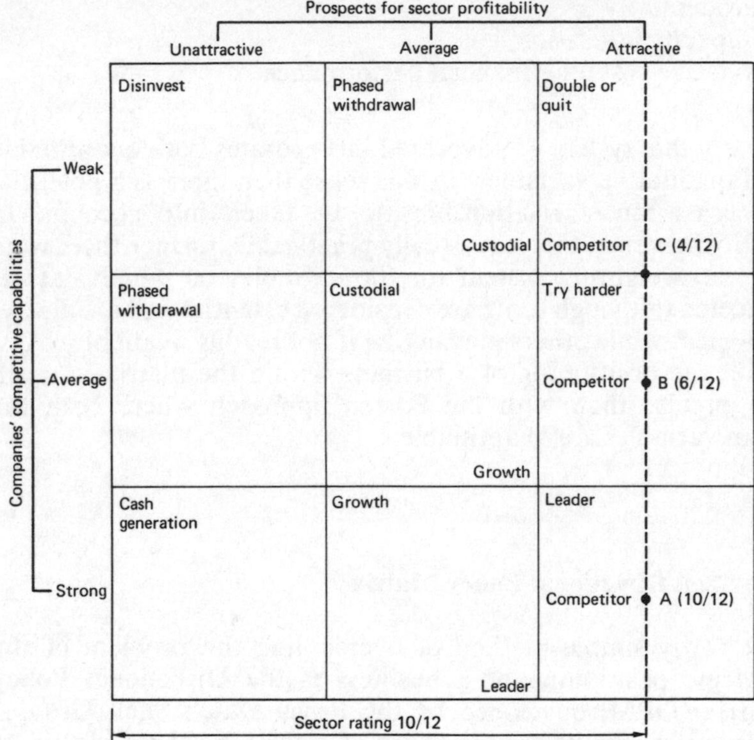

Fig. 4.7 Shell Directional Policy Matrix – Product X
Source: Royal Dutch Shell Group, *The Directional Policy Matrix,* company publication, 1975

needs of particular industries, thus for example industry feedstock is not appropriate in industries such as engineering and would probably be replaced with some suitable alternative. The two factors of market growth and market quality are, however, fundamental to any business sector analysis.

Each of the factors is then rated and scored for individual businesses. For the chemical industry, for example, the centre point or average market growth rating corresponds roughly with the five-year average growth rate predicted for heavy organic chemicals in Western Europe. This position is allocated three 'stars' – a visual display system being used to give more impact than numbers – and steps from one to five stars are established on either side of the average. Market quality is a more difficult area to quantify and in order to arrive at a sector rating a number of criteria are considered such as the sector profitability record; margin/capacity historical relationship; number of competitors; number of customers; value added; risk of product substitution and the like. Positive positions on most of a list of variables such as this would attract a four or five-star rating. The remaining factors are similarly scored and the business assigned a star rating on a one to five scale.

Competitive capability is determined on the basis of three factors, *market position, production capability* and *product research and development*. Market position is determined essentially as relative market share. Thus a five-star rating would apply to a leadership position where relative market share was strong and the business also occupied a price and technical leadership position. At the other extreme a one-star rating would signify a negligible current position.

The ratings for each of the main factors making up the primary dimensions are usually drawn up by specialists from the business area in conjunction with planning staff, although more sophisticated sampling techniques and computer-based methods have also been developed. From the assigned star ratings for each of the factors a numerical score is established by translating one star to 0, two stars to one and so on. It is also possible at this stage to weight the factors if desirable. Ultimately the two sector scores can be deduced and the business plotted on to the matrix. The relative capabilities of the three competitors illustrated in Figure 4.7 are thus shown in Table 4.1.

From these relative positions alternative strategies emerge. Competitor A is in a leadership position and thus equates approximately with a BCG star, and would receive absolute priority in resource allocation to ensure market position is maintained. The Avis or 'try harder' position of competitor B is a useful extension of the BCG matrix, implying that such a business is beyond the question mark phase and can be moved towards at least a leadership equality position by the correct allocation of resources. Without such an allocation, however, this type of business in the long term could be vulnerable. The double or quit zone occupied by competitor C conforms closely with the BCG question mark, with a similar philosophy advocated of the careful selection of a few such businesses for investment and the effective abandonment of the remainder.

Table 4.1 Companies' Competitive Capabilities Analysis (Competitors A, B and C)

Market position	*A*	*B*	*C*	*A*	*B*	*C*
Market share, Western Europe	65%	25%	10%	★★★★★	★★★	★★
Production capability						
Feedstock	Manufactures feedstock by slightly out-dated process from bought-in precursors.	Has own pre-cursors. Feed-stock manufac-tured by third party under process deal.	Basic position in pre-cursors. Has own sec-ond process for feedstock.			
Process economics	Both A and B have own 'first-generation' process supported by moderate process R & D capacity.		C is licensing 'second-generation' process from Eastern Europe.			
Hardware	A and B each have one plant sufficient to sustain their respective market shares.		None as yet. Markets product imported from Eastern Europe.			
	Overall production capability ratings:			★★★★	★★★	★★(★)
Product R & D (in relation to market position)	Marginally weaker	Comparable	Stronger	★★★★	★★★	★★(★)
	Overall competitors' ratings			10/12	6/12	4/12

Source: Royal Dutch Shell Group, *The Directional Policy Matrix*, company publication, 1975.

Matrix positions in the middle column are in general those for which market growth has fallen to around the industry average. The growth zone usually applies to products in oligopolistic markets with no outstanding leader where sufficient rates of return are available to justify commensurate investment to maintain position in line with market growth. Such businesses are also usually cash positive. The custodial/withdrawal zone is actually the most populated sector of the matrix. Typically custodial situations apply to the weaker competitors in sectors with too many participants. The indicated strategy in such situations is to maximise cash generation, without further commitment of resources, but the density of products means that clear guidance is often difficult to obtain and the matrix positions provide only indicative estimates.

Business sectors falling in the below-average industry growth and quality zone should be harvested or divested. These sectors generally conform with the BCG cash generation or dog positions.

The DPM thus provides one solution to the problems of incorporating a richer mix of quantitative and qualitative variables in assessing portfolio positions. Further, the three by

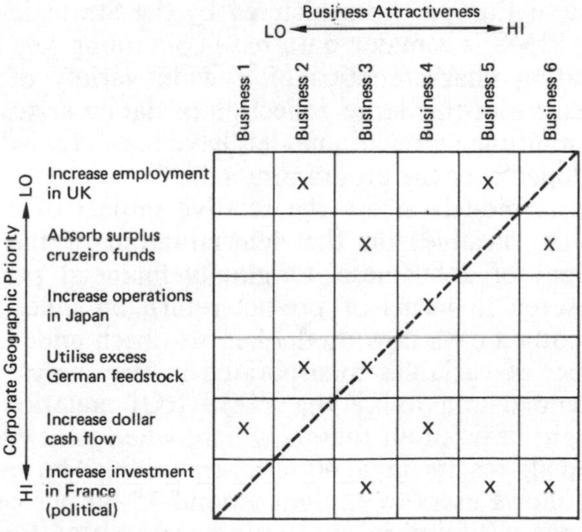

Fig. 4.8 Product/Geography Second-order Directional Policy Matrix

three matrix does help to reduce the sharpness of the BCG matrix positions which can actually be somewhat misleading in practice. In addition, the DPM has been extended to a series of second-order transition matrices which permit a reconciliation between product and geographic or socio-political variables. Such a matrix is shown in Figure 4.8 which illustrates *business attractiveness* on one axis and *corporate geographic priorities* on the other. The investment possibilities for each business are indicated by the crosses. Using the matrix it is possible to produce a relatively optimal allocation of investments so as to fund those businesses which are most attractive while at the same time fulfilling corporate financial/political geographic objectives.

The PIMS Approach[6]

The most powerful approach to portfolio planning yet devised is that of the PIMS programme. This emerged from the early attempts at General Electric to discover the 'Laws of the Market Place' and today embraces data on well over 1000 businesses drawn from over 100 major corporations in the USA and Western Europe. Administered by the Strategic Planning Institute, PIMS is a major data base containing key details of the operating characteristics of a wide variety of different businesses. From this large collection of data a series of cross-sectional multiple regression models have been gradually refined and developed over the programme's life.[6]

The basic models assess the relative impact of a series of quantifiable variables on the determination of the financial performance of a business. Originally financial performance was measured in terms of pre-tax return on investment but more recently a cash flow model has also been added. Further, the number of variables incorporated in the analysis has also been extended and today the PIMS ROI equation includes twenty-eight basic profit factors which, when joint effect terms are included, results in a 40-term equation. The use of this equation allows users to explain around 75–80 per cent of the performance variation in any business submitted for analysis. More importantly, for strategy makers PIMS also incorporates a strategy sensitivity and optimisation model which permits the impact of forward strategic moves to be assessed, isolates the effectiveness of individual strategic changes under varying environmental conditions and suggests optimal combinations of moves to meet specific performance measures.

The Par ROI Model

For any business the PIMS Par ROI model generates an estimate of the normally expected or par rate of return on investment given the market attractiveness, conpetitive differentiation, capital/production structure and discretionary budget expenditures of the business. In addition, the model also provides a comparison of the trend in actual ROI relative to the Par ROI, a diagnosis of strengths and weaknesses deduced from the relative impacts of the major profit determinants for the business and a sensitivity analysis of the change in the Par ROI for variations in the data inputs.

The 28 basic factors in the model are grouped into six major classes of profit influences and these together with the key profit determinants in each category are set out below:

INDUSTRY MARKET ENVIRONMENT
Key profit Determinants
- Long-run industry growth rate
- Short-run industry growth rate
- Stage in the product life-cycle

COMPETITIVE POSITION
Key profit determinants
- Market share
- Relative market share
(your share ÷ share of your three biggest competitors)

DIFFERENTIATION FROM COMPETITORS
Key profit determinants
- Relative product quality (excluding price)
- Relative price
- New product introductions

CAPITAL STRUCTURE
Key profit determinants
- Investment intensity (fixed capital + working capital ÷ sales)
- Fixed capital intensity

PRODUCTION PROCESS
Key profit determinant
  Vertical integration (value added/sales)
BUDGET ALLOCATION
Key profit determinants
  R & D/sales ratio
  Marketing expense/sales ratio

The most powerful overall terms are market share and relative market share and investment intensity and, although a subjectively measured variable, product quality. The close relationship between return on investment and relative market share and investment intensity are illustrated in Figure 4.9 (i) and (ii).

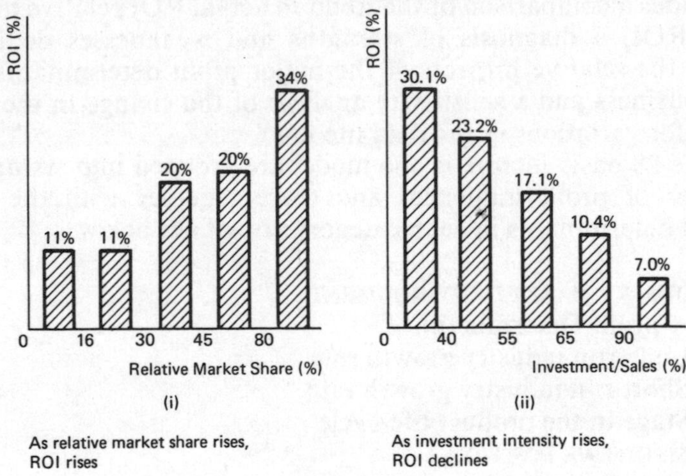

Fig. 4.9 Relationships between Relative Market Share, Investment Intensity and Return on Investment

Source: The Strategic Planning Institute

For PIMS subscribing companies, the data on any business is compared with the all-business mean for each profit factor and its value indicated relative to the mean. The impact of the difference between an actual business and the average business is also shown as an effect on ROI. Thus a strong market share would have a positive impact since high share has a positive effect on ROI. The size of the impact varies according to the relative factor strength, and the deviation of the actual business from the average. These impacts indicate the relative strengths and weaknesses of a business but do not necessarily suggest management action, since the cost of remedial treatment is unknown. The Par ROI for a business is then assessed as the PIMS mean ROI plus the sum of the individual key factor impacts and the combined effect of the support factors. From this data strategic indications are developed such as those in Table 4.2 which shows the general cross-impact relationships of other key profit indicators on different market share and investment intensity businesses.

Table 4.2 PIMS Indicated Cross-impact Relationship Effects on ROI

	Given Market Share			*Given Investment Intensity*	
Impact of HI	*LO*	*HI*	*Impact of HI*	*LO*	*HI*
Product Quality	Vital	Helpful	Marketing Expense Level	Indifferent	Avoid HI
Purchase Frequency	HI best	MED/LO best	R & D Effort	Favourable	Favourable
Manufacturing Intensity	Avoid Desperately	Avoid Strongly	Capacity Utilisation	Favourable	Vital
Relative Price	Average	High	Market Share	Favourable	Vital
			Sales per Employee	Favourable	Vital

The PIMS Par ROI has been recalculated six times to date covering a total longitudinal period from the mid-1950s to the mid-1970s. The key factors have tended to remain stable throughout these separate evaluations although there has been significant change in a number of lesser variables. Overall, however, the explanatory power of the model has tended to remain broadly the same, around 75–80 per cent.

The Par Cash Flow Model

In response to the changing needs of strategic planners in the mid-1970s PIMS introduced a cash flow par model in addition to the ROI model. For, while ROI remained the principal corporate financial measurement, in the early 1970s the oil crisis, leading to high inflation rates and increased interest rates, has led to a transformation in corporate thinking and a concentration on liquidity and cash flow.

The PIMS cash flow par model has a shorter history than the ROI model, which partially explains why it is somewhat less successful, accounting for only around 70 per cent of the observed variation in cash flow across the PIMS businesses. Par cash flow is deduced from 19 cash flow influencing factors, the key variables of which tend to be similar to those that influence ROI. The key factors influencing cash flow are set out below together with the relative direction of their effect for an increase in the respective factor:

Factor	*Effect on Cash Flow*
Percentage point change investment/sales	(−)
Real market growth, short run	(−)
Market share growth rate	(−)
Investment/sales	(−)
Selling price growth rate	(−)
Market share	(+)
Vertical integration	(+)
New product sales (% of total sales)	(−)
Marketing expense/sales	(−)
Marketing expense growth rate	(−)

Like the ROI model, the cash flow par model estimates the normally expected cash flow for a business, a diagnosis of the factors generating or absorbing cash and an indication of the sensitivity of cash flow to changes in the key factors.

While the principal focus for analysis in the PIMS programme is the business unit, the capacity for developing portfolio planning models covering the whole range of the corporation's businesses is now beginning to be exploited. Two forms of portfolio model have thus far been developed. In the first of these the cross-impact characteristics between PIMS variables for all portfolio businesses can be explored and the relative effectiveness of corporate policies evaluated. For example, if most businesses were shown to be relatively high in terms of research and development costs compared with the PIMS mean this would imply a research-intensive strategy for the corporation. If, however, this finding was coupled with the fact that relatively few businesses showed as leaders in either product quality or market share this would imply that the corporation's research policy was not effective in translating technical spending into product performance results. The second form of PIMS portfolio modelling allows corporations to develop optimal strategies for each business so as to produce the best corporate performance in terms of return on investment, corporate cash flow or some predetermined combination of these two factors.

For any company the understanding of the impact of the underlying dynamics of the businesses in its portfolio in both return on investment and cash flow terms is useful even if the full value of the PIMS analysis is not available. This type of analysis thus complements the portfolio planning techniques already discussed above.

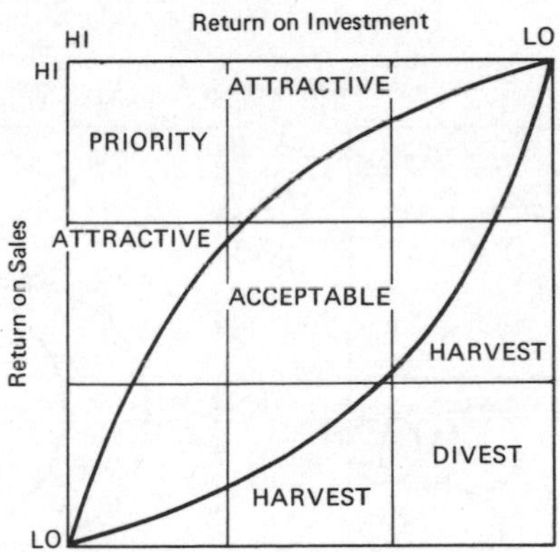

Fig. 4.10 Financial Ratio Matrix

Finally, it is often useful to develop overall financial portfolios which highlight the ratios chosen by management as the key measurements of the business. Illustrated in Figure 4.10 is a matrix using return on sales and return on investment. Those businesses which are to receive priority tend to perform well on both dimensions. The matrix also shows some businesses which may have high investment returns but low sales returns which may fall into the acceptable band. Businesses with both a low return to sales and low return on investment are candidates for divestment.[7]

PRACTICAL PROBLEMS WITH PORTFOLIO PLANNING SYSTEMS[8]

There is no doubt that for top management strategic portfolio planning provides a useful tool for decision-making in the diversified corporation. In use, however, a number of problems have emerged, some of which are fairly readily overcome, others of which are not. However, these problems do not usually apply equally to each of the techniques but must always be borne in mind by management. These techniques are an aid to decision-making and not a substitute for it.

The Problem of Market Definition

The first and one of the most serious problems which does potentially affect all the techniques is the problem of market

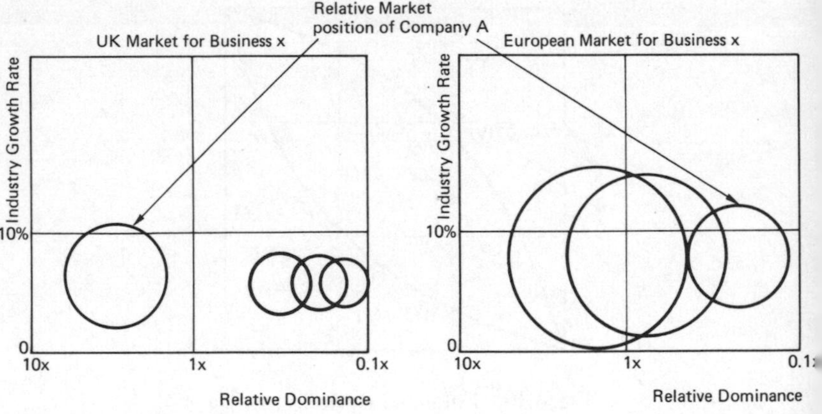

Fig. 4.11 Importance of Geographic Market Definition for Business Analysis

definition which, if not correctly identified, makes the measurement of market share and/or market growth rate unreliable, as shown in Figure 4.11. It is a problem that is often especially important for MNCs. This example shows that when measured in the UK market Company G, a major industrial chemicals producer, had a clear position of relative dominance against its nearest competitors. When measured against the context of the European market, however, Company G's business has been transformed from an apparent cash generator to being a dog. In reality, despite the fact that the European Market leader did not compete in the UK market at all, the implied threat that its potential entry generated was sufficient to significantly reduce the cash flow potential of Company G's business since the prices it charged were affected by the position in Western Europe as a whole.

A further problem which illustrates the importance of accurate market segmentation is shown in Figure 4.12 which in the first case shows Company H's position as a major distributor of records, music cassettes and cartridges, which is shown as a high-growth market. In the second, the market is actually segmented into three types of records – popular, classical and budget – and into cassettes and cartridges, which reveals quite different positions for Company H in these sub-segments both in terms of market share and industry growth rate. Decisions thus made universally on the basis of the first business positioning could therefore be in serious error when taken in the light of a more careful segmentation. Care must also be taken to distinguish between market segmentation and product differentiation, otherwise it may well bc that undefendable segments will be incorrectly identified.

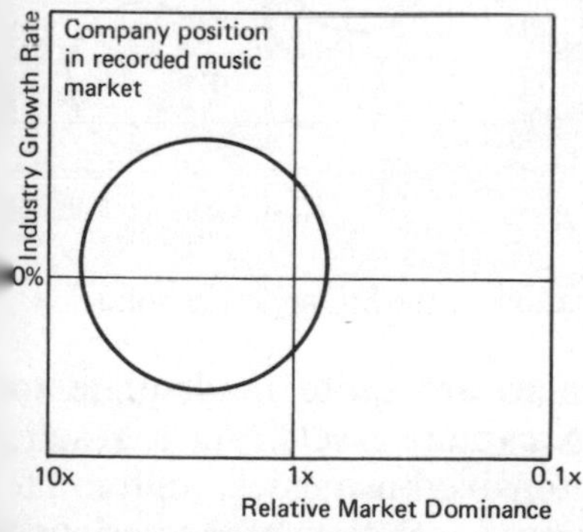

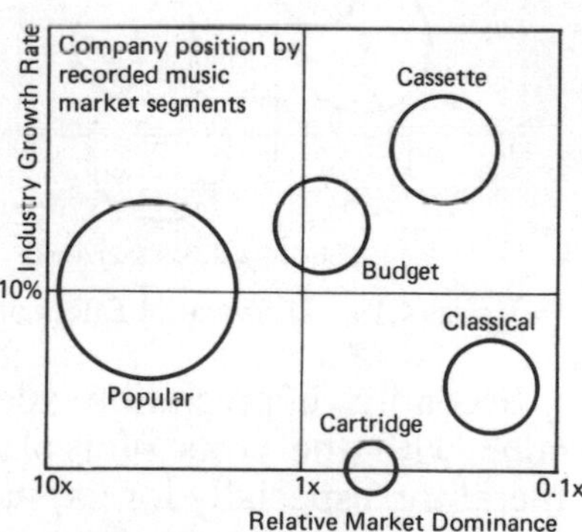

Fig. 4.12 **Importance of Market Segment Identification for Business Analysis**

The Problem of Inflation

In recent years high rates of inflation have had a serious affect on the cash flow and profit characteristics of any businesses. The effect of inflation is fclt in several ways. Firstly, under conditions of inflation price and cost changes can affect different businesses in different ways as shown in Figure 4.13, which shows the different chemical business units of Company B under deflated and undeflated market conditions. One general effect of inflation is that it tends to make even low-real-growth businesses into apparent high-growth operations. Thus, in real volume terms the portfolio of businesses operated by Company B is largely balanced in terms of cash flow generation. Under conditions of high inflation, however, growth rates in money terms rise rapidly. As a result the working capital requirements of even low-real-growth businesses tend to escalate rapidly and cash generators can become cash users. The effect is not uniform, however, and in the example shown a significant change in the structure of the portfolio takes place, with the relative positioning of a number of the businesses changing markedly.

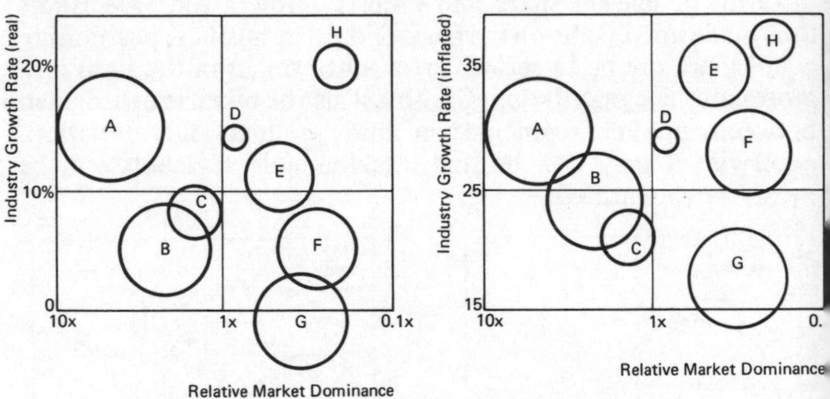

Fig. 4.13 Differential Effect of Inflation on the Strategic Portfolio

Secondly, depreciation allowances are quite inadequate to cope with the costs of replacing capital assets. As a result, therefore, especially for capital-intensive businesses, high inflation can seriously transform the actual cash flow characteristics of a theoretically balanced portfolio, resulting in potentially dangerous liquidity positions.

Problems of Economic Growth

While the difference between real and inflationary growth rates represents a problem, a further difficulty can occur in identifying the actual growth rate of a business. Many businesses are cyclical and unless such a cycle is clearly understood and a long enough time-span used in assessing growth rate again all the systems can give potentially misleading positioning. In practice, for large multibusiness firms it is not unusual for external consultants to incorrectly identify the real growth position of specialised cyclical businesses.

Strategic portfolio planning systems must not be used, therefore, as short-term or even medium-term forecasting models. It is important for management to understand the basic business cycle of the markets they operate in and to adjust the relative merits of each business accordingly. The portfolio planning approach can be useful in highlighting imbalances in an overall portfolio of businesses operating with different cycles but the approach should not be used for short-run operating decisions which are inconsistent with long-run strategic objectives for any particular business.

The Problems of Foreign Exchange Variation

One problem which has become increasingly important with the growth of multinational operations and interpenetration of geographic markets has been that of exchange rate variation. The effect of foreign exchange rate variation can totally transform the relative experience curve effect. Thus in the case of Figure 4.1 when costs are measured in, say, a weaker currency like sterling the slope of the curve reverses and a real cost increase takes place. For markets where global relative cost positions are important, therefore, experience curves must be modified to account for exchange rate variation in order to measure relative cost advantage.

Foreign exchange rates can also affect the relative capital intensity of a business when this is measured in a second currency. Many US and other US quoted multinationals have found recent SEC-imposed changes in accounting treatments of overseas assets and earnings have significantly affected their balance sheets when these have been measured in dollars. For multinationals operating production assets for example in strong-currency-based environments and supplying to weak currency areas where it is not possible to maintain the relative exchange rate differential, margins can be reduced, capital intensity increased and relative cash flow significantly cut back.

A further set of complications occurs in multinational transactions which can change the relative economics of a business. Increasingly multinationals are centralising their treasury management functions as described in Chapter 5 in order to optimise group cash flow and post-tax profitability and to minimise foreign exchange exposure. Indeed a number of organisations are actually managing their foreign exchange positions as a profit centre and in some cases up to 50 per cent of corporate profitability has been generated from this source.

For multinationals therefore the amount, location and form of post-tax income is usually paramount rather than pre-tax ROI or cash flow – the main measures for present portfolio planning techniques. The optimisation of post-tax income, therefore, often distorts the position of various businesses as measured in pre-tax terms and must be taken into account when assessing the strategic position of any business.

The Problems of Organisation and Motivation

Although significant technical problems do occur in practice with portfolio planning the most serious area of difficulty emerges when the implementation of a portfolio strategy is attempted. Such problems surface in a variety of ways.

Firstly, it is rare that the SBU or the division of a corporation into businesses will conform to its formal organisation structure. Thus, it is often possible to find elements of a strategic business unit located in two or more product or geographic divisions of a multimarket firm. Moreover, there is a tendency for top management to assess a corporate portfolio in relation to the formal structure rather than account separately for cross-divisional businesses. As a result, therefore, odd aberrations can and do transpire. For example in Company I, a major European chemical producer, seriously dysfunctional behaviour occurred when one half of a high-growth business was located in a product division identified by top management as a cash generating operation while the other half was located in a regional geographic division singled out for heavy investment. In the first case the business unit management were reluctant to make any investment which did not show an extremely high rate of return, rapid payback and low cash usage, while in the second managers were prepared to accept low rates of return, provided an investment contributed to improving the business unit growth and share position. As a result the managers responsible for operating elements of the same business within the different divisions were attempting to pursue almost totally opposite strategies.

Although logically such situations clearly should not arise, major reorganisations are usually painful and must be introduced against the wishes of many of the vested interests within the existing structure. Significant reorganisation does not, therefore, occur in an evolutionary manner but rather takes place periodically when it becomes clear that strategy and structure have diverged significantly. The models described provide little or no help with regard to implementation and as a result organisational discrepancies can be common when SBU-based strategies are introduced.

Surprisingly perhaps, a number of companies that have endeavoured to adopt a portfolio-based strategy have lacked the cash control systems to ensure even that resources are collected from those businesses to be harvested so they may be redeployed to other businesses which are cash users. In many organisations the traditional pattern has been that cash generating operations have first call on the funds they create. In Company J, a diversified building materials, engineering and construction company, for example, a clear cash generating division which was producing cash from a depleting asset was allowed to invest these funds in overseas acquisitions rather than be forced to redeploy them to the organisation's developing activities in construction and engineering. This case was made possible by the tolerance of central management to allow divisional cash balances and high investment discretion levels. Successful redeployment, therefore, usually requires central resource allocation for strategic investments and cash availability is ensured by such features as central bank accounts, global or regional cash pools, and capital charge systems on managed assets.

A third common problem occurs when a business is identified as a cash generator or dog or placed in a harvest/divest category. For most organisations there is a fairly common value system amongst managers that growth and progress is normal for all businesses. Where a business is therefore identified as one to be run down for cash generation, this is alien to accepted management values. Moreover, the harvest position is soon recognised by the workforce, who tend to become demotivated and resistant to management policies. Industrial relations

Table 4.3 Alternative Organisation Structures and Management Styles for Different Portfolio Positions

Strategy	*Invest/Grow*	*Selectivity/Earnings*	*Harvest/Divest*
OBJECTIVE	GROWTH	EARNINGS	CASH FLOW
STRATEGY CHARACTERISTICS	Intensive pursuit of market share Earnings generation subordinate to building dominant position Focus predominantly on long-term results and payout Emphasis on technical innovation and market development	Intensive pursuit of max. earnings Focus balanced between long and short term Emphasis on complex analysis and clear plans Emphasis on increased productivity, cost improvement, strategic pricing	Intensive pursuit of max. positive cash flow Sell market share to max. profitability Intensive pruning of less profitable products/segments Emphasis only on short term
ORGANISATION CHARACTERISTICS	Must enable future growth Product or venture operations Separate 'futures' from operations Build technical competence Strong international focus Highly competent staff functions	Must provide flexibility at moderate cost Matrix organisation (balance cost and people development) Centralised product planning Overseas sourcing operations Pooled sales and distribution utilisation Centralised finance	Must be low-cost/no frills Functional structure (lowest cost) Collapse product depts. into functionally organised division Reduce/eliminate labs. and forward engineering Maximum pooling where cost-effective Combine mfg/eng. operations

MANAGEMENT CHARACTERISTICS	Emphasis on entrepreneurs Young ambitious, aggressive Strong development and growth potential High risk tolerance Highly competitive by nature	Emphasis on 'solid businessman' Tolerates risk but doesn't seek it Comfortable with variety and flexibility Careful but not conservative Trades off short-term/long-term risk/reward	Emphasis on 'hard-nosed operators' Seasoned and experienced Seeks high efficiency Low change-tolerance Wants instant results, doesn't look ahead

problems often accumulate in a bid to maintain job security and it is now becoming increasingly difficult to shed labour in a casual manner. Strong pressure mounts, therefore, for reinvestment in the cash generating business which may be exactly the reverse of central management's intended strategy.

This problem becomes especially acute in dominant business companies where one core activity constitutes the major profit earning potential. In these cases not only does the business unit management resent being asked to pass on cash generated to new businesses in which they often do not see the logic, but is in a much more powerful position to press its case since it is the principal profit earner. Moreover, in such companies it is common that central management itself has largely been promoted from within the core business and is also relatively unsure about the new activities such concerns enter into in order to regenerate themselves. There are a large number of examples of this situation and in many of these a far from theoretically optimal strategic solution has been adopted – a fact that is more consistent with behavioural reality. One implementation device that has been occasionally used is the adoption of alternate management teams, objectives and controls for businesses in different strategic positions. The characteristics of the approach used in one major US electrical products manufacturer are illustrated in Figure 4.14. In this system management teams are matched to business needs and a number of US corporations are now moving to using such a concept.

CONCLUSION

The development of portfolio planning techniques over the past decade has provided an increasingly valuable tool for the management of multibusiness firms. In particular it permits top management to identify the basic characteristics of each of its businesses and to plan the strategic future of the total corporation accordingly. It also permits management to begin to take a rational account of other variables which are of particular importance to the MNC, such as achieving a suitable geographic and socio-political balance amongst its operations.

Despite the important gains these tools have made to strategy formulation, problems do occur in their practical usage. A number of these are technical and can largely be overcome with suitable modification or provision of additional checks. Unfortunately the more intransigent problems occur in gaining organisational acceptance of the strategic messages portfolio planning sometimes reveals. Unless derived strategies are therefore implemented with much care and sensitivity the economic strategic improvement that might be expected from the use of portfolio planning can be, and probably will be, largely dissipated in employee and line management resistance to changes advocated.

5 Multinational Corporate Treasury Management

The task of financial management in the multinational corporation is of particular importance. Today it has become a key determinant for the corporate profitability of the MNC to have its financial resources in the right form in the right place at the right time. The task of ensuring that this is achieved is that of corporate treasury management. It is a relatively thankless task for if it is not done then management is accused of ineffectiveness, and bad planning. On the other hand success leads to accusations of being a corporate speculator. Nevertheless, since the introduction of floating exchange rates, short-term money management has become so important that in a number of cases earnings from good treasury management have accounted for up to 50 per cent of corporate profits.[1]

As a result it is becoming increasingly important to develop adequate systems for international financial planning and, in particular, mechanisms for coping with both short- and long-term money management and tax planning arrangements. In addition, it is necessary to integrate, on a post-tax basis, the expected financial returns from capital investment with the requirements of the corporation's product market strategic plans and to establish a suitable long-term capital structure for the global operating group.

Treasury management in the multinational enterprise is substantially different from that of the purely domestic operating concern. The multinational treasurer must cope with an additional range of problems not faced in one-country trading, such as international taxation rates, remittance policies, foreign exchange exposure, variations in local capital markets, exchange control restraints and specific legal and accounting convention constraints prevailing in individual countries. Moreover, the international financial executive faces a number of non-technical difficulties, notably time, distance and culture, which complicate his task. Thus distance results in delays and reduced reliability in communication. Similarly, time-zone differences result in significant problems for short-run foreign exchange and cash management, while culture leads to problems of custom, tradition and language.

TREASURY ORGANISATION FOR THE MNC

There is no one right way of organising the corporate treasury of the multinational, but as with planning systems the task of financial management tends to vary according to the complexity of international operations and the type of organisation structure adopted. Three particular phases have been identified in the evolution of multinational operations.[2] These phases are partially a function of size, but also of the degree of complexity caused by increased product and geographic coverage.

Phase 1 Elementary Treasury Organisation

Conditions favouring this structure

1. Low level of international activity
2. Little or no intercompany trading across geographic borders
3. Domestic structures functional or possibly divisional overseas holding company structure, or for European MNCs – mother–daughter structure

Unfortunately, as a firm moves beyond exporting and first develops international operations it usually fails to take adequate care in modifying its financial policies. This often creates serious problems later when it is much more difficult to amend arrangements established during this unplanned stage. In large part such difficulties occur due to a lack of knowledge of the differences involved between domestic and international financial management.

At this early stage in international activities when an overall functional or possibly a domestic divisional organisation applies, the finance function still tends to be managed at corporate headquarters, although specialist skills are seldom available. Rather, an inadequate staff tends to have neither the time to closely manage the activities of overseas operations, nor the specialist skills to design and monitor adequate corporate decision rules. Further, the size of the business at this time seems not to justify the expense of adding a specialist international finance function.

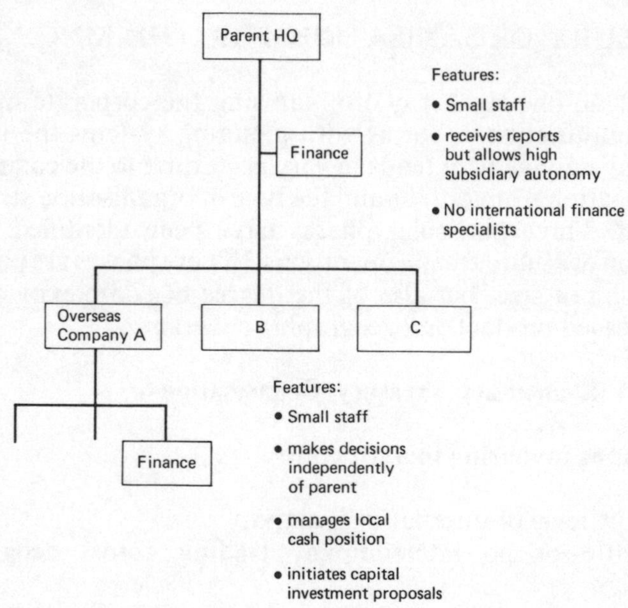

Fig. 5.1 Elementary International Treasury Management Organisation

As a result the financial managers of overseas operations operate without adequate direction from the parent and each subsidiary tends to be treated independently of all others. There is little or no attempt to take advantage of intercompany trading potential and where this is done it tends to be on an arm's-length basis, with each subsidiary seeking to optimise its own performance irrespective of the impact on the corporation as a whole. It is at this time too that legal entities become established without usually any thought of the desired ultimate fiscal and legal structure, so making for significant later difficulties in taxation planning and the like. The financial management of an enterprise in the early stages of a multinational strategy is shown in Figure 5.1. Many European-based MNCs with mother–daughter structures tend to allow a phase 1 financial management structure to persist much longer than their American counterparts despite high levels of overseas involvement.

Phase 2 Intermediate Treasury Organisation

Conditions favouring this structure:

1. Modest levels of international activity (circa 15–40 per cent of sales) with some intercompany trading activity
2. Found with all forms of international organisation structure but common with international division structures
3. Often installed after a serious international financial loss in a subsidiary especially due to foreign exchange losses, or uncovered devaluation
4. Corporate financial staff have responsibility for both domestic and international operations. Global financial planning is *not* conducted.

As the corporation expands its overseas operations it rapidly becomes apparent that international financial management is different from domestic. Financial skills are developed within the overseas subsidiaries, while growing intercompany trading activities often lead to the central consideration of foreign exchange risk management and tax planning. This move to add central office international finance skills is enhanced by the growing importance of overseas operations, which, for many European corporations, where home market sales tend to be relatively small, can soon dominate the overall activities of the corporation. Ironically, however, it has been suggested[3] that it very often takes a significant shock to the system, such as serious losses in an overseas subsidiary or foreign exchange problems on a devaluation, before a strengthening of the central financial management occurs.

The decision to strengthen international treasury management having been taken, it still requires a substantial period before new control and planning systems can actually be implemented. This can easily take up to two years, dependent upon the complexity and comprehensiveness of the systems introduced and the time requirements for establishing new legal and fiscal systems. When established, the organisation of financial management in such a system is depicted in Figure 5.2. The enlarged central financial staff make most of the financial decisions of significance and overseas subsidiaries are allowed very little autonomy even in local financial decision making.

The transition point between Phase 1 and Phase 2 systems of financial management is imprecise. In a study of 187 US multinationals it was reported that of the 75 firms examined, with total sales between $100 million and $500 million in 1969, 80 per cent had centralised their international financial management.[4] Foreign sales in these firms usually represented some 15–30 per cent of total world sales with each firm operating manufacturing plants in 10–20 countries. This type of treasury management can, therefore, exist with any form of overall structure, but tends in the main to be found in firms with an international division structure or an area structure based on low product diversity.

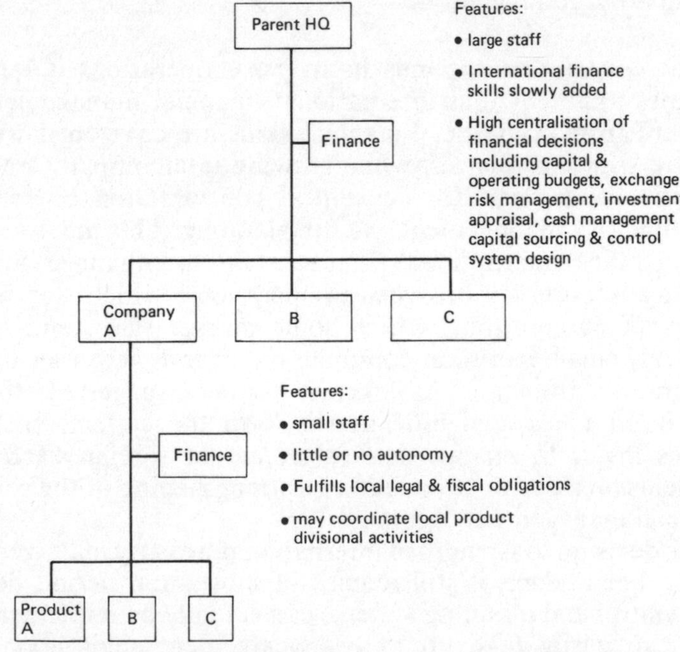

Fig. 5.2 Intermediate International Treasury Organisation

The adoption of a policy of centralisation means that the central financial unit usually takes on responsibility for the preparation of capital and operating budgets for international operations, development and administration of systems to manage exchange risk exposure, international investment appraisal, cash management, overseas capital sourcing and control over the collective group capital structure, tax management and the design and implementation of standardised financial control procedures for overseas subsidiaries, together with financial consolidations on a global basis. Caterpillar Tractor Company provides an example of such a tightly centralised treasury management system. Caterpillar, which has a global-regional form of organisation, centralises all aspects of financial management for both domestic and international operations, from policy-making to administration and supporting services. The overseas regional operating managers do not have financial staffs of their own, but rely instead on the corporate financial unit. This unit provides all the necessary support and advice in connection with line management decisions with financial implications. Each senior member of the corporate financial department, irrespective of his functional responsibilities, is concerned with both foreign and domestic affairs.[5]

Phase 3 Advanced Treasury Organisation

Conditions favouring this structure:

1. High levels of geographic and product diversity. High intercompany trading activity between overseas subsidiaries as well as with parent
2. Controlled decentralisation within a well developed set of corporate rules
3. Found with matrix area based organisation structures. Finance function becomes three-tier
4. Large international financial skills including specialist tax advice, treasury and controllership

Continued growth in overseas activities brings a new dilemma. While growth in the size and scale of overseas operations increases their importance and the development of a core of international finance experience at the central office are both pressures for continued headquarters management, new forces emerge which pull in the opposite direction. These include the growing complexity of operations and the increase in financial options open to the firm. When the number of overseas subsidiaries grows large and where transaction possibilities can exist not merely between the subsidiaries and the parent but between subsidiaries themselves, the managerial task of optimisation becomes impracticable, especially from a central management department.

As a result, therefore, there is a move to delegate more autonomy to operating subsidiaries or to regional headquarters units. This autonomy, however, is only permitted under tight control. Central management produces an extensive code of conduct which sets out in considerable detail the decision rules to be adopted by local treasury managers. This structure is depicted in Figure 5.3. Within the framework of these standard operating procedures, which often extend to several volumes, local management is permitted freedom to act in certain areas of financial management, although some activities tend to be retained at the central office.

The Singer Company, one of the most international of US firms, operates a Phase 3 system. The chief financial officer has worldwide responsibility for financial policy, planning and financing. The office of the treasurer has five departments – planning, foreign finance, cash management, insurance and treasury services. The office of the corporate controller has four departments, all of which have both foreign and domestic responsibilities, and cover profit planning and financial analysis, accounting operations, corporate auditing and management information systems.

Singer is organised into a series of eight operating groups on a product line basis, all have some international activities, and each group is subdivided into regional or product divisions. Some have their own financial staff, but most do not; but all country management teams do, although the extent depends upon the size of local Singer operations. Neither domestic group nor divisional financial staffs, however, have international financial executives. In some countries where Singer has units reporting to more than one operating group, a special finance committee is set up to coordinate local financing.

The formulation of policy for overseas operating units is

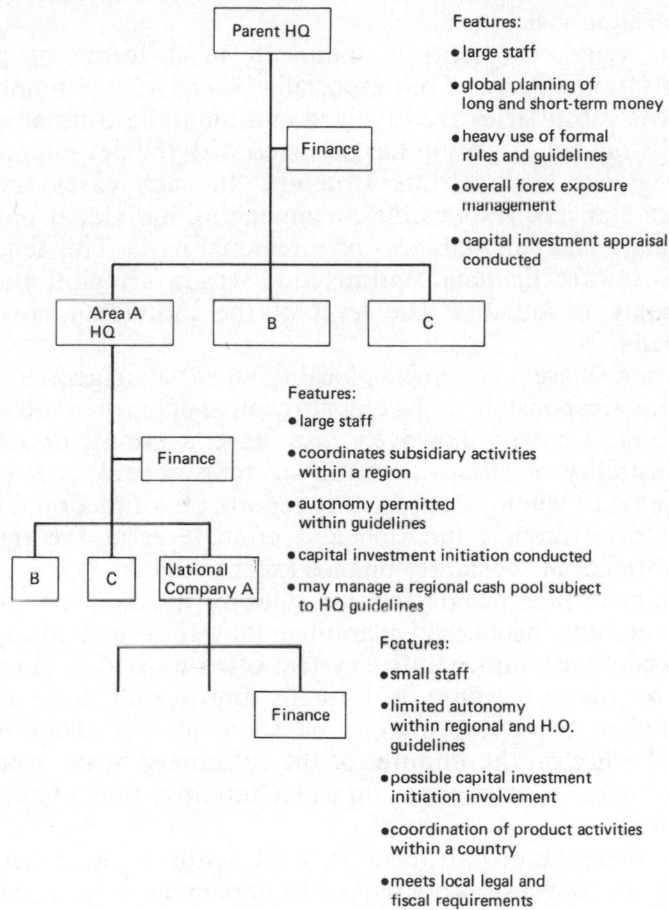

Fig. 5.3 Advanced International Treasury Organisation

clearly the responsibility of the corporate centre. These policies, guidelines and procedures are spelt out in a financial manual which is divided into treasury and controllership sections. The treasury section, for example, covers cash management, credit and collection, foreign exchange transactions, dividends and royalties and bank relations. The controller's section lays down detailed guidelines on accounting policies and procedures; preparation of budgets, and the contents and format of information reports. This manual provides local management with clear-cut directives and limits the necessity of excessive central supervision.[6]

This type of system is found in most forms of global organisation structure, but especially where a large number of overseas subsidiaries are involved and umbrella companies are used. A further extension has occurred with the development of the regional headquarters structure. In such cases regional finance staff are responsible for managing individual national subsidiary company finances on a regional basis. This tendency moves toward financial optimisation within a region and less autonomy is found at the level of the individual operating company.

With a Phase 3 system the local financial management tends to be line-responsible to the chief executive of his own subsidiary company. He will, however, also have a strong dotted-line responsibility to the international treasurer of the parent company, to whom he effectively reports on a functional basis. The central finance function also often reserves the right of appointment of subsidiary finance executives.

The mere presence of decision rules in such systems are not, however, any necessary guarantee that they will always be followed. One simple control system often utilised is to require local boards of directors to formally approve all those actions required by the central finance decision rules. A check by the central office on the minutes of the subsidiary board meetings thus provides a cross-check on when authority limits have been exceeded.

The presence of partnerships, joint ventures and other non-wholly-owned subsidiaries makes the implementation of centrally controlled financial management systems more difficult. This is especially true in politically sensitive investments, where managerial control may well be shared with governments or their agencies or where local participation is a prerequisite of investment, as in much of the Middle East. In some cases all possibility of complete financial control from the centre is lost, as in investments in associates.

In these situations the management of a group capital structure alone is fraught with difficulties, as each subsidiary and associate tend to pursue independent policies. Further, distribution policies also become subject to greater risk and equity positions are threatened as individual companies use their own paper for raising cash, making acquisitions and the like. Most companies, therefore, endeavour to restrict their positions in uncontrollable finance situations. The wholly-owned majority activities may then be treated with a high level of central control, either directly or via detailed decision rules. The remaining minority of semi-independent local equity positions, joint ventures and the like are treated on an advise-and-consent basis only, although certain rights with regard to financial management will usually be sought at the outset of any such relationship.

Despite the difficulties and the initial move to decentralisation, those firms which have very extensive overseas operations tend again to endeavour to develop global policies for finance, leading to increased central control. This has resulted largely from a recognition of the importance of short-run financial planning to the profitability of the MNC. It has also come about due to improvement in systems which, for example, do enable group cash and foreign exchange exposure positions to be managed globally.

Some indication of the increasing tendency toward recentralisation is shown in Figure 5.4, drawn from analysis of treasury management in a number of European MNCs. Those companies which operate an international division structure tend to have fewer overseas operations than those which have moved to a more complex divisional form of organisation. The latter firms tend to be managed by a system of worldwide product divisions or a mixture of product divisions coupled with a series of regional geographic divisions. Finally, the third form of regional/product matrix organisation is usually associated with a high level of international activity in terms of both product and geographic diversity.

THE MANAGEMENT OF INDIVIDUAL FINANCE FUNCTIONS

Long-term Financial Planning

The locus of responsibility for long-term financial planning in multinational corporations tends to be at the centre. There is a somewhat greater degree of autonomy given to those firms

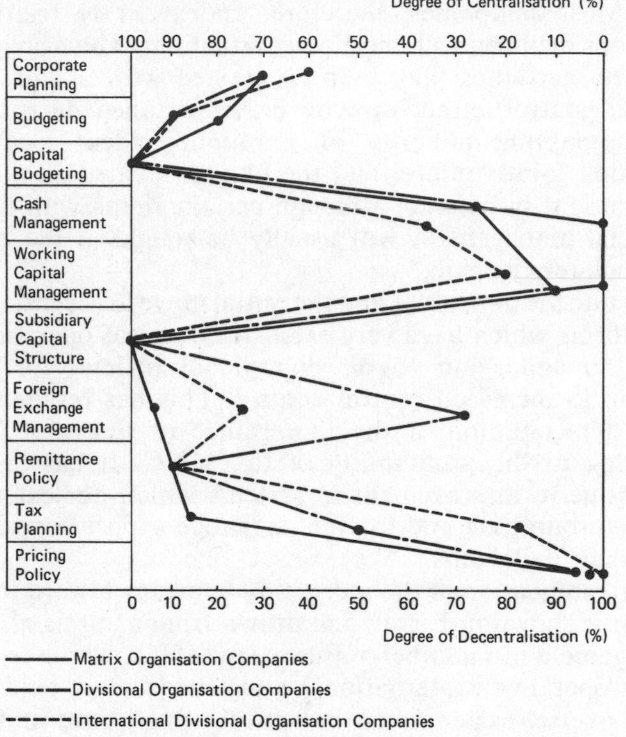

Fig. 5.4 Structural Profile of Responsibility for Financial Tasks
Source: J. C. S. Kimber, op. cit. p. 167.

managed with an international division structure than either those with a divisional or matrix form of organisation, reflecting somewhat the lower degree of overseas involvement and a relative lack of knowledge concerning overseas operations.

Long-term financial planning tends to emerge largely as a result of an aggregation of subsidiary unit plans which lead to the identification of financial needs for a period ahead. The central finance unit then usually plans ahead for changes in capital structure, type and location of new money sources and the like. Nevertheless, these forward plans are often contingent only in that the high levels of uncertainty in many businesses make it impracticable to undertake firm financing commitments for long periods ahead. The actual period forecast in detail, as with strategic planning systems, is a function largely of the nature of the business.

British Petroleum, for example, tends to plan its fund raising in 'pipe dreaming' form up to ten years ahead. Skeleton finance plans are made for three to five years ahead, but these too are contingency plans because of the high levels of uncertainty as to the timing of new major investments which can have a significant impact on overall financial needs. Firmer plans are laid for the next one to two years, as the group control department is able to identify and collate worldwide plans and, from operational plans, determine probable cash and borrowing requirements both locally and centrally.[7]

In BASF the forward planning system covers the next five years. Like many others it is initiated by the definition and establishment of corporate objectives by top management. These incorporate not only operative terms such as volume, sales growth, market share and the like, but also various financial standards, for example, financial security as expressed by certain balance sheet ratios. All the operating divisions within the group prepare a plan embracing sales, cost of goods sold, operating results, capital expenditure requirements and financing needs for a five-year period. These are consolidated at headquarters and amended where necessary.

The group treasury makes recommendations based upon the plans, concerning items such as the absolute level of borrowing desired on a worldwide basis or in a specific market. In addition financial standards are proposed covering the level of gearing, liquidity and certain cash flow ratios. These recommendations for a financial framework serve as a flexible set of guidelines which can then be applied or modified to fit specific situations.

The five-year plan is not rigid, but is naturally updated on a rolling annual basis. The annual plan covering the first year of the five-year projection is drawn up and discussed in the late autumn of each year and becomes binding towards the year-end. Because more detailed and accurate information is available the action programmes identified in this plan are more precise. The financing programmes incorporated thus specify the volume of funds required, the expected cost, the expected timing for obtaining them, the instruments to be used to raise them, the capital markets to be used and so on. A detailed programme of this nature is drawn up for every member company of the group together with an overall consolidation.[8]

Financial Budgeting

The budgeting process tends to be slightly less centralised in more complex multinationals than in those with a lesser international involvement. Local management tends to be allowed somewhat more flexibility in negotiations in such firms, but at the same time the budgetary control systems and standardised reporting relationships are the most developed in the matrix organisations. These firms tend also to have the greatest level of financial expertise located in subsidiary operations. In Exxon for example the central treasurer's department devotes itself to broad planning, funding investments, planning research, planning finance and planning the executive development of management. Its operating unit managers produce their own budgets and operating plans and are responsible for day-to-day decision-making subject to an extensively developed, but flexible, reporting manual.[9]

By contrast the central office input in international-division-organised firms tends to be highly operational and central office executives often participate actively in the preparation of subsidiary level plans. Divisional firms tend to be closer to the matrix organisations, with an increased reliance on systems laid down by the central finance staff.

In many planning systems, the annual budget is derived from an expanded version of the first year of a long-term plan which specifies in detail the operational activities of each subsidiary for the coming year as described in the BASF system. This, however, is not always the case. In a considerable number of companies budgeting takes place outside the planning cycle and may well have a separate responsibility line, often to the controller's office, inside the central treasury, rather than to the corporate planning unit.

Capital Budgeting

Detailed consideration of some elements of the capital investment process are handled elsewhere, but in all types of organisation this critical function is strictly retained at the centre. While discretionary limits are established they are generally too low to enable any subsidiary to make any significant investment which might have any strategic impact. The scale of discretionary limit usually varies according to size, both of the total group and the individual subsidiary, but also according to the characteristics of a business. Thus discretionary limits tend to be higher in capital-intensive industries such as petrochemicals than in, say, food processing. For example in Company K, a multi-billion dollar oil company, the upper limit on discretionary expenditure is $1m, providing the sums concerned are contained within the annual capital budget, while in Company L, a European engineering concern with sales around $300 million in 1974, the upper discretionary limit is $100,000. In each case, despite the difference in scale, the size of the discretionary limit is too low to enable the subsidiary unit management to commit the group to any new activity of any significance. Blanket limits tend to be utilised for minor items, but the total amounts concerned form part of the annual budget and further sanction is needed for any expenditure in excess of the agreed limits. Some firms not only require approval of individual capital requests, in addition to incorporation and justification in an annual capital budget, but also require further authorisation before actual cash disbursements are made. This latter tendency applies mainly to smaller firms where operational centralisation still prevails.

The responsibility for investment planning is not always a treasury management function. Indeed in one recent survey the planning function was the most common single responsible unit.[10] In the main, however, the initiation of the majority of projects comes from within the operating divisions subject to either formal or informal guidelines established by the central office. Most MNCs do have a system of formal investment guidelines although very rigid policies are uncommon. Those firms with only informal guidelines tended to develop a system of known acceptable norms which identified acceptable strategic areas of investment and some idea of a corporate investment return norm.

Acquisitions, investments in new countries or markets and very large investment projects are usually initiated at the centre. In the main acquisitions especially are conducted without divisional involvement although the initial identification of overseas candidates often originates within subsidiaries. Very large capital projects tend to be experienced in markets with substantial economies of scale requiring investment on either a regional or global scale.

All the MNCs studied use discounted cash flow methods for investment appraisal almost invariably based upon the internal rate of return. All also used payback, whilst less frequently working capital needs and cash flow were treated as important criteria. Most companies also conduct sensitivity analyses but complex decision-tree and mathematical models are not widely used. However a growing number of companies are beginning to adopt a portfolio method as a working technique.[11]

Nearly half the companies examined had some form of formal 'post-audit' procedure while a number of others had less formal procedures applied to particular projects. In reality, little use was made of post-audit data since projects tend to change as they are implemented and the final result is therefore often significantly different from the original proposal, so making comparison difficult.[12]

The measurement of risk for overseas operations is not well developed. This topic is developed at length in Chapter 9; but financially most companies expect either a premium over the normal investment return rate, a fast payback or a combination of both these factors.

Cash Management

Day-to-day cash management tends to be largely decentralised, although this is an area where significantly increased autonomy passes to local management with growing complexity. In Company M, a major European chemical and textile manufacturing firm, for example, the overall group cash position is monitored monthly for each profit centre in Europe, but geographically distant operations are much more self-contained. This is especially true of the group's North American and Australian operations, which are relatively large and operate with a high degree of autonomy.

In the international division organisation the monitoring of subsidiary cash positions formally takes place usually on a weekly basis, but in addition there is a substantial degree of informal communication. Absolute limits on net cash positions are usually established on a per country basis, and any deviation has to be approved by the central finance staff.

Cash management in divisional concerns is similar, with relatively frequent monitoring of subsidiary cash levels on a country-by-country basis. By comparison, the matrix companies, having established clear decision rules, tend to allow much more decentralisation, utilising the remittance policy and foreign exchange management systems as controls over cash levels. In those firms where regional headquarters systems have been built up, regional cash pools tend to be a feature which is managed by local financial staff within central guidelines. In Company N, a European multinational consumer products manufacturer, for example, all cash requirements for group companies operating in Western Europe come from a series of central cash pools and balances are sent to divisional centres daily where they are utilised for group purposes or placed on the foreign exchange markets. There is also an informal examination of the cash and working capital positions monthly and a formal detailed examination on a quarterly basis embracing cash balances, net debtor/creditor position, stocks, tax payments, dividends, raw material prices and exchange rates. Non-European operations tend to work again essentially in geographic groupings, where local regional management groups manage their own day-to-day cash, reporting to the corporate centre in detail on a quarterly basis. The determination of the currency balance in which cash pools are held may remain localised, but advice and in some cases clear rules come from the central treasury function.

The management of cash in those multinationals which combine a mixture of wholly owned, partially owned and strongly nationalistic subsidiaries tends to be complex and involve an amalgam of centralised and decentralised control. Imperial Chemical Industries, for example, has over 400 subsidiaries and manufactures in more than 40 countries. Its system of global cash management has evolved in large part from the pragmatic extension of UK methods suitably modified.

With the exception of certain large, non-wholly-owned subsidiaries, all cash in the UK is centralised at the corporate headquarters. By a variety of methods this is passed through London-based banks daily. The operating divisions use their own bank accounts for limited purposes only, such as wage payments and the like, operating as closely as possible to a nil balance by transferring surpluses to the centre or obtaining central funds to cover deficits.

Export proceeds arrive in more variable form and more complex arrangements are used to optimise cash flow. External customers are encouraged to remit by cable or airmail to specific City banks or their overseas correspondents, while group subsidiaries remit by cable transfer, so allowing sterling export proceeds to become cleared funds on the day of receipt. Other major receipt items such as royalties, loans, commissions, sales proceeds of investments and the like are controlled as to timing and account destination by the group centre.

Cash outflows for invoices are handled by central computer facilities with all divisional purchases from one supplier being consolidated into a single payment. Something like 75 per cent of these are posted on the penultimate working day of the month, thus allowing the centre time to arrange cover. All currency payments pass through the central office, so allowing for planned currency purchasing.

Detailed cash forecasts form an essential link in the control of these operations. A detailed month-by-month projection is made for the year ahead and a general forecast for the following two years. These forecasts indicate the expected liquidity position and indicate short, medium or even long-term financing needs. A second forecast covers the short term and is built up from daily advice passed to the Treasury from sales and purchases accounts department, overseas accounts and foreign exchange sections, and operating divisions. Disbursements, such as dividend and interest payments made from the centre, are added and the whole collated to produce a forecast for the next few days ahead.

A separate finance subsidiary has been established to handle centrally all short-term borrowing and depositing of funds. Sales proceeds are routed through this subsidiary in such a way that any surplus or deficit arises in this unit, which is also responsible for foreign exchange exposure management and advising overseas subsidiaries on their money management systems.

Overseas, where the ICI equity stake is less than 100 per cent and local shareholdings exist, such as in Canada, Australia and India or in joint venture situations, short-term policy is controlled locally. This is usually within limits established between local management and the centre, the local treasurer then arranging his own funds transfers, borrowings, deposits and exchange risks.

In the case of wholly owned subsidiaries central advice is provided to local management to ensure a group perspective is taken. Cash arrangements are centralised to create one cash centre in each country in which more than one subsidiary operates, and in Europe coordination on a regional basis occurs in Brussels. Cash management is also integrated with foreign exchange risk management. Short-term cash forecasts sent to London by subsidiaries thus contain detailed estimates of currency receipts and payments arising from both intra-group and external transactions, thus allowing the centre to examine the matrix of cash centres, each with a currency exposure position. This permits action to be taken on forward cover both at the centre and in the subsidiaries.

The cash forecasts provided from each cash centre when aggregated enable the central treasury to construct a group policy for short-term borrowings, surpluses and internal fund transfers such as dividends and other remittances to the parent. Each cash centre not only indicates its expected surplus or deficit position, but also indicates its short-term borrowing facilities and local money market conditions. Thus, in addition to giving advice on currency risks, it is possible for the centre to reduce group currency risk exposure, interest rate differentials and the like, subject to exchange control regulations. This is achieved by means of a computer model which is programmed to indicate an optimum financing strategy.

Working Capital Management

Non-cash working capital management also tends to be decentralised in all forms of multinational organisation, although central office interventions tend to be more direct in the international division concerns. In grid structures decision rules govern working capital positions with policy implementation being handled by local staff. In these firms, however, central office changes in the ratio positions of working capital categories tend to be relatively frequent, since this often forms an integral component in foreign exchange management.

The principal method of control over working capital stems from the planning system, most organisations agreeing limits with individual subsidiaries according to the needs of the business, local financial conditions and the like. Ideal ratio targets are often utilised and modified to suit specific situations. Actual performance is then monitored regularly against plan, usually on a monthly basis.

The performance of individual subsidiaries is normally measured, at least partially, in terms of return on investment or assets managed, and this is considered to provide a further check on working capital levels, especially where reward systems are performance-related. A number of companies also charge interest on working capital increases, especially when these are obtained from central funds. More recently somewhat greater central attention has become focused on net working capital positions as with cash flow due to central interest in the management of currency exposure positions.

Subsidiary Capital Structure

In virtually all firms no discretion is permitted in the capital structure of overseas subsidiaries and any changes in such structures must normally be agreed with the central finance function. The choice of capital structure for an overseas subsidiary is dependent on many factors, and no one universal system is appropriate. One recent study has indicated the substantial differences that prevail in capital structures for particular industries in different countries, as shown in Table 5.1.

The reasons for these differences are many and various, but amongst the more important are:

Most capital markets outside the USA and the UK are too small to absorb major security flotations, although the capital markets in Western Europe are improving. There has also been a general lack of interest on the part of individuals, insurance companies, pension funds and the like in large equity portfolios. Most corporate security issues of both debt and equity tend to be placed privately with banks and private lenders. In a number of important countries, including Japan and West Germany, the major banks also combine the role of lender and stockholder, increasing perhaps the

Table 5.1 Debt Ratios in Selected Industries and Countries*

	Alcoholic Beverages	*Auto-mobiles*	*Chemicals*	*Electrical*	*Foods*	*Iron and Steel*	*Non-ferrous Metals*	*Paper*	*Textiles*	*Total*
Benelux	45.7	—	44.6	37.5	56.2	50.0	59.2	35.9	54.2	47.9
France	35.8	36.0	34.3	59.1	24.7	33.7	55.0	35.5	20.9	37.2
W. Germany	59.2	55.1	54.8	67.5	42.5	63.8	68.1	71.8	44.9	58.6
Italy	64.9	77.3	68.2	73.6	66.4	77.9	67.5	—	66.6	70.3
Japan	60.9	70.3	73.2	71.1	78.3	74.5	74.5	77.7	72.2	72.5
Sweden	—	76.4	45.6	60.1	46.8	70.0	68.7	60.7	—	61.2
Switzerland	—	—	59.7	50.8	29.2	—	26.3	—	—	41.5
UK	43.8	56.5	38.7	46.9	47.6	44.9	41.7	46.6	42.4	45.5
US	31.1	39.2	43.3	50.3	34.2	35.8	36.7	33.9	44.2	38.7
Total	48.8	58.7	51.4	57.4	47.3	56.3	55.3	51.7	49.4	

* The number in the matrix represents average total debt as a percentage of total assets based on book value. Each company is weighted equally, i.e. the individual company debt ratios are summed and divided by the number of companies in each sample.

Source: Stonehill and Stitzel. (See Chapter 5, note 13.)

desirability of high leverage and thus explaining the high debt ratios of companies in these countries.

Tax treatment variations between countries explain some structure differences, thus tax treatment of interest, royalties, management fees, depreciation and the like vary greatly between countries.

National attitudes toward financial risk vary. Debt levels acceptable to bankers in Sweden and Japan would often be totally unacceptable in the USA.[13]

Table 5.2 lists, in order of relative importance, those factors which according to a recent study amongst major British and European multinationals were cited by corporate treasurers as principally influencing their choice of capital structure for subsidiaries. Most frequently mentioned were taxation rates, including withholding taxes, remittance possibilities, political stability and local capital availability. These could be interpreted as meaning that firms were concerned about reducing the amount of money invested in foreign countries, maximising returns, and keeping a careful eye on the long-term security of any assets held abroad by an evaluation of likely political developments.[14] Clearly the structures adopted for individual countries varied, but all firms tended to consider a number of the factors listed in making their decisions, although the more sophisticated firms had well-established procedures, while still treating each case separately.

While individual cases were treated on their merits a number of generalisations are possible. Most of the multinationals surveyed disliked granting foreign equity participations, although a small number actually encouraged them, having considered that they were becoming inevitable in many countries. Nearly all the firms utilised local capital whenever possible, both to reduce foreign exchange and political risk.

Overseas companies in smaller multinationals tend to be relatively undercapitalised, to avoid capital levies and reduce political exposure. Intercompany debts may be allowed to increase and loans be left outstanding, as it is argued that there is a better chance of removing money through current account indebtedness and loans. These policies become more difficult as overseas operations grow bigger. Further, some countries,

Table 5.2 Principal Factors affecting Subsidiary Capital Structures

Average number of factors used by each company = 3.3

	Relative weight of individual factors % used
Government constraints	8
Interest rates	6
Political stability	11
Group capital structure	7
Future forex movements	4
Remittance prospects	15
Local capital availability	13
Degree of ownership	2
Managerial motivation	2
Other	15
Total	100

Source: J. C. S. Kimber, op. cit.

notably in Latin America, pressurise for the capitalisation of reserves to ensure that capital size stays in line with growth of the business.

Foreign Exchange Management

The management of foreign exchange exposure is rapidly becoming one of the most important managerial tasks for international financial executives. In the international division organisations relatively limited overseas operations permit a close central supervision of net exposure positions on a reasonably frequent basis. Growing complexity makes this task increasingly difficult, and largely for this reason many divisional companies have still not developed adequate central systems, due usually to a shortage of specialist management. As a result such firms are often relatively decentralised, utilising decision rules on a country-by-country basis. By contrast the matrix organisations have tended to develop sophisticated short-term foreign exposure risk management mechanisms. This area has increasingly become the key responsibility of central management in establishing decision rules in areas such as working capital and cash levels.

Foreign exchange management involves the minimisation of risk and the maximisation of any potential gains. Practical risk minimisation at the lowest cost needs centralised management on a global or regional basis. The presence of non-wholly-owned subsidiaries thus presents a difficulty.

Among the European multinationals researched, those with a developed foreign exchange (forex) management system tended to conduct their own investigations and constantly monitor overseas currencies as well as using the services of banks and other specialists. The main variables monitored by one such corporation are shown in Table 5.3.

Table 5.3 Foreign Exchange Rate Indicators

Macro-economic	*Local Financial*	*Local Political*
Balance of payments	Change in the money supply	Government stability
Balance of trade	Bank credit position	Party economic policies
Level of overseas borrowings	Local interest rates	Election dates
Foreign exchange reserves level	Forward exchange rates	National budget policies
International bank position	Commodity and property price indices	Government exchange rate intervention policy
Comparative rate of inflation	Local collections trend	
	Relative bankruptcy rate	

Source: Business International Money Report, 18 March 1976.

In Company O, a major Anglo-Dutch multinational, the group's exposure is considered with respect to four yardstick currencies, sterling, Dutch guilders, deutschmarks and dollars. Future exchange rate movements are forecast by the central finance group, utilising inputs from local sources, a central economics and statistics department and a top management overseas committee. These assessments are compared with expert advice from foreign exchange dealers in London, Hamburg and Rotterdam against a background of general economic development. Regular studies of macro-economic trends are conducted covering trade flows, balance of payments figures, purchasing power, local political activity, interest rate pressures and others.

Exposure minimisation is achieved mainly via local borrowing to net assets to liabilities, and by use of forward cover. The company does not attempt to speculate and opportunity costs of funds are largely ignored. The company does, however, take a position to avoid expected significant exchange rate changes, such as devaluations.

The company in this last respect is fairly typical of the multinationals examined. The main methods utilised by firms in exchange risk reduction are shown in Table 5.4. Nearly all firms utilise forward cover. Most firms collect forward cross-border cash forecasts on a monthly basis which itemise such factors as export receipts, import payments, dividends, interest, royalties, management fees and loan repayments. These figures are made available currency by currency from all subsidiaries. The centre can then decide what to do about the overall risks revealed. These are largely dealt with by matching, with entry into spot or forward markets being made in respect of the balance of receipts or payments. While this is the normal pattern and most firms took the view that they should not engage in speculation, a few have begun to hire experienced foreign exchange dealers and have made profits, some significant, from forex operations.

Table 5.4 Foreign Exchange Risk Reduction Mechanisms

Average number of instruments used per firm = 2.7

	% of sample companies using
Forward cover	85
Leads and lags	61
Trade payments	31
Equate Assets and liabilities	31
Management fees, etc.	15
Loan structuring	23
Loan timing	15
Other	8

Source: J. C. S. Kimber, op. cit.

After hedging, leads and lags tends to be the main route utilised for coverage. Over 60 per cent of the European and

Table 5.5 Limits on Leads and Lags and Netting in Select Countries* (periods given below are maximum possible terms)

Country	*Export lag*	*Export lead*	*Import lag*	*Import lead*	*Netting*
Argentina	180 days	Allowed – no limit	180 days[1]	Not allowed	Not permitted
Australia	180 days[2]	30 days	180 days[3]	180 days	Permission required
Belgium	180 days[4]	90 days[4]	180 days[4]	90 days[4]	Permission required
Brazil	Not allowed	Allowed – no limit	180 days	Not allowed[5]	Not permitted
Canada	Allowed – no limit	Allowed – no limit	Allowed – no limit	Allowed – no limit	Permitted
France	180 days	Allowed – no limit	90 days[6]	Not allowed[7]	Permission required but difficult
Germany	Allowed – no limit	Allowed – no limit	Allowed – no limit	Allowed – no limit	Permitted
Ireland	180 days	Allowed – no limit	Allowed – no limit	Not permitted	Permission required but readily available
Italy	120 days[8]	360 days	360 days	80 days	Not permitted[9]
Japan	180 days	180 days[10]	120 days[11]	120 days[11]	Not permitted[12]
Korea	Permitted but not encouraged	Permission required	Permitted but not encouraged	Permission required but rare	Permitted
Mexico	Allowed – no limit	Allowed – no limit	Allowed – no limit	Allowed – no limit	Permitted
Netherlands	Allowed – no limit	Allowed – no limit	Allowed – no limit	Allowed – no limit	Permitted
New Zealand	180 days	Allowed – no limit[13]	Allowed – no limit	Not allowed[14]	Permission required[15]
Philippines	60 days[16]	Allowed – no limit	Allowed – no limit	Not allowed	Permission required but authorities flexible
South Africa	180 days[17]	Allowed – no limit	180 days	Not allowed[18]	Not permitted except with special permission
Spain	90 days	180 days	180 days[19]	Not allowed[20]	Permission required but difficult
Sweden	180 days[21]	Allowed – no limit	180 days[21]	Not allowed[22]	Permission required[23]
Switzerland	Allowed – no limit	Allowed – no limit	Allowed – no limit	Allowed – no limit	Permitted
Taiwan	Generally not permitted[24]	Tolerated[24]	Tolerated[24]	Permitted in some cases[24]	Not possible
UK	180 days	Allowed – no limit	Allowed – no limit	Not allowed	Permitted
US	Allowed – no limit	Allowed – no limit	Allowed – no limit	Allowed – no limit	Permitted

* Based on information primarily obtained locally from finance ministries, central and commercial banks.

[1] But longer lags are permitted for capital goods; [2] Deferred terms are approved for export of capital equipment and in some instances where goods are sent abroad on consignment; [3] Longer periods may be granted by central bank if normal commercial practice with goods is involved; [4] As of mid-February, the Belgium/Luxembourg Exchange Institute requires permission for all commercial payments above Bfr10 million. Permission is now being refused for transactions involving a time lag between payment and billing dates; [5] Except with special permission from exchange department of central bank for a maximum of 25 per cent of value of imports; [6] Except for imports of raw materials that have a maximum lag time of 180–360 days; [7] Except for 30 per cent down payment on imported capital goods and 10 per cent down payment on imported noncapital goods; [8] Once payment is received, Italian exporters can only hold foreign exchange denominated accounts for 15 days as opposed to 30; [9] Italian exchange office of Foreign Trade Ministry can authorise exceptions. Offsetting debts and credits can be affected by banks only when two different firms are involved, except for oil companies; [10] But exporters are allowed to receive advances for up to 12 months on export contracts less than $500,000; [11] But importers are usually bound by the contracted time of payment; [12] Except for 'invisible' trade-related items, such as harbour charges and warehouse fees, etc.; [13] But not customary, except in the wool trade; [14] In special cases, the reserve bank will allow early deposits – down payments – on capital equipment where called for by usual trade practice; [15] But is not usual – precise status in law is unclear; [16] The full value of exports is normally required to be remitted within 60 days; however, lags of up to 180 days are allowed for new exports or sales to new markets; [17] Once payment is received, exporter can hold foreign exchange for seven days as opposed to 30; [18] With exchange control approval, and after specially designed equipment is ordered, up to 40 per cent of the value of the order may be paid in advance; [19] Includes 90-day grace period; longer lags are permitted; [20] Except with special permission or if 25 per cent down payment is required for placement of order; [21] 180 days or customary conditions of payment, whichever is shorter; [22] Except for one-third down payment on machinery and related goods, and consignments of under Skr50,000 with permission; [23] Must be based on current payments and is authorised only if it involves balancing out of accounts between Swedish parents and their direct foreign subsidiaries (i.e. multiparty netting is banned); [24] Technically, these practices are allowed since there are no specific regulations concerning leads and lags; however, the country's all-embracing exchange control system ordinarily makes leads and lags impractical.

Source: Business International.

British companies surveyed utilised leads and lags, while it has been estimated that as much as 50 per cent of all US corporate hedging activity is conducted in this way.[15] An example of how this type of method works is shown in Figure 5.5, which shows intracompany cash flows under normal trading conditions and when a currency realignment is feared. Countries vary substantially in their tolerance of leads and lags techniques. The regulations prevailing in a number of major countries are shown in Table 5.5.

In addition to simple leads and lags transactions a number of variations can be applied to increase the scope for reducing forex exposure, including the following:

1. Invoices should be denominated in a hard currency whenever possible.
2. Weak currency receipts can be offset by purchases of physical goods whenever possible.
3. Build up stocks of imported goods in countries where devaluation is likely.
4. Tighten credit terms and introduce penalty charges for late payment on weak currency receipts. There are limits to this policy due to competitive reaction.
5. Cover net exposed local assets by offsetting local borrowing. There are many ways of achieving this with costs varying according to the source of finance.
6. Minimise locally held weak currency holdings by transferring excess funds to regional cash pools and the like.
7. In the case of blocked local funds try and convert weak currency cash into time deposits or claims in hard currencies or assets unlikely to be affected by devaluation.
8. Consider the sale of forward weak currency receipts on the forward exchange market.
9. Consider buying exchange forward for debts likely to accumulate in hard currencies.
10. Consider the use of special currency risk insurance in extreme cases.

Remittance Policy

The determination of remittance policy is consistently highly centralised, the key difference between different types of

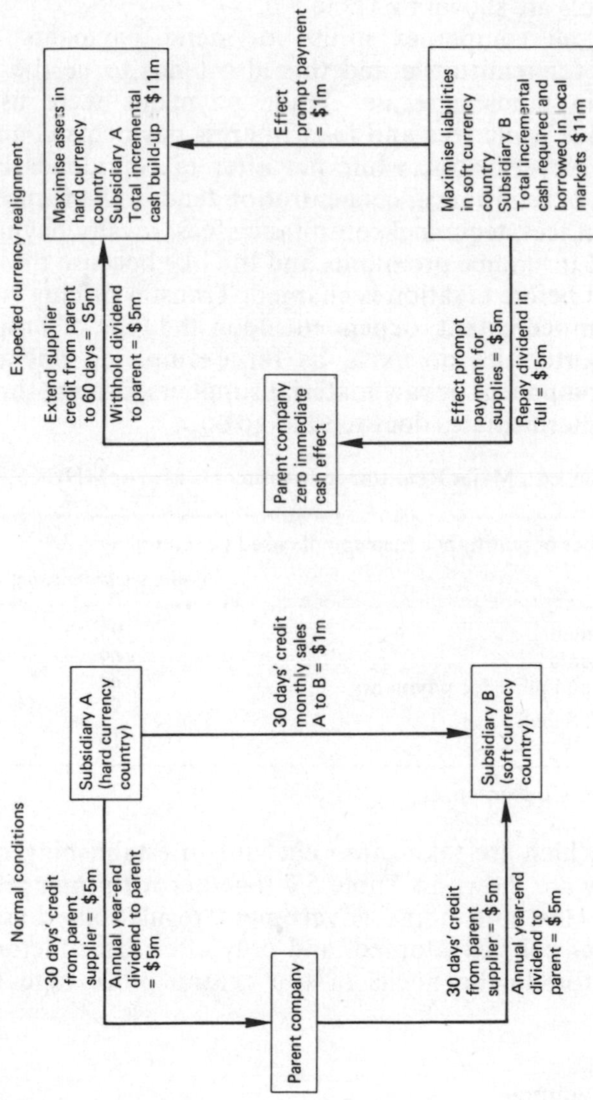

Fig. 5.5 Leads and Lags in Hedging Technique

Source: Wooster and Thoman, op. cit.

organisation tends to be in the degree of sophistication adopted in the financial methods used and routes adopted. The principal methods of remittance observed in European and British multinationals are shown in Table 5.6.

Virtually all companies utilise dividend payments as a mechanism for remittance and this also tends to be the most important in terms of scale. Trade payments were usually second in size while fees and loan interest payments count for much less. Nevertheless, while net after tax dividends is the largest item of remittance, concentration tends to be focused on management fees, technical consultancy fees, royalty payments, licence fees, insurance premiums and the like because these are remitted net before taxation is charged. Transfer pricing is used to only a limited extent, dependent upon the type of business. Where opportunities do exist, as for example in operations involving component or raw material suppliers, pricing through tax haven intermediates does tend to go on.

Table 5.6 Major Remittance Instruments used in MNCs

Average number of remittance instruments used per company = 2.9

	% of companies using
Dividend payments	95
Interest payments	69
Management and other fee payments	90
Transfer pricing	31
Loan repayments	13

Source: J. C. S. Kimber, op. cit.

Factors which are taken into account in establishing remittance policy are shown in Table 5.7 together with their relative weighting. Host and home government regulations dominate the choice of policies adopted, and only after these factors are accounted for do the needs of the central office tend to be optimised.

Taxation Planning

Taxation planning tends to become a more important financial management interest as the scale of overseas operations develops.

Table 5.7 Key Factors governing Remittance Policy

Average number of factors considered = 3.9

	% of total number factors cited
Host government regulations	25
Home government regulations	18
Central office requirements	13
Financing needs	13
Tax planning	10
Political image	8
Other	15

Source: J. C. S. Kimber, op. cit.

It is almost inevitably a central office responsibility when it is seriously undertaken, with the creation of specialist tax departments as part of the treasury function. While this subject is dealt with more extensively elsewhere, amongst the European multinationals researched it was found that the tax planning arrangements are still poorly integrated with the corporate planning system, which still tended to examine overseas operations on a pre-tax rather than post-tax basis.

CONCLUSION

The potential impact of international financial management on the profitability of the MNC is so large that it must command high priority in developing suitable managerial expertise to fulfil the task. Although many multinationals are rapidly becoming aware of this, many others have still to develop adequate financial systems for the global management of a complex organism. The growth of overseas operations suggests that for those companies which have underdeveloped systems they should compare their own position with that of some of the corporations described above with regard to each of the main tasks of international treasury management and be prepared to amend their procedures accordingly.

6 International Tax Planning

The planning of the international tax position in the MNC has become a vital factor in investment decisions, capital structure, working capital management and overall corporate profitability. Tax planning is an extremely complex management task since the rules are constantly changing. It is not possible therefore in this chapter to cover the subject in detail since the topic is too large and the results would be obsolescent almost as they were written. Rather the intention is to examine briefly the main mechanisms used for tax reduction and to illustrate the effects of some of these. Detailed considerations for the individual corporation must be developed on a unique basis, to meet the specific strategic needs and objectives of the enterprise concerned.

The importance attached to tax planning in making major investment decisions in the MNC varies from firm to firm. One recent survey covering 140 multinational companies based in the USA, France, Germany and the UK invited firms to rank in order of importance some 78 possible influences on investment location decisions.[1] Among these were five relating to tax treatment, which were rated as shown in Table 6.1.

Table 6.1 Effect of Tax Variables on Investment Location Decisions

MNC Home Country	*US*	*UK*	*France*	*W. Germany*
Tax rate differentials	17	5	9	23
Tax incentives	32	12	30	19
Joint tax treaties	39	67	65	28
Tax loss carry back and forward	41	24	53	30
Tax of export income and income earned abroad	49	48	52	47

The most important factor overall in determining the choice of investment location was political risk, followed by supply considerations. When the 78 factors were grouped into nine clusters, the tax factor was ranked third overall. The survey revealed, however, that European-based MNCs were more concerned with taxation, which they ranked second to the supply factor, with political risk third. US firms, in contrast, ranked political risk first, followed by the supply factor, the labour factor and, fourthly, taxation.

Apart from the rates of tax and incentives prevailing in individual countries, however, the main area of concern to the tax planner is that of taxation resulting from international, as opposed to domestic operations. In general, no international tax complications occur from domestic operations, but rather they arise when income from one country accrues to an operation resident in a second country. Should this income be taxed in both countries a double taxation situation would arise. The basic aim of tax planning is to avoid such occurrences and, by a variety of techniques, to reduce the level of profitability created in high-tax countries while increasing profits in low-tax ones, including tax havens. There are two basic techniques in tax avoidance, each of which raises different problems and which must be used in conjunction with normal commercial considerations for prudent managerial action. These techniques are:

Diversion: in which profits are diverted from high-tax to low-tax countries, usually by trading.

Extraction: in which pre-tax profits in a high-tax country are reduced by charges such as interest, royalties and the like.

DIVERSION TACTICS

The With or Within Decision

Diversion can be employed not only for intracompany operations between manufacturing centres but for trading operations. In this it is important to distinguish the differences between trading *with* a country and establishing a presence *within* a country. For tax purposes therefore it is important to understand the legal definitions of what constitutes a permanent establishment within a particular country since only such operations are normally subject to local taxes. Merely trading with a country, therefore, does not usually incur a local tax liability. Most domestic tax laws approximate to the OECD model tax treaty definition of a permanent establishment. This includes a place of management, a branch, an office, a factory, a workshop, a mine or quarry and a building site which exists for more than 12 months. A number of LDCs, however, dislike this definition since they argue it is possible to carry out profit-making activities involving their countries, without establishing a permanent establishment.

One frequently used such method of operating without a permanent establishment is by use of a representative office. Representative offices, warehouses and display facilities, purchasing offices and information collecting centres are specifically excluded from the OECD definition of a permanent site. Representative offices and service subsidiaries are therefore frequently used as a cheap method of overseas entry with significant tax advantages, although precise treatments vary from country to country. This method has been especially widely used by banks in developing overseas operations and in some countries, for example Hong Kong, is the only method of establishing a local presence.

For normal trading activities the establishment of a conduit company for diversion of profits is a widely practised technique and is illustrated in Figure 6.1. The company, instead of selling

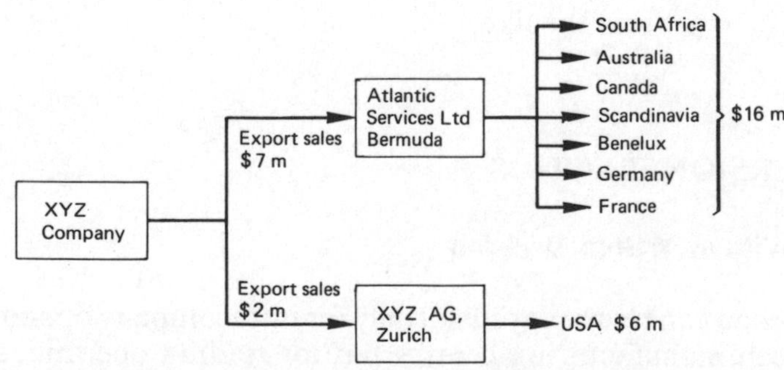

Fig. 6.1 Sales Conduit Subsidiary Operation

its products direct to its customers in other countries, operates through two conduit companies.

If, for example, the sales to the USA are made direct, some US source income would be subject to a 30 per cent withholding tax. It would therefore be useful to structure this trade through a 'conduit' country with a bilateral tax treaty with the USA, such that the aggregate tax burden suffered in the conduit would be less than 30 per cent. Two such countries are the Netherlands Antilles and Switzerland.[2] For other countries this may not be the best alternative and in the illustration XYZ Company utilises a Bermuda conduit for the bulk of its overseas sales. This route is, however, not useful for servicing US sales since there is no suitable bilateral tax treaty.

Tax Incentives for Exports

Not only is conduiting of some export traffic used for diversion but it is not uncommon for governments to sanction or even encourage artificial pricing, so reducing taxation, if this will encourage exports. Non-tax incentives, such as insurance, special grants, low interest rate loans, overseas market intelligence and the like, are almost universal. Although both the articles of GATT and the EEC specifically rule out most fiscal incentives, many countries operate significant tax-saving schemes. France and the USA for example have comprehensive export incentive schemes which allow manipulated transfer prices to create non-taxable income.

US companies may qualify as a domestic international sales corporation (DISC) when 95 per cent of income or more is derived from export-related activities, such as exporting or providing services in respect of those exports. US manufacturing firms, therefore, normally create a separate legal entity, the DISC corporation, to handle exports. From the profits of this DISC corporation, 50 per cent are deemed to be those of the parent and are taxed whether or not they are distributed. The remaining 50 per cent of the DISC's profits are not taxed in the US, and this situation can continue indefinitely until the DISC makes a distribution to its parent or is in some way disqualified.

Moreover, in arriving at the taxable income of a DISC, the normal US revenue insistence upon arm's-length pricing need not be applied. However, the internal transfer prices used must be such that they do not result in the DISC income exceeding specific limits. The tax-deferred income of a DISC may then be loaned to the company's parent or any other US export manufacturing corporation to finance an increase in its export operations. Such a loan is termed a 'producer's loan' and must have a maturity not exceeding five years and be made to a US-based export product manufacturer.[2]

In late 1975, the House Ways and Means Committee voted to allow DISC tax benefits only for the gain in average export profit over the 1972–4 period. The base would be 75 per cent of the annual average export profit in the 1972–4 period. Tax on half the income over that base would be deferred as under the existing law. Some restrictions were also imposed on product area and military exports and some raw agricultural products were ineligible for DISC treatment.

Apart from DISC corporations, the US government operates a number of special tax incentive corporate forms, notably the less developed country corporation, which allows certain tax incentives to firms operating in less developed countries, the possessions corporation, offering incentives for operations in US overseas territories such as the Canal Zone, Guam and American Samoa and the Western Hemisphere Trade Corporation which allows a special deduction for US tax purposes for corporations specifically engaged in business with Western Hemisphere countries. The House Ways and Means Committee in late 1975 voted to phase out the special benefits of Western Hemisphere Trading Corporations over a four-year period.

The French system of fiscal incentives for exports is less formal than that of the US but specifically allows firms to manipulate intracompany prices for export sales. For domestic activities intracompany trading is expected to adopt arm's-length pricing for tax purposes. In addition to pricing flexibility, French companies establishing an export office can create a deductible reserve to cover losses incurred by such an office for the first five years with no limit on the amount of capital to be invested.

Many other countries offer fiscal incentives for exports, including Australia, South Africa, India, Japan and Sweden. Ireland is especially generous charging no tax on profits derived from exports at all, while Spain has a provision enabling tax-free reserves to be built up to cover overseas market development.

Transfer Pricing

The area of transfer pricing, while clearly offering the main route for profit diversion, is also fraught with dangers and must be taken into account for all MNCs whether their intention is tax avoidance or not. In most countries tax authorities have the power to substitute 'arm's-length' prices for those prices claimed by companies in their dealings with affiliates. The US authorities have been especially aggressive in this respect and one study of 871 cases where the US IRS considered making adjustments to international transactions in 1968–9 revealed that these cases led to 1706 potential adjustments being made. Of these, the largest single area, involving 591 cases or 34 per cent of the total, were pricing adjustments. Only 29.5 per cent of these potential adjustments were, however, actually made but those then involved the largest average sums, of $1.8m compared with an overall average of around $850,000.[3]

The tough line adopted by the US authorities to maximise the level of US-based corporate profits, has prompted a reaction from other countries where US subsidiaries operate, who claim that taxable profits were made there, thus often creating a double tax claim. This often leads to an international dispute between the relevant tax authorities, leaving the MNC as an injured bystander and largely unprotected by dual tax treaties, which normally exist to prevent this type of dual claim.

In large measure the problem arises from the difficulty of defining an 'arm's-length' price. Only the US and French tax authorities have actually endeavoured to do so, and both of these methods are technically suspect or not applicable for export trade purposes. The scope and difficulty of the problem is highlighted by the case of the Swiss pharmaceutical manufacturer, Hoffman La Roche and the UK Monopolies Commission. Although its internal transfer price was accepted by the UK Revenue authorities, the company was investigated by the Monopolies Commission regarding the supply of two tranquilliser drugs, Librium and Valium. The authorities argued that the generic active ingredients for these could be purchased from Italian manufacturers for about £9 and £20 per kilo respectively, compared with the company's internal transfer price of £437 and £979 per kilo respectively. As a result the company was forced to reduce its prices in the UK, which were already amongst the lowest anywhere in the world, and was subjected to similar attacks by other anti-trust agencies in different countries.[4]

While this case clearly demonstrated enormous variation in open market and internal prices it is illustrative of some of the difficulties, since in justification the company claimed that prices were fixed not on a cost plus basis, but rather on the grounds of what the market would bear. Further, the company had substantial overheads, such as a high research and development commitment, not required in a low-cost manufacturing company copying patented products. All MNC's will find themselves with transfer pricing problems, if not from a chosen policy of tax reduction, then from conflicting reallocations from the tax or other authorities in both home and host countries. It is, therefore, essential for all MNCs to adopt a planned approach to intracompany pricing transactions across national boundaries, which takes full account of tax practices whether or not the objective is tax reduction.

For the tax minimiser, the optimum tax strategy would be to locate in a tax haven and centre all business from there. This has been done by a number of banks and financial institutions, but is impracticable for most manufacturing MNCs. A number have, however, located in countries offering tax holidays or substantial capital and investment grants. Ireland is especially attractive in the EEC, offering tax exemption on export profits, substantial cash and other grants, good repatriation guarantees and useful double taxation treaties. Elsewhere in Europe the Mezzogiorno region of Italy, West Berlin, and the development areas of the UK all offer potential attractions to the foreign investor. In countries therefore where substantial tax relief for export-derived profits applies, it would be useful to avoid setting up permanent establishments in the countries where sales are made. Should it be desirable to operate local sales subsidiaries, transfer prices from the low-tax manufacturing site should be maximised, and, where possible, the sales companies' profits restricted to a service fee or limited level of sales commission. For companies manufacturing in high-tax centres the feasibility of supplying components from or doing local assembly in low-tax countries should be explored.

The most simple form of diversion by transfer pricing is the establishment of a tax-haven-based sales subsidiary to which goods are invoiced at cost, before being sold at high prices to a third subsidiary or other parties operating in a high-tax area. The largest profit would then accrue to the sales subsidiary in the low-tax country. Purchasing subsidiaries can be established for the same purpose, the subsidiary buying at a low price and selling on to a manufacturing subsidiary in a high-tax location at a high price so as to leave manufacturing profits at a minimum. A variation of these methods is to allow the offshore subsidiary a commission for all sales or purchases channelled through it. Commissions, providing they are reasonable, are hardly ever subject to withholding taxes and are often preferable to extracting royalties and the like. All these transactions are effected by simple cross-invoicing procedures. More sophisticated variants can incorporate tacking on high interest charges to the price of goods sold or purchased to reduce pre-tax profits in a high-tax country. Similarly, goods may be sold as part of a package including royalties, management fees and the like. In each case, however, it is necessary to calculate the optimum tax strategy taking different tax rates and local attitudes into account. The principal locations for such subsidiaries are Switzerland, the Netherlands, Panama, Venezuela, the Channel Islands, Bermuda and US-based DISC corporations.[5]

It is important, however, that tax haven sales subsidiaries, especially for US-based multinationals, should actually operate, rather than be letterbox concerns, unless the operation is a DISC. This prevents difficulties with revenue authorities in high-tax areas such as the home country. This can be achieved by ensuring the sales company assumes a level of commercial risk and operates premises, employs people and so on. An alternative may be to locate a sales company in a country which has a low tax rate or to combine it with a servicing company.

Despite the opportunities offered for tax savings, a number of important potential disadvantages do occur from the use of diversion tactics; and these should be borne in mind before the adoption of such a policy. These disadvantages include:

1. It may become extremely difficult to evaluate the true profitability of individual subsidiaries.
2. Significant behavioural problems may occur when local management see all their efforts syphoned off, especially in performance related reward companies.

3. Serious difficulties usually occur with joint ventures.
4. The cost of administration may not be justified by tax savings.
5. Unrealistic prices may lead to accusations of dumping or substitution of prices by local authorities, so negating the value of the exercise.

EXTRACTION

Financial Structure

There are a number of major extraction mechanisms, the most important of which, in terms of scale, and an essential ingredient of any multinational strategy, is by adequate attention being paid to the determination of subsidiary financial structures. Ideally, high debt structures should apply in high-tax countries with loans being made from tax haven operations. In this way the maximum income flow, subject to withholding taxes, would accrue in the low-tax environment. Multinational firms, therefore, make substantial use of special finance companies located in low-tax countries which either lend on funds accrued from the parent or other group subsidiaries, or enter the capital markets and raise funds themselves. Such a finance company then operates as an internal corporate bank. Indeed, many industrial companies including Dow, Firestone and Nestlé, have established authorised banks, which have particular advantages as financing vehicles.

In addition to potential tax advantages the establishment of a separate finance subsidiary tends to concentrate attention on the need to develop global corporate treasury techniques such as those described in Chapter 5 with regard to cash, working capital and forex management. It is even possible to convert such an operation into a profit centre, and a few finance companies have begun to take on work for third parties, having developed a range of sophisticated international financial services. The clear use of such finance corporations as profit centres actually improves their tax position markedly since it is accurate to claim that the subsidiary is not merely a letterbox tax convenience.

A major reason for the early formation of offshore finance

subsidiaries was to gain access to the Eurocurrency markets. Many countries impose restrictions on offshore interest payments and, to gain access to the world's largest capital market, offshore finance corporations have been formed by many US, German, British and Italian firms. In order to float Eurocurrency loans the main locations for offshore finance corporations tend to be the Netherlands Antilles, which has an especially favourable tax treaty for US companies in that no US withholding tax is levied on interest payments to them; Luxembourg, which is the centre for the Eurobond market and widely used by German MNCs; the Netherlands, often in conjunction with a Netherlands Antilles affiliate; and Panama and Liberia are also used.

The optimum position for a finance corporation is seldom if ever achievable. It is rare that a tax haven finance subsidiary will be allowed to lend at the highest rates to a high-tax-country subsidiary and receive gross interest payments. More likely there will be a series of withholding and other taxes and exchange control regulations in force. In addition, if the rate of interest charged by a tax haven subsidiary seems unreasonable, this may well lead to the imposition of anti-avoidance procedures, which substitute an 'arm's-length' interest rate.

Restrictions on capital structure and hence on excessive use of debt are commonly used by revenue authorities to limit interest payments to offshore finance corporations. Such systems operate in Canada and the USA. Other countries limit the rate of interest payable abroad irrespective of the lending source. Thus in Belgium the tax code prohibits the deduction of interest where this exceeds the central bank interest rate for advances to public securities, plus 3 per cent or 9 per cent when rates are below 6 per cent. The UK provides that interest paid by a UK subsidiary to a foreign parent is not an allowable tax deduction and will be treated as a distribution, unless tax at a standard 30 per cent is withheld. This rule is only waived under UK double tax treaties and even these are subject to some exceptions. However by means of such treaties, zero withholding tax rates apply between the UK and a number of countries including Germany, the Netherlands, Switzerland and the USA.[6]

With care, most restrictions can, however, be avoided. The most important methods used for this purpose involve conduit arrangements or the use of third party intermediate organisations.

Under such a system use is made of double tax treaties or interest payments in respect of financial operations to reduce effective withholding tax rates. The location of such conduits is dependent on three main factors, namely a system of favourable double tax treaties, local tax rules which accept that the conduit company will only take a small turn on transactions and finally no withholding tax on the payment of interest to the lender.

An alternative to the use of an internally owned conduit company is to use a third party agency, and in particular local banks, to broke transactions in conduit countries. Banks may also qualify for withholding tax exemptions which apply specifically to banks in many double tax treaties. An illustration of such a back-to-back bank conduit transaction which also provides a method of reducing foreign exchange risk exposure is shown in Figure 6.2.[7]

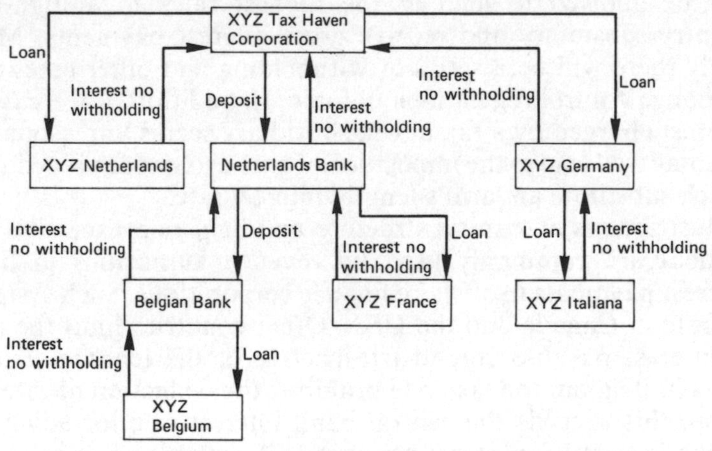

Fig. 6.2 Combined Back-to-Back Finance Corporation Extraction Operations

This shows how to avoid withholding taxes and extract interest from a series of European subsidiaries. Assuming the tax haven original lender is a UK non-resident corporation, the Belgian withholding tax on interest for direct loans is 20 per cent, in France 10 per cent, West Germany and the Netherlands zero and Italy 35 per cent. However, a zero rate of withholding normally applies if interest is paid from a Belgian bank to a Dutch bank. The tax haven company could therefore lend to a Netherlands bank which would on-lend to a Belgian bank which in turn could lend to the Belgian subsidiary. This would involve two bank profits but might well be less than the 20 per cent withholding.

Lending to France normally involves a 10 per cent withholding tax but under a French/Dutch tax treaty no withholding applies to interest payments to financial institutions. Thus use is again made of the Dutch bank to provide funds to the French subsidiary. Italy represents a situation which requires different tactics since a withholding tax is levied on interest payments to Holland. No withholding applies to interest on loans from Germany, however, hence funds for Italy should be conduited through the German subsidiary, which like the Dutch, could be funded directly, since neither country normally applies withholding tax on interest payments.

The use of banks as illustrated, while increasing flexibility, can also lead to difficulties. Firstly, relative expense is significantly increased, secondly banks usually require full security for any lending they undertake, hence the terms back-to-back loans, credit swaps and switching deposits. The company must also normally bear any exchange exposure which might occur, although on occasion this can be used to advantage. For example, consider a swap deal whereby a finance subsidiary makes a hard currency deposit with a multinational bank and is provided with a corresponding facility in a soft currency country. The transaction is completed when the bank pays back the original deposit in its hard currency and the local subsidiary its soft currency loan. The intervening exchange exposure in this case tends to be in the company's favour.

Leasing

Leasing offers a relatively new and presently little developed method of extraction. A lease contract, as distinct from a hiring contract, normally exists between a lessee and lessor with the latter providing the finance to purchase an asset, the ownership of which is retained, but the precise nature of the asset is specified and used by the lessee for its working life, in return for a series of payments which are calculated to produce a return on the original outlay. As yet anti-avoidance measures covering leasing are rare in most countries. Leasing, which first developed in the USA, where now it is a major vehicle for financing capital investment, is still a relatively new means of financing in most other countries, although it is growing fast, encouraged by the spread of US multinational banks. It is a much more flexible method of finance than conventional lending techniques, although third party leasing is generally more expensive unless tax advantages are present. Nevertheless, lease payments can be adapted to take account of both the lessee's and lessor's respective profitability, cash flow and tax positions.

The domestic treatment of lease agreements varies greatly between countries and provides the basis for attractive potential avoidance procedures. At its most simple a tax haven subsidiary could borrow money from its parent to purchase an asset, which would then be leased at a high price to a high-tax-country subsidiary. Further, it might also be possible for the parent or other group subsidiary to purchase an asset, reduce its own taxable profits by claiming high local depreciation allowances or alternatively selling the benefit of these allowances to a third party, and then to lease the asset for a low rent to a tax haven subsidiary which in turn could on-rent at a high rate to another group company resident in a high-tax country. In such a case one would capitalise on the benefits of 'tax leverage', as shown in Figure 6.3, by reducing high tax rates twice over and channelling funds into a tax haven.

It may also be possible to claim depreciation allowances on behalf of both the lessor and lessee, due to the differences in local tax treatment. In Germany and the Netherlands, for example, the right to depreciation lies with the lessee rather than the lessor. Leasing also provides a method for overcoming a country's poor depreciation rates which might extend over an asset's life. By leasing from a group company in a generous depreciation policy country, the lease terms can be arranged to ensure that the depreciation period is much shorter than the life of the asset.

Lease payments are also very useful in reducing political risk exposure, especially if local borrowing cannot be found to finance capital investment. Rental payments may well not be restricted, as other technical services may be, and in the event of confiscation assets do not belong to the local subsidiary, but to a foreign parent. Alternatively, a back-to-back type arrangement may be possible so that ownership resides with a third

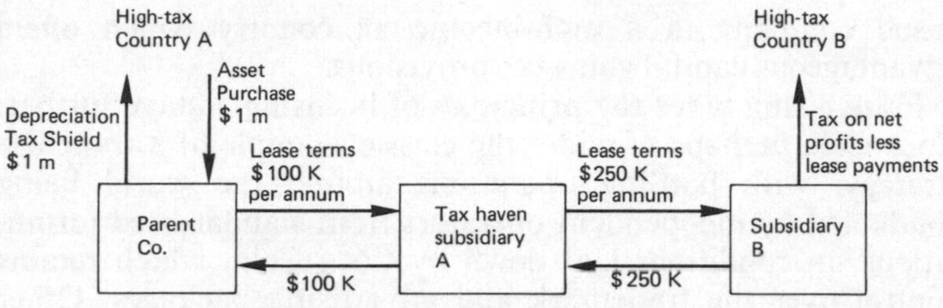

Fig. 6.3 Tax Leverage Leasing Operations

party. Leasing may also be used to counter debt equity ratio restrictions and contracts may be written in hard currencies to reduce exchange risk exposure.

While tax treatments vary considerably there is a growing tendency for countries to treat rental income in the same way as royalty income. In the absence of a permanent establishment, therefore, rental income might suffer the withholding tax applicable to royalty and applied to the entire amount of the lease payments, making the establishment of a permanent presence in a country a potentially necessary step.

While a tax haven-based subsidiary may be used to locate a leasing company the situation is more complex than most tax-saving areas. In many cases it may be preferable to take advantage of generous depreciation provisions and a strong tax treaty position. For many international leasing companies, therefore, the UK may be an optimum location possessing good depreciation policies, a wide range of double tax treaties and access to the Eurocurrency markets. Switzerland is also a favoured location for similar reasons.

Licensing and Technology Payments

Licensing and technology payments are a widely used method of extraction. The optimum tax strategy is generally to offset research costs against profits in a high-tax country and locate patents and the like in a low-tax environment. A tax haven company could then sell or license its technology at a profit to group subsidiaries or third parties. Withholding and other taxes on the income of the low-tax company could be reduced by conduiting. In practice the situation is seldom this simplistic and it may actually be advantageous to locate a technology-based company in a high-income-tax country which offers advantageous capital gains tax provisions.

Franchising takes the principles of licensing a stage further. Coca Cola perhaps provides the classic example of a franchise strategy, with bottling operations around the world being conducted by independent operators from standardised formulations, in conditions laid down by Coca Cola, which retains control over the trademark and advertising packages. Other examples include Kentucky Fried Chicken and Holiday Inns. In general, franchising can lead to profits from both royalties and management fees. However, because of the relative newness of the concept, the rules for tax treatment are somewhat less established than for royalties, and it is occasionally found that greater flexibility prevails.[8]

The tax treatment of licensee and royalty payments varies substantially. Royalty payments normally are accepted as tax-deductible, but capital sums paid out for patents and the like are usually considered as capital expenditure and are therefore not deductible from profits. Correspondingly, royalty revenues are normally treated as income and taxed accordingly, while capital sums may be treated as capital gains. It is therefore imperative to ensure that any income received by one company must be treated as tax deductible by the payer. On occasion it is, however, possible to improve this position. For example, the payment from a sale may be classified as a deductible expense for the payer and as a capital gain which is either untaxed or taxed at a low rate for the seller.

It is becoming increasingly difficult, however, to pass on parent company research costs to subsidiaries in the form of royalty fees or research contributions. At the same time, home base tax authorities are increasingly insisting that at least part of such costs are actually allocated to overseas subsidiaries. The MNC, therefore, tends to be caught in a tax trap brought about by conflict between tax authorities. The prior registration of licence agreements is, therefore, generally a requirement to ensure a favourable tax treatment. Care must also be taken to avoid unreasonable charges since many countries will also include 'arm's-length' imputation provisions, to guard against excessive royalty or research contributions.

Having established deductibility, the main tax problem is then one of avoiding the withholding taxes which are often imposed. These rates, too, are highly variable and are affected significantly by double tax treaties. This is illustrated in Table 6.2, which shows the rate of withholding tax deducted on royalties, first in the absence of a double agreement and secondly where the recipient is a resident of three countries with a network of such tax agreements.

Table 6.2 Tax Treatment of Royalty Payments for Selected Countries

Royalty payments from	*General rate (%)*	*Rate on payments to* UK (%)	USA (%)	Switzerland (%)
Belgium*	20	Nil	Nil	20
Canada	15	10	15	15
Denmark	Nil	Nil	Nil	Nil
France*	18.2	Nil	5	5
Ireland	35	Nil	Nil	Nil
Italy*	24.75†	3.3†	3.3†	24.75†
Netherlands*	Nil	Nil	Nil	Nil
Spain*	14‡	14‡	14‡	5
Sweden	43	Nil	Nil	Nil
Switzerland	Nil	Nil	Nil	
UK	41.25	—	Nil	Nil
USA	30	Nil	—	Nil

* Turnover taxes levied as well
† Includes approximate allowance for local taxes
‡ Reduced to 6 per cent in certain circumstances

Source: John F. Chown, *Taxation and Multinational Enterprise,* (Longmans, 1974), p. 83.

This normally means making use of double tax treaty conduits, and the Netherlands Antilles and Switzerland have been traditional favoured locations for technology-based companies. An alternative which has been growing rapidly is to avoid the royalty classification, and hence usually withholding taxes, by charging for 'knowhow' rather than patents although many countries now tend to allocate knowhow a similar tax treatment to royalties.

Management and Service Fees

The MNC operates a series of central services for its subsidiaries at the corporate headquarters. These cover a wide range of activities but normally include such areas as planning and organisation, legal and finance, control and coordination. Functional activities such as marketing, production and research and development may also be serviced partially from the centre. These services cost a substantial amount and means must therefore be found of fairly allocating these costs to overseas operations, quite apart from any tax avoidance considerations.

The area of management and corporate services has become, therefore, a significant area for the extraction of payment from subsidiaries. For tax purposes it may be possible to charge fees which are not subject to withholding taxes, unlike many royalty payments. Similarly it may be possible to locate service or headquarters companies in beneficial tax areas, in order to extract fees from high-tax countries and accumulate them in tax havens. Unfortunately many tax authorities take an especially suspicious view of internal service fees. In EEC countries for example it is becoming a growing trend that expenses will only be allowed if it can be shown that services have actually been performed and if possible have led to demonstrable benefit to the subsidiary.

On the other hand revenue authorities in many home base countries are insisting that MNCs charge out that part of their central costs which in no way relates to income generated locally. Thus many companies would be satisfied merely to ensure their legitimate expenses are tax-deductible, rather than attempt to use this area as a tax avoidance device.

A number of guidelines can be established which should be adopted to improve the chances of deductibility:[9]

1. The services must be shown to have been actually performed under a contractually binding contract for future services, and not a retroactive agreement.
2. The service must directly relate to, and benefit, the payer. This will often be difficult to prove unless the services increased the payer's revenue or produced other tangible benefits.
3. The agreement should emphasise the 'good business reason' which the payer has for entering into the agreement, except where such agreements should be widely drawn to allow room for manoeuvre with the local tax authorities, as in Italy.
4. It should be clear that those performing services are

giving valuable advice of a kind that could be sought from a third party, such as technical or marketing services. Pure management or controlling advice such as financial control and coordination will be regarded normally as an intangible advantage which should accrue without charge.

5. The services to be rendered should not be capable of being regarded in any way as costs which would normally be included in the intercompany prices of tangible goods.
6. Because the battle for deductibility will be fought locally, local management and auditors must willingly accept charges and argue for their deductibility in discussions with tax authorities.
7. Above all the charge for management services should be on an arm's-length basis and, to the greatest extent possible, reasonable in relation to local prices.
8. When calculating an arm's-length price it is vital to ensure that the services are reasonable in relation to the payer's (and its competitor's) financial position.
9. Arbitrary methods of fixing the basis of charge are not usually very successful, both because they are more difficult to substantiate and hence deduct, and from the viewpoint of flexibility. Thus the calculation of fees should not refer to profit levels or be based on a flat percentage of subsidiaries' sales, assets or turnover.
10. In order to substantiate costs, detailed records of the services provided and expenses incurred should be kept, showing the tangible benefits to the company concerned.

TAX HAVEN LOCATION

The traditional tax havens are seldom used as holding company locations for the receipt of dividends. They are more widely used for the receipt of royalty payments and cross-invoicing profits as well as providing special manufacturing bases in some cases. In general the choice of a tax haven location should be made as part of an overall strategic analysis of the needs of the firm. Without this, the usage of such operations may often not only be inappropriate but may actually increase the net tax burden.

Nevertheless, MNCs arc growing increasingly sophisticated

in their use of offshore tax haven locations for financing vehicles, intermediate holding companies and revenue collecting operations. One recent survey amongst European and British multinationals revealed that on average each MNC interviewed operated between two and three tax haven subsidiaries. In order of importance these firms made the most use of subsidiaries located in the Netherlands, and to a lesser extent the Netherlands Antilles, Bermuda, the British Channel Islands and Switzerland.[10] Other locations were much less widely used, although this reflects to some extent the sample, as North American companies make much greater use of Caribbean and Panamanian locations.

The Netherlands

Although not a tax haven, for many companies the Netherlands represents the most favoured location for an intermediate holding company. In general, Netherlands companies are exempt from tax on income or capital gains attributable from a foreign branch. Moreover, under participation provisions Netherlands companies are generally exempt from all Netherlands taxes in respect of dividends, and capital gains in respect of 'qualifying participations'. Such a participation must have been used by a Dutch holding company since the beginning of the year and must represent at least a 5 per cent holding. In addition, for foreign participations, any foreign dividend-paying company must be subject to *some* corporate tax on its profits (no matter at how low a rate) in the state where it is resident, and must be regarded as a portfolio investment. However, losses or expenses of qualifying foreign participations are not deductible from Netherlands taxable profits.

In general therefore a Netherlands holding company can receive dividend income which, if already taxed, is not taxed further upon receipt. Other trading income, such as interest, royalties and the like are subject to full Netherland taxes and therefore it may be optimal to first flow royalties or interest payments to an intermediary company, wholly owned by the Netherlands company. Such income should then be subject to a low tax rate in the intermediary's country of residence, and then paid out as dividends to the Dutch parent. This technique is often combined with Switzerland or the Netherlands Antilles.

An additional advantage of a Netherlands holding company

is that it is not forced to make a distribution, so allowing capital to accumulate locally. When such a company does pay dividends to its foreign shareholders there is a standard 25 per cent withholding tax. This rate, however, is substantially reduced or eliminated by a widespread network of double tax treaties. Similarly, many of the dividend flows to the Netherlands, which would also normally be subject to withholding taxes, are also protected by these treaties.

An example is shown in Figure 6.4 of Company O, a US multinational which shares the ownership of a Dutch holding company with its British subsidiary, which in turn is partly owned by local shareholders. By manufacturing in the UK and utilising a low price to its European subsidiaries which are wholly owned by the Dutch company, profits can be accumulated in the EEC operating subsidiaries. Part of these profits are then extracted via a Swiss-based management services company and, after paying local tax, flowed back as dividends to the Dutch holding company. In this way the US parent is able to show an extremely high rate of return on the share of capital it puts into its UK subsidiary, while leaving a sufficient return in the UK to maintain the local company's position with its British shareholders.

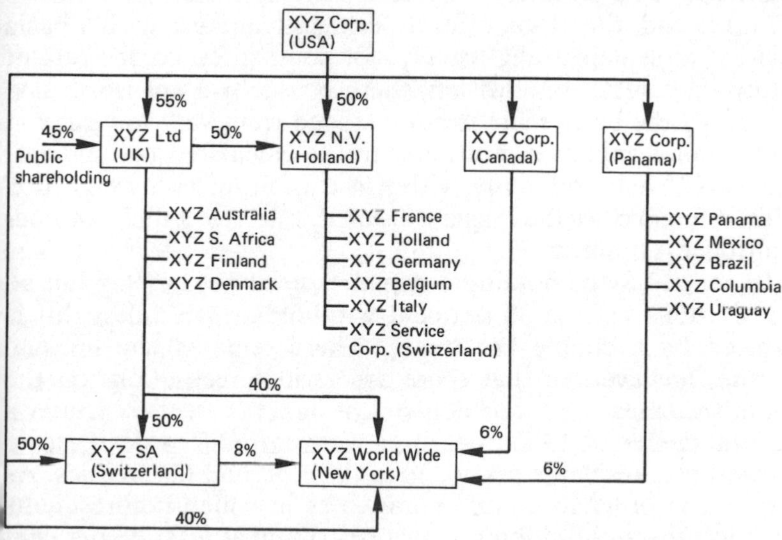

Fig. 6.4 Global Fiscal Structure using Intermediate Holding Companies

The Netherlands Antilles
These are a useful and widely used tax haven, whose advantages derive mainly from a special tax position for investment companies, coupled with the assistance of double tax agreements, expecially with the USA and the Netherlands. Historically, under the USA-Netherlands double tax treaty, which was extended to the Netherlands Antilles, the rate of withholding tax on dividends was reduced from 30 per cent to 15 per cent, while on royalties and interest payments it was reduced from 30 per cent to nil. Excess exploitation led to a change in the treaty rules and as from 1967 a company can no longer take full advantage, but it is still possible to obtain the benefit of the double tax treaty and pay local tax on net profits.[11] A further advantage offered is the possibility of using the Netherlands Antilles' extensive free port facilities for local manufacturing, assembly and processing.

Switzerland
The Swiss tax system is complex and not always low. Three taxing authorities are involved, the federal government, the canton and the commune or municipality. The top rate of federal tax is around 8 per cent and there is also an annual wealth tax at a nominal rate. The individual cantons compete for taxes and, therefore, offer differing advantages with a basic scale of rates depending usually, for companies, on the rate of return on capital. In addition, there is usually a net worth tax. Generally the basic scale is not changed from year to year, but each canton applies a multiplier to the calculated tax and this can vary. Each commune within a canton levies its own tax, with reference to the basic cantonal rate, to which another multiplier is applied.

In general Swiss holding companies need not pay tax but all distributions suffer a 30 per cent withholding tax unless this is reduced by a double tax treaty. There remains one unusual feature, however, in that there are serious restrictions on the use of the extensive Swiss network of dual tax treaties. Under a Federal decree of 1962, measures were introduced designed to prevent non-residents taking advantage of dual tax treaties. As a result, in order to qualify companies in which non-residents have a 'substantial interest' must distribute at least 25 per cent of the gross treaty protected income. Further, not more than 50 per cent of the gross treaty-protected income can be used to satisfy, directly or indirectly, non-resident 'claims', including royalties, research and development fees and the like. In addition, financing of a Swiss company must not be unorthodox in that loans must not exceed 600 per cent of equity, while interest must not exceed a 'normal' rate fixed by the Swiss authorities.[12]

The Channel Islands

There are no capital gains, estate, wealth or gift taxes in the Channel Islands and a flat 20 per cent income tax rate applies. The main attraction for companies centres on the 'corporation tax' registered company which is neither 'controlled and managed' in 'nor carrying on business within' Jersey or Guernsey. Such companies pay only a flat annual corporation tax of around £300, which is high by international standards.

The Channel Islands are widely used for tax planning purposes especially for individuals. Such use tends to revolve around the use of discretionary trusts when, providing neither the settler nor the potential beneficiary are residents of Jersey or Guernsey, a trust can usually escape all tax. The use of the islands as a staging post for UK 'remittance basis' money is also growing, and a corporation tax company can also be linked to a Dutch holding company system with remitted funds avoiding UK corporation tax, since Channel Island funds are within the Sterling Area and qualify as overseas investment remittance, for the Bank of England. There are disadvantages, however, in particular the fact that the islands are within the UK exchange control area.[13]

Bermuda

Bermuda is a highly respected tax haven, having carefully nurtured a selective image, unlike the Bahamas which, following independence in 1973, have become somewhat less popular due to fears of political instability. There are no taxes in Bermuda apart from a flat fee company registration. Under the Exempted Undertakings Tax Protection Act 1966, the Finance Minister is authorised to give assurances that no taxes for up to 30 years will be imposed on 'exempted companies'. Such concerns can do no business in Bermuda, nor invest in local shares or real estate. An exempted company must have a registered office in

Bermuda and at least three local directors, generally bankers, accountants and the like. Bermuda is therefore somewhat expensive as a tax haven but in return has a reputation for respectability and excellent service.[14]

The Bahamas

Despite fears for its stability and the imposition of exchange controls on funds held by Bahamanian residents, which led to a number of banks and corporations relocating, the Bahamas still offers the widest range of banking, legal and other services, with over 12,000 companies registered, about half of which are engaged in financial services in the Caribbean.[15] It also has good communications with the USA, by comparison with the Cayman Islands. As in the Cayman Islands and Bermuda, there are no income or other taxes although companies must file an annual return, but no detail is required of financial operations or profits. The Bahamas are considered to be a good location for a sales company, and Freeport offers an attractive potential manufacturing and distribution base, being only 50 miles from the US mainland.

The Bahamas has suffered from its image of providing a base for fraudulent and dishonest operations. A number of deals, offering tax shelter to US citizens, resulted in fraudulent conversion and the avoidance of SEC regulations. There has, therefore, been a move to improve the quality of banking institutions with the objective of eliminating the undesirable fringe.

Panama

Widely used by Western Hemisphere MNCs, Panama corporations pay no tax on income received from abroad. Even if a Panama corporation has an office in Panama, it does not pay local income tax if the transactions from which the income was generated were consummated outside the country. Further, managing and directing companies in Panama, whose operations take place outside the country also does not constitute a local source of income. As a result Panama tends to be used frequently as a sales or corporate headquarters location. Local company law is also extremely flexible. Officers and directors may be non-resident, shareholders' and directors' meetings may be held anywhere in the world, no yearly registration taxes are levied and capital registration tax is relatively low.

The Cayman Islands

The Cayman Islands are geographically inconvenient, but offer a number of significant tax planning advantages. Firstly, the islands only became independent in the early 1960s and took the opportunity to rewrite their tax laws to be tailor-made for international corporate and trust transactions. Secondly, they are politically stable and the tensions between the community and the financial institutions observable elsewhere are low.

There are no taxes on income, profits, capital gains or dividend distribution and no estate, gift or succession duties. Exempted company trust formation is possible for periods generally of fifteen years. Such companies pay a registration fee of 0.1 per cent, with a minimum fee of $400 and a maximum of $1000, and an annual fee of 0.045 per cent of capital and a minimum of $200 and a maximum of $1600. Exempted companies also have other privileges, notably that they can issue no-par-value shares or bearer shares and do not need to file an annual return of shareholdings.[16]

Other Locations

Apart from the favourable tax locations briefly discussed above there are many other countries which claim to be tax havens. Most of these are of relatively limited interest, although a number may offer specific attractions for particular geographic territories, such as Hong Kong, the New Hebrides, Liechtenstein and the British Virgin Islands. Nauru, a former Australian dependency, is attempting to stimulate its position as a tax haven in the Pacific Basin but, as with many other island operations in the Caribbean and the Pacific, competition is high. In general, many tax havens come and go as legislation is introduced to stimulate or discourage such activity. Unless, however, some inherent commercial advantage applies, it is usually possible to obtain similar, if not better facilities, in one of the already established environments.

CONCLUSION

Tax planning is a complex topic requiring specialist skills, but it has become a vital ingredient in planning in the MNC. Normally the function of tax planning forms part of the responsibilities of the corporate treasurer's department. All too often, however, the decisions and policies that are pursued by tax planners are not well integrated with the activities of the corporate planning and capital budgeting functions. Frequently, these activities are decided first, with expected financial performance being determined on a pre-tax basis, and it is only after the essential decisions have been made that tax considerations are taken into account. While clearly commercial considerations must normally dominate strategic decision-making, it can be vitally important to take account of tax implications at the time major commitments are made, in order to avoid the possibilities of taking the wrong decision and leaving an unfavourable net return on investment situation.

7 Investment Planning and Entry Strategies

THE CAPITAL INVESTMENT PROCESS

Control over capital spending and decisions on the type, timing and location of strategic investments are the key areas of decision-making that are strictly centralised in most MNCs. This does not mean that all such projects are initiated at the centre because most capital investment requests are actually first identified as a result of planning gaps or opportunities observed at the level of the local subsidiary or regional office. Further, capital investment planning in the multinational is not a wholly rational process in several ways. Firstly, companies do not usually conduct an extensive search to determine the full range of opportunities open to them, but rather they conduct only a limited search until an opportunity is identified which meets the required standards. Secondly, capital investment decisions are taken largely as a result of a behavioural and political process rather than an economic one.

The capital investment process in the MNC can be subdivided into six stages, from the development of the proposal to the project audit, shown in Figure 7.1. While formal procedures are common for the appraisal, budgeting and authorisation stages, the process itself is characterised by informality. The sequence

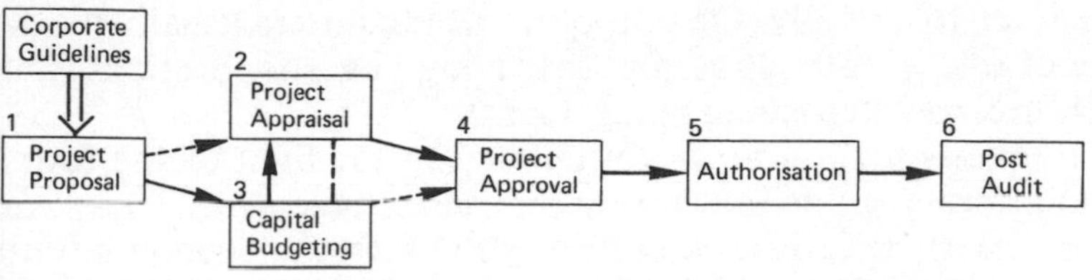

Fig. 7.1 Stages in the Capital Investment Process

is predominantly a bottom-up one, with proposals for most projects being generated at product divisional, regional or local subsidiary levels of the organisation. Since considerable organisational effort is required to develop a detailed project proposal, the support of superiors is sought by lower-level managers early in the process to provide an early warning of the project and to obtain an initial reaction.

1. Project Proposal

The majority of capital expenditure requests involve relatively small amounts of spending and are proposed by subsidiary management on the basis of opportunities for cost reduction or because replacement has become desirable. Expansion proposals emerge as a result of the planning process which identifies gaps between the forecasts generated and the current capability. Most of these proposals are aggregated to form a combined request for funds which is passed up the chain of approval to regional or product division management and ultimately to corporate headquarters.

The corporate head office is responsible for the initiation of certain types of capital investment. These include major acquisitions, although the identification and evaluation of suitable candidates may involve regional or national managements. This topic is discussed at length in the next chapter. Secondly, corporate involvement is high in the development of projects for very large investments such as production units capable of supplying several countries, although the initial proposal and the details of the project are worked out at regional or product divisional level. Thirdly, investments in new products are usually closely supervised by head office development staffs or product coordinators, as discussed in Chapter 10. Finally, the corporate headquarters usually plays a major role in entry strategies involving new site locations, joint ventures and licensing arrangements.

Requests for funds are formulated in the light of the formal and informal guidelines set by central management. These vary from clearly specified objectives, strategies and spending limits – an approach favoured by US companies – to general indications of strategic parameters and investment levels. The strength of corporate cash flows has an important effect on the approach to investment guidelines. Companies with surplus resources, for example those with very profitable core businesses, impose fewer restrictions on investment proposals and this tends to lead to more proposals being generated.

Where no investment guidelines are provided by corporate headquarters informal rules become established based upon what has proved acceptable in the past.[1] Where expectations about appropriate investment levels have become established over several years, subsidiaries may be unwilling to make requests for more funds than they would normally expect to get, and thus suppress potential investment opportunities. Similarly, in situations where corporate interference is low because a steady level of investment has been maintained from cash flow, local management may be unwilling to risk asking for extra cash for fear that limits will be established from the centre.

2. Project Appraisal

For the majority of proposals, the initial appraisal is carried out at local level. The standards adopted for appraisal criteria, such as rates of return on investment, are strongly influenced by previous experience, i.e. projects rejected earlier by corporate management as unsatisfactory are taken as benchmarks. Local management usually has some flexibility in setting acceptability criteria, and may indeed choose high rates in order to impress central management. Corporate expectations for different kinds of investment are likely to vary according to product, location and project type. For example, Company L requires a higher rate of return for expansion proposals (20–30 per cent) than cost reduction or replacement projects (around 15 per cent).

Overseas investment in countries considered to be in the 'high risk' category needs to show additional returns. The required rate is set partly on a subjective basis by international division or regional management based on their local knowledge and partly on specific assessments of such key factors as political stability, wage rates, market size, income per head, taxes and financial controls, local incentives and the like. For the case of 'risky' countries, the corporate headquarters may propose reduced-risk entry techniques, such as joint ventures, licensing or turnkey contracts, or impose fast payback requirements. In general where a company already has production operations in a particular country, proposals from the subsidiary are treated in the same way as domestic projects. Strategic moves into new countries and/or new businesses are strictly centrally controlled, although regional and subsidiary management may play an integral role in preparing the case for such projects.

Most companies specify detailed formats for appraisals, and indicate specific calculations required. In a recent survey of multinational companies,[2] all the sample companies used discounted cash flow methods and an Internal Rate of Return measure. Payback was a widely used criterion, with two years regarded as a fast payback period. Over half the companies carried out sensitivity or probabilistic analyses but many had found OR techniques, including decision-trees, inappropriate for the kinds of complexity involved in capital projects. The use of computer routines to assist both the assessment of the project and its impact on business profitability was widespread among US multinationals. One purpose of this analysis was to avoid putting money into a business with a poor return, even though the particular project was acceptable.

The timing of the project appraisal varies according to the kind of project. Small 'routine' capital investment requests from existing businesses are typically incorporated in the capital budget prepared as part of the corporate planning process. Where medium or long-term capital spending projections are included in the planning process, they act as an early warning system for a subsidiary's overall intended level of investment. As the operating year approaches, detailed appraisals are carried out before projects are formally included in the corporate capital budget.

In the case of larger projects which may be 'strategic' for the local subsidiary but still involve relatively small financial sums relative to the corporation, the project is not included in the budget until the idea has been checked in outline by the top management of the subsidiary for consistency with strategic plans, and until a detailed appraisal ensures that the project is acceptable. Once they enter the capital budgeting process they are likely to be scrutinised by regional or corporate headquarters and to be worked on still further before inclusion in the annual profit-budget. One major US multinational refers to this process as 'progressive appraisal'.

3. Capital Budgeting

Capital budgeting is formalised in most multinationals. A medium/long-term investment budget is prepared as an input to plan projections and capital spending is included in the annual budget estimates. As in the case of business plans, the time-horizon for investment budgeting varies considerably between companies. The longest horizons are adopted by firms with substantial investment lead times such as oil, automobile and chemical companies. Some highly formalised companies undertake new ten-year projections annually, while others are content with a one-off exercise every few years. In all cases the detail diminishes as the plan looks further ahead: only large expenditures are identified in distant years with a lump-sum estimate of other investments.

A typical example of an integrated business and investment planning system is to be found in Company P, a US chemical company. Capital investment planning is closely linked to the planning process and is carried out over the same planning cycle. The capital plan is projected over a five-year period and aggregated at business unit, regional and corporate levels. A more detailed capital expenditure forecast is prepared two years out with quarterly reviews and with details of major projects. Projects tend to be initiated by the manufacturing function as a result of capacity gaps identified during the planning process and are passed up through the worldwide product group management. The process is normally bottom-up but the corporate headquarters occasionally initiates projects where it has identified a major strategic opportunity for a new product area. The capital budget is coordinated at regional level by a regional director of planning, who reconciles product and national plans for the area and who reports to the international division planning group in the US.

Although the investment estimates are integrated into the business plan, capital budgeting and planning are to a large extent separate and parallel processes. In many companies, plans are the responsibility of line managers or planners, while the capital budgeting and authorisation process is supervised by the finance function. In Company Q, a European engineering products company, for example, there are separate planning and capital expenditure departments. Capital proposals emerge from corporate plans, but then enter a separate capital planning process with a five-year horizon. The next time that capital and investment plans meet is at the annual budget approval stage, when corporate finance staff check that investment plans still conform to strategic objectives.

The parallel processes are illustrated in Figure 7.2 using a five-year planning horizon. In the planning process, early estimates

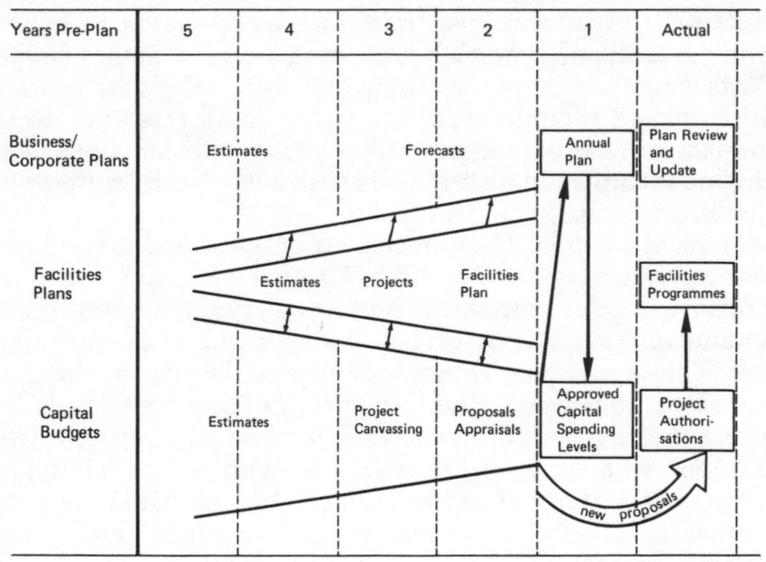

Fig. 7.2 The Parallel Processes of Business Planning and Capital Budgeting

of business unit performance are narrowed down to specific forecasts and future strategies which form the quantitative framework for the annual plan. The capital investment estimates and, subsequently, proposals, should also be generated within these strategies since they are likely to be crucial to implementation. For many businesses, routine or replacement investment is fairly easy to predict and can be treated as a recurring cost. These expenditures are incorporated in a facilities plan. Investment projects, however, particularly those which involve innovations or new departures, are generated outside the business planning process. In these cases, since the capital budgeting and appraisal processes are carried out by the finance function, they often act as integrators between the two systems.

Three fundamental problems affect the smooth integration of the two systems, however:

1. The phasing of investment projects is frequently out of cycle with the planning system.
2. In a changing environment new opportunities involving capital commitment can occur at any time and may require urgent approval.
3. Integration between product, geographic and functional activities is very difficult.

The behavioural dynamics between the corporate head office and the operating unit also impose important constraints on the management of capital budgeting. Since the corporate headquarters is likely to be more favourably disposed towards highly predictable cash generating businesses, a key objective of the local manager is to build up a rolling commitment to spending in his investment estimates which do not surprise the system by the fluctuations. Once an investment level norm is established relative to the cash flow he generates, he then has some flexibility to use the capital expenditure system to bring forward special projects which he favours. Reducing internal uncertainty for the corporation is an important part of the capital budgeting game.

4. Approval

In companies with developed planning systems, the approval of the bulk of capital investments takes place during the resource allocation phase of the corporate planning process. Much of the financial data has already been aggregated and overall spending levels for divisions are reviewed in the light of their overall strategy. Spending discretion levels in most MNCs are actually very low and formal approval for all save minor capital requests must normally be obtained from the corporate headquarters. Moderate spending authority is sometimes granted at regional and/or product division level, but this is not normally adequate to enable these units to make any fundamental change in the strategic position of a business. However, although formal approval must be obtained from the centre, when a region or product division is strongly committed to a particular project, it is unusual for this not to be approved. In reality the formal act of approval is not usually the key determinant of the investment process. Rather it is the informal soundings which take place between the corporate headquarters and the capital project initiating units that largely determines which projects actually reach the stage of seeking approval.

In some companies the integration between the approval for capital spending and for corporate and business plans is carried out by a capital expenditure review committee. This body has the responsibility for vetting individual projects before they can be included in the plan. It usually has the same or an overlapping membership with the corporate plans review board.

An important aspect of the approval process is that for reasons of external and internal confidentiality the corporate rationale for the investment decision is often not formally communicated to the business unit manager making the project proposal. Thus 'interpretation' of corporate or divisional decisions is important for considering future submissions. Distance and cultural differences add to the problems of interpretation and make investment initiation for overseas businesses difficult.

5. Authorisation

The authorisation stage of the capital investment process is the later procedure by which permission to begin spending on a project is obtained. Since cash is involved, a hierarchy of authorisation levels exists in the company to control spending. Again, formal control of relatively minor expenditures at board level is common. Authorisation is usually limited to projects specified in the capital budget.

However, as a result of the timing and behavioural pressures indicated earlier, the capital expenditure review committee may be used as an additional court of appeal for new or substitute projects – to which at least some of the members of the committee have already become committed. Such 'late entrants' can cause significant problems. One major UK engineering firm found recently that only 16 of 62 significant projects in the capital expenditure budget for the year were actually brought forward, while 21 new projects had been admitted.

The emergence of non-budgeted investment proposals leads to the adoption of formal or informal ranking procedures so that, for example, all budgeted items receive first priority and additional strategic investments second priority. However, this is seldom practicable and the solution adopted by one US automobile products company is to move away from a capital expenditure authorisation procedure towards a budget cash limit system.

6. Post Audit

Although post auditing procedures for investment projects are in widespread use, at least on a selective basis, the changes between the intended project and its implementation are frequently so great that comparisons are not very useful. Since action is taken early on if a project is in trouble, the procedure also has little action value for management. They are, however, of some value to the finance function in the preparation of further proposals.

The Capital Investment Process and Manufacturing Strategy

Many investment proposals involve the improvement and/or expansion of existing facilities in one country and require local knowledge alone. For the multinational company with interdependent manufacturing establishments in several countries, however, complex questions of sourcing and logistics also need to be resolved when, for example, a significant plant addition is contemplated. The technical assessment of such projects then requires the coordination of several kinds of expertise in different countries. The pattern of international manufacturing operations, therefore, has a strong influence on the way that investment proposals are handled. In addition, the ability of the organisation to transfer knowhow from one manufacturing unit to another significantly affects the spread of technological and operating improvements and the quality and quantity of projects initiated.

In many multinational companies the domestic product

divisions are the source of operating innovation. Local production policies need to be adapted to prevailing industry practice. Many of the home country assumptions about inefficiency need to be modified in the light of local work practices, skill availability, technological sophistication and the like. The trade-offs between service levels and efficiency also vary due to different levels of expectation in the market place, among suppliers and the like. Longer delivery times may be acceptable, for example, but suppliers may be less reliable. Production policies will also differ in various parts of the world. The more advanced Western nations will have like standards of efficiency and service and thus broadly similar production policies are appropriate. In less developed countries where markets and plant sizes are smaller and skills and infrastructures less advanced, a variety of production styles is necessary.

THE PLANT LOCATION DECISION

The location of a new plant is one of the key strategic decisions for any company. It represents a major investment in physical and human assets which changes the geographical spread of the enterprise. It involves considerable risk. Although a new site has the potential to operate efficiently, it may be many years before cost targets can be realised. Under operating conditions prior assumptions about production logistics may prove to be invalid. If performance is unsatisfactory withdrawal or liquidation is costly and difficult. The consequences of a bad location decision which puts a new plant in the wrong place with high operating costs remain with the firm for many years.

For most companies the new location decision arises infrequently. Typically the need for a new plant emerges as a result of production capacity problems and a branch operation is set up not far away if extension at the present site is impossible.[3] The multinational company on the other hand can face several different types of location decision due to its size and geographical spread.

Capacity shortages, cost reduction opportunities, technological advances, new products and the like result in proposals for new manufacturing establishments in various countries around the world. Some of these proposals originate at head office; many are initially generated by overseas subsidiaries, area offices, or product divisions. In all cases detailed local knowledge needs to be combined with an appreciation of the global implications for the corporation before an informed location decision can be made. The challenge for the multinational corporation is to develop appropriate expertise at the various levels of the organisation and to establish the formal and informal processes which will ensure the best possible allocation of new manufacturing resources.

The evaluation of overseas investment opportunities is often a cascade process. Once an opportunity has been identified it is first necessary to select between countries where such an investment might be located in the case of plants which can service several markets. This involves the detailed evaluation of the investment climate in several countries in order to reach a rational decision. Having selected which country the firm might wish to invest in, several sites might be available within the country and detailed site appraisals should be conducted to evaluate them.

In comparing the investment climate of particular countries a number of factors are important. These include the following:

Market Characteristics

This factor is important if the local market is considered to be a vital element in plant viability. The size of market for the company's products and its rate of growth need to be known in detail, together with the competitive situation, expected market share and the like. Detailed market evaluation is discussed further in Chapter 10.

The economic stability and expected economic future are also relevant factors in comparing countries since a more promising environment tends to reduce the risk of the project. The introduction of protective tariffs is also often an important influence on the choice of a plant location. National laws may encourage inward investment by the promise of such tariff barriers or the MNC may decide to invest locally to protect an established market threatened by such a government move after the development of local competitors.

Local market characteristics are not always of high importance, however, notably in situations where the firm wishes to take advantage of other favourable characteristics such as low labour or tax rates.

Macroeconomic Factors

In addition to the detailed knowledge of the local market, it is also important to examine the basic macroeconomic trends in alternative countries, for it is usually much less risky to invest in a growing, healthy economy than in one in depression or beset by long-term economic problems. Typical indicators are the level of gross national product and its growth rate trend; the balance of payments situation; income per capita and, if possible, some indication on actual income distribution; the size of the population and its socio-demographic make-up; and a number of key economic indicators which may be chosen to be particularly relevant to the business being considered, for example number of households, television ownership, telephone ownership, steel consumption per capita and suchlike.

Political Factors

Political risk is an area of growing concern for most multinationals. Political factors include general political stability, attitudes to different types of foreign investment, demands for control and participation, efficiency and honesty, and record on discrimination. Methods are evolving for assessing the political risk of a particular country and these are discussed at length in Chapter 9.

The general legal environment governing business operations, both for domestic and foreign firms, should also be identified. This might include price controls, attitudes to monopoly and restrictive practices, resale price maintenance, consumer legislation, product liability obligations and insurance requirements and costs. The possibility of insuring all or part of the proposed investment against government action should also be investigated. For companies that initially decide to invest in assembly operations, the requirements for local content in the finished products should be cleared before commitment, together with some indication of how this might be changed in future and what sanctions might be imposed on imports and exports, remittances, cash grants and investment incentives and the like.

Infrastructure Characteristics

It is important to consider the infrastructure of each country although these characteristics are considered in greater detail for the comparison of particular sites. Key points that should be checked include transport facilities, port facilities, ease of exporting and importing, availability of local supplies of raw materials and packaging, availability of energy supplies, geographic distance between plant and suppliers and customers, local laws governing pollution and environmental factors, availability and costs of suitable sites, and ease of planning permission. The infrastructure must also be considered from the viewpoint of key employees and their families, both at the country and individual site levels. The availability of suitable housing, educational facilities, social and recreational facilities, the type of climate, crime rate and so on will be important influences in attracting executives and their families and are also significant for labour relations and employee motivation. Too few companies really consider the needs of employees, believing that adverse environmental conditions can be overcome by additional payments. For some industries such as process plant engineering and oil exploration, harsh environmental conditions are common, but for most industrial and consumer goods companies the infrastructure needs of employees should form an important component in site evaluation.

Labour Factors

Labour is an increasingly important determinant of location. The first factor which must be checked is that adequate labour is available in the mix of skills required. In LDCs this is often not the case and the MNC should therefore be prepared to introduce a substantial amount of job training and in some cases basic literacy education. It will also be necessary in most cases to use local nationals in the majority of the managerial positions. Again, in many LDCs there is a serious shortage of skilled manpower which can well mean the development of extensive educational programmes in order to develop the necessary technical and often linguistic skills. Further, because such skills are short in many LDCs it is extremely difficult to keep and motivate such national executives, who are often offered attractive alternative opportunities. In developed countries the use of home country nationals in senior management positions is often still possible, but the practice is usually expensive and in countries such as Switzerland work permits for non-nationals may be difficult to obtain.

In addition to availability, labour relations should be carefully investigated. The structure and attitude of the local trade unions, their record for restrictive practices, unofficial disruptions and strikes, and their ability to maintain discipline amongst their members are important considerations. In some industries, notably automobiles, labour relations have become so unreliable that companies are sacrificing possible economies of scale in order to try and reduce possible risks from strikes at key production and component plants. As a result dual sourcing of major components has become the norm, with alternative suppliers being located in different countries. In addition, in some cases assembly lines are also being duplicated in alternative locations within a region.

Labour law in many countries is also tending to impose increasing restrictions on business decisions. In some European countries, for example, worker participation at board level is now required and this is likely to become common practice in most developed countries. Employment protection legislation in many countries also severely restricts the right of employers to hire and fire or establishes expensive rules for severance pay. Finally, the social security and fringe benefit requirements laid down by legislation in many countries can almost double the actual cost of wages paid.

Labour costs are also an important consideration, especially in labour-intensive businesses. The rising cost of labour in the developed countries has led to the widespread growth of satellite plants in less developed countries with ample supplies of relatively cheap labour. Manufacturing or assembly facilities are established in such countries for the production of products designed for supply to other developed nations or to the MNCs home country.

These satellite plants are not necessarily located close to developed country markets but may be geographically remote. Tariff barriers are equally important and the rapid expansion of the number of free trade associates with the European Economic Community, for example, has substantially increased the

Table 7.1 Factors influencing Satellite Plant Spread and Location

Change Factor	*Present Situation*	*Future Outlook*	*Planning Implications*
1. Movement of plants to low-wage countries	A few major European firms have established satellite plants for European markets	Sizeable trend toward satellite plants, particularly in Eastern Europe	Plants established outside target markets, especially in labour-intensive, high value to weight ratio type product
2. Tariff barriers	EEC tariff preferences extend to over 50 countries	European-wide free trade in most industrial products	Tariff preferences obtained outside EEC member countries opening up new locational opportunities while maintaining EEC preference
3. Marketing benefits of plant location	Influence of marketing variables now more important than wages and other cost elements for many firms	Development of European mass market conditions and competition	More emphasis on facilities for investment versus exports in consumer-oriented industries. Less emphasis on import agents
4. Regional differences	Substantial differences remain in regional aids, wages, taxes	Gradual elimination of regional differences, but some will persist	Regional differences will continue to influence locational cost picture
5. Attitude towards environment	National and *ad hoc* measures influencing plant location and pollution control equipment in new plants	Regional legislation defining pollution and other environmental standards	New element raising plant costs in more highly industrial areas
6. New energy sources	Traditional sources, located in Northern European countries still provide the bulk of industrial energy	Shifting emphasis on oil, nuclear fuel and other forms of energy largely independent of geographic constraints	Greater freedom to locate areas calculated to attract the most valuable resources of the future – human, technical and managerial

Source: J. Leontiades, op. cit.

potential location possibilities for satellite production units to service European markets. The list of European multinationals making use of such units include Germany's Rolleiwerke, which has established camera-making subsidiaries in Singapore to export its products on a worldwide basis; Volkswagen, which produces components for its European and US operations in Mexico; Britain's Plessey Company, which has set up satellites in Malta, Portugal and Singapore to produce a wide range of products for European markets; Olivetti, which supplies its worldwide needs for desk calculators from Latin America; and many electrical appliance producers who have established component and assembly operations in Singapore, Hong Kong and Taiwan to supply products for their global markets.[4] A number of the environmental factors affecting the spread and location of satellite plants to service European markets are shown in Table 7.1, together with their planning implications.

Financial Considerations

The relative state of development of the local capital market, sources and costs of finance, the stability of local currency and policies towards remittance and exchange control are amongst the key financial dimensions that need to be considered for each country. A further factor that can have a significant influence is the availability of government financial incentives such as investment grants, low-cost loans and the like. Often such incentives are coupled with fiscal concessions. Almost all governments offer incentives to foreign investors, although these may differ substantially from region to region within a country and they must be considered in the context of government attitudes in other areas, for example, with regard to taxation and remittance. Unless care is taken it is quite possible for investments to be made which, when investment incentives are taken into account, appear to offer a rate of return acceptable to the corporate headquarters yet are quite unacceptable in terms of the after-tax remittable income expected by the parent. In many developing countries with a weak exchange rate or tight exchange control regulations, it is therefore advisable to extract profits as quickly as possible.

Investment incentives come in many forms and their payment

may be made at varying times during the project life. Initial capital investment is often stimulated by the use of outright cash grants toward the cost of plant, land or buildings. On occasion such incentives can take the form of free buildings and land provided to the company's specification. Alternatively, low or zero-interest rate loans may be provided. Further incentives may be available once the project has commenced operation, such as special grants to cover employee training, wages subsidies, rapid depreciation allowances or tax holidays.

The timing of investment incentives is especially important under conditions of high interest and inflation rates. Thus at the beginning of a project incentives in monetary form or free factories, plant and equipment will usually be substantially more valuable than future depreciation allowances or tax holidays on profits unless the company has other profit-making operations within the country against which the allowances can be used. The stability of incentives is a further point that should be examined carefully. There is no point investing in a new location on the expectation of future incentives only to find that by the time these come to fruition the original basis has been changed. Some countries make frequent changes in their systems of incentives, the United Kingdom for example, and this must be regarded as an important negative consideration.

The use of investment incentives is particularly useful for moderate and high-capital-intensive businesses, or those that employ substantial numbers of people. Nevertheless, unless investment is being made purely to service a local market, care should be taken to ensure that transportation economics are low enough and transfer pricing opportunities are adequate to ensure the required level of profitability. Within the developed countries a number of areas have especially attractive investment incentives. These include the development areas of the UK, the Mezzogiorno region of Italy, the area of West Berlin in Germany and, for US companies, Puerto Rico, where the special tax advantages of a US possession corporation applies.

Fiscal Considerations

The final area for investigation in comparing countries is that of taxation. This includes both corporate and personal, direct and indirect tax rates, tax treatments on dividends, interest payments, technology, management fees and the like, tax treatments for depreciation and other expenses, treatment of losses, and rates of excise duty. It is also important to consider the tax morality of each country since in many the official level of taxes and that which is actually paid differ markedly. Unless the MNC is therefore prepared to adopt local custom and practice, possibly contravening the law, then certain countries should clearly be avoided. The cases where it is considered necessary for companies to keep several sets of books are numerous.

Tax concessions are also an important form of investment incentive. Alternative investments should always be investigated in after-tax terms, although of itself tax is seldom the most critical determinant of investment location. The main exception to this is for those operations which it is attractive to locate in tax-free zones. Further, the treatment of other factors, such as a slack supervision on inter-company transfer prices, can often be as significant as straight tax exemptions on export profits.[5]

Local tax holidays are a common form of incentive. These are especially useful for low-capital-intensity firms which expect to show high profits quickly from their investments. Such operations therefore are usually involved in industries such as pharmaceuticals, speciality engineering and consumer electronics, which are assembly, mixing, blending and packaging operations. In the EEC, the Republic of Ireland, for example, has one of the most attractive systems of tax incentives. These consist of a tax holiday to 1990 for profits generated from exports, a good network of tax-saving double tax treaties and credible repatriation guarantees. These concessions are also supported by a generous system of cash and other investment grants.

In addition to tax holidays many countries operate customs-free zones. These are of less use to manufacturing firms, consisting usually of warehousing facilities to which goods can be imported without incurring local duties and taxes. Transport costs may therefore be reduced by bulk shipment to such a location conveniently situated close to the final market from where products can be repacked or assembled and then re-exported duty-free to their ultimate destination. Only when products are therefore formally imported into a country do they become liable to local tax and duties. There are some 200 such customs-free zones around the world and they are therefore relatively common.

Less common are zones which are tax-free as well as customs-free. These are the free port areas around the world and in effect are mini tax havens. Profits made in such areas from manufacturing, assembly and processing escape local taxes and may also qualify for investment incentives. Vital factors to consider in possibly locating in a free trade zone are transportation economics and the cost of storage. Many satellite plants are located in such zones, with Taiwan and South Korea being the main sites in the Far East. In addition, Singapore is establishing itself as such an area, while Hong Kong, with its low tax rates and being wholly customs-free, has become the most successful single free trade zone. Dow Chemical, for example, has chosen Hong Kong as the site for the construction of the world's largest polystyrene complex. Other important free trade zones include Freeport in the Bahamas, the Colon Free Zone in Panama, Mexico, the Dominican Republic and the Shannon Airport Free Zone in Ireland.[6]

The investigation of the investment climate of a country is therefore a complex procedure and many factors must be taken into account. A comprehensive abbreviated checklist which may be useful is shown in Figure 7.3. The importance of each

---

Market Characteristics
Size of market and growth rate
Key market characteristics
Industry structure and competitive position
Product adaptation needs
Any price controls?
Level and type of price competition
Channels used, controls and availability
Media used, costs and availability
Advertising controls, spending patterns
Tariff position. Is protection available?

Macro economic Factors
Size of GNP and growth rate
Inflation rate
Balance of payments position, historic? future?
Stage of economic development
Income per capita, historic? future?
Size and demographics of population
Number of households; percentage home ownership

Political Factors
Type and stability of government
Any dangerous internal strife?
Any particular ethnic, social class problems?
Economic ideologies of major political parties
Historic attitude toward MNCs. Any nationalisation? unfair discrimination?

Attitude to private enterprise?
Fairness and honesty of administration of accepted standards of morality, corruption present or not?
Fairness and honesty of legal system
Efficiency and operating speed of bureaucracy
Details of corporate law affecting the MNC; monopoly control? restrictions on ownership? legal obligations? consumer law? product liability? pollution control?

Infrastructure Characteristics
Geographic distribution of industry and population
Availability, cost and efficiency of transport systems
Availability, cost and efficiency of port facilities
Availability, cost and reliability of raw materials
Availability, cost and reliability of energy and utilities
Site location prospects and proximities to raw materials? markets?
Site costs? building costs?
Climatic conditions?
Housing, educational, social/cultural facilities?
Ease of foreign trade imports? exports?

Labour Factors
Availability of managerial, technical, linguistic and skilled and unskilled production labour
Labour productivity, historic? expected?
Educational and skill levels
Level of unemployment, historic and expected trends
Degree of union membership
Trade union structure and attitudes
Record of industrial relations
Labour laws affecting the MNC; trade union participation? employment protection? social security payments? hire and fire regulations? redundancy costs? other fringe benefits expected costs?
Wage rates, historic? trend?
Attitudes to profit sharing?

Financial Considerations
Stage of development of local capital market
Sources and type of funds available; costs?
Stability of local currency, historic? future?
Exchange control regulations
Treatments of leads and lags
Investment incentive schemes available
Stability of investment incentives
Depreciation treatments
Accounting and financial reporting requirements
Availability and cost of risk insurance locally? in home country?

Fiscal Considerations
Tax rates (corporate and personal, income capital gains, withholding, excise duties, payroll tax, VAT rates, other direct and indirect taxes)
Tax treatments on dividends, interest payments, technology, management fees, transfer policies and other means of extractions
Tax incentives for investment
Customs and tax-free zones
Joint tax treaties
Treatment of losses
Import-export tax drawbacks
Attitudes to avoidance? evasion?

Fig. 7.3 Checklist for Assessing Country Investment Climate

factor will vary according to the particular characteristics of the individual business unit and corporation, and in a somewhat more sophisticated version of the evaluation procedure clusters of factors can be weighted to reflect their relative importance and in order to rank countries by a quantitative score.

ALTERNATIVE ENTRY METHODS

Apart from direct investment into a green-field site there are several other important strategies for entry into a new geographic market. Cross-border mergers and acquisitions are discussed in the next chapter, but two other strategies which need consideration are the use of licensing and joint ventures. These two strategies will probably become increasingly important even for established MNCs in the next quarter-century as many nations move to favour alternatives to local subsidiaries wholly owned by foreign MNCs.

Entry by Licensing

Advantages and Problems of Licensing

Licensing may offer substantial advantages for some MNCs. Firstly, the level of capital investment required is usually much less than in establishing a green-field site and as a result the degree of risk is much lower. Secondly, management requirements are reduced since it is not necessary for the MNC to actually buy a site, install plant, hire and train a workforce and so on. As a result, licensing may be especially useful to smaller organisations unable to tackle a large number of markets simultaneously or unaccustomed to overseas operations. Thirdly, it may provide the most economic method of servicing a market which would be considered too small for the MNC to establish a company-owned plant. Fourthly, licensing tends to present fewer exchange risk problems than a full-scale manufacturing operation, and by the careful use of tax planning can actually offer high levels of net profitability. Fifthly, licensing may be the only way into some markets, for example, Eastern Europe, or offer the best method of entry for an acceptable level of risk. Finally, licensing may be an integral element in a more complex strategy, such as the sale of a key component or ancillary product, or as a means of obtaining knowhow from overseas companies via reciprocal licensing technology agreements.

Licences do, of course, also have immediate or potential disadvantages. Firstly, every licensee can be a potential competitor to the licensor. This is especially true if the licence agreement does not carefully specify the territories in which the licensee is able to operate. Thus if care is not taken the MNC may find itself in competition with its own licensees in third-world countries. This problem has become especially difficult in Western Europe as a result of the gradual widening of the European Economic Community. Under the competition clauses of the Treaty of Rome many licence agreements with restrictive territorial clauses have effectively been nullified when new countries have joined the Community. Secondly, it is not easy to maintain control over a licensee and hence it is possible that trademarks and brand names can be damaged as a result of inferior quality control, after-sales service and the like. Thirdly, it is possible for a licensee to build up a substantial business using a licensor's trademarks and technology. Since many licence agreements contain sliding scales on royalty rates dependent on turnover the licensor can find that much market success does not result in significantly improved royalties. Further, the licensor will be prohibited from entering this market or will only be able to do so after an expensive renegotiation of the original agreement. Inflation is also a potential problem in licence agreements which do not allow for product volume. Without tying royalty payments to volume as well as turnover, the licensor can find a declining royalty level for similar volumes as inflation increases turnover levels and triggers lower royalty rate thresholds. Finally, there may be problems in eliciting payment from licensees as a result of deliberate refusals to pay, exchange control restrictions, currency risks, local withholding taxes and such like.

Company R provides an example of an interesting use of licensing as an integral element in an international strategy. A major chemical specialities manufacturer, the corporation has adopted an international strategy based on direct investment in the developed countries, a decision which first led to the dissolution of a number of old-established agreements set up before the company elected to expand overseas. In order to reduce the level of risk, keep the amount of management time-committed within bounds and yet still take advantage of opportunities, the company has adopted a licensing-based strategy to cover developing country markets. The licence agreements established for these countries contain a number of different features from the company's traditional method of exploiting its technology. First, countries are selected on a regional basis where substantial governmental advantages could be expected from the establishment of local manufacturing, such as the introduction of tariff barriers against imports. Second, Company R in return for a management fee, which usually takes the form of an equity participation in the venture, will establish a turnkey plant under licence for a small, popular range of products with an established local company. The capital cost of the plant is paid for by the licensee. Technology requirements are reduced by Company R supplying essential ingredients in masterbatch form, so reducing the production task in the new venture to blending and filling operations. The sale of masterbatch is made through a low-tax overseas subsidiary, as are imports of additional product lines for which local demand is inadequate to justify local production. Finally, the licensee must use Company R's brand names and trademark on all products produced and pay a running royalty on all production. In return, Company R provides its licensees with a continuing technical and local marketing support service, including assistance in developing export sales to other countries within the same region.

Licensee agreements are usually drawn up between two independent companies; but, increasingly, the licensee might be a state-owned company in socialist countries. Companies may also take a minority or other shareholding in their overseas licensees and it is not uncommon for MNCs to sign a licence agreement with their own wholly-owned subsidiaries as a means of profit extraction. Licensee agreements in their simplest form usually cover the use of a patent or trademark, while more complex variants often include one or more of the following features:

A patented product or process
A trademark or tradename

Manufacturing techniques and other proprietary rights generally referred to as knowhow
Components materials or equipment essential to a manufacturing process
Technical advice and services of various sorts
Marketing advice and assistance of various sorts
Financial and/or management participation in the foreign company[7]

Licence agreements are not always successful, however, and a number of factors have been identified which are associated with success and failure. These are listed below:

Factors important for Success[8]

1. Choice of a reliable, competent and compatible licensee
2. Inherent value of the patents, trademark or knowhow licensed
3. Thorough advance research and understanding of the market
4. Mutual confidence and respect for each other's interests and objectives
5. Some participation in ownership and/or management
6. Close personal contact and public relation efforts with licensees
7. Prestige and favourable reputation of the licensor and the licensed product
8. Margin of technical and research lead maintained by the licensor
9. Provision of merchandising and sales assistance to licensees
10. Organised supervision and servicing of licensees by a special licensing staff
11. Scale of activity and amount of effort and attention devoted to it
12. Active support of top management
13. Correct timing and pacing of licensing activity
14. Anticipation and detailed spelling-out of contract obligations and relationships
15. Effective coordination with other elements of international strategy.

Factors leading to Failure[9]

Thirty per cent of licence arrangements in a recent survey had failed in some important way. Most of the reasons for failure were the company's own fault and in order of frequency these reasons were:

1. Inadequate market analysis by licensor
2. Product defects not known or understood by licensing executives
3. Higher start-up costs than licensee anticipated
4. Insufficient attention, interest and support from licensee's top management, marketing, engineering and production executives
5. Poor timing
6. Competition
7. Insufficient marketing effort on the local scene by licensor and/or licensee
8. Inadequate licensee 'after-sales' effort
9. Weakness in licensee market research and competitive intelligence

The Licence Agreement

The licence agreement establishes the terms binding the two parties. The precise terms and conditions will vary according to the particular needs and desires of both parties and the specific characteristics of the business. Not only are the bargaining positions of each partner involved in arriving at a suitable agreement, but it is important to ensure that local legal requirements covering such areas as trademarks, patents and monopoly/competitive rules are duly taken into account. A checklist of questions which should be carefully considered in drawing up a licence agreement is shown in Figure 7.4. The area of taxation requires special attention since, as shown in Chapter 6, there is substantial variation between countries in the treatment of royalty and capital payments for patents, trademarks and knowhow. As a result there is substantial scope for tax saving from the judicious use of inter- and intra-corporate licensing.

1. How many patents, processes or trademarks to be used?
2. How will technical assistance be rendered?
3. Which products are included in the agreement and to what extent?
4. What territory is to be covered by the licence?
5. How should the licensee be compensated?
6. What happens if compensation cannot be paid by the licensee?
7. If sub-licensing is permitted, how should it be carried out?
8. What are the provisions as to duration and cancellation? What provisions exist for licence recapture in the event of royalty default, bankruptcy, etc?
9. What are the assignment possibilities?
10. What rights does the licensor have in developments by the licensee?
11. What visitation and inspection privileges are held by the licensor, and on what terms and conditions are they to be exercised?
12. Can the parent company inspect accounts?
13. What provisions are there for satisfactory promotional and sales performance and for adequate quality control?
14. What governmental approvals are required?
15. What tax factors are involved?
16. How is inflation dealt with?
17. What are the royalty terms? How do these compare with others in the industry?
18. What provisions?

Fig. 7.4 Checklist for Establishing Licence Agreements[10]

Entry by Joint Ventures

Advantages of Joint Ventures

Despite the reluctance of many MNCs to participate in them and their relatively high failure rate, joint ventures are becoming an increasingly common entry strategy. There are many reasons for this. Firstly, for the smaller organisation with an inadequate supply of finance and/or specialist management skills, the joint venture can prove an effective method of getting the necessary resources to enter a number of markets. This is especially true in attractive developing countries where local contacts, market knowledge or political requirements may make joint ventures the preferred route. Secondly, joint ventures can be used to reduce local nationalist prejudice against foreign-owned companies. Indeed, in many developing nations nationalism has gone so far as to make 100 per cent foreign ownership impossible, making joint ventures with a local partner a prerequisite for entry. Somewhat less extreme legal measures include specific discrimination in favour of local firms, through the placing of government contracts or discriminatory taxes and restrictions against foreign firms importing key raw materials, components and the like. Thirdly, joint ventures may provide specialist knowledge of a local market, entry to required channels of distribution, supplies of raw materials, access to government contracts and local production facilities. Fourthly, in a growing number of countries, joint ventures with host governments are becoming increasingly important. This is especially true in extractive industries such as oil and minerals where nationalisation has been followed by the creation of joint ventures between local governments and foreign multinationals so that the latter can provide the necessary technology required to exploit natural resources. Fifthly, the creation of consortium companies has been growing in recent years in order to undertake particular projects which are too large for the industrial partners to undertake alone – this is true of many mining consortia such as Queensland Alumina in Australia owned by a group of aluminium producers; provide access to markets in which the participants require a mix of skills – for example, a number of consortium banks aimed at penetrating markets in the Arabian Gulf; or to provide particular political benefits such as the Swedish-American consortium formed to exploit iron ore deposits in Liberia, where a wholly US venture would have been unacceptable. Finally, exchange controls may stop a company exporting capital and thus prevent the formation of an overseas subsidiary. The supply of knowhow alone may, however, be sufficient to enable such a company to obtain an equity stake in a joint venture with a local partner.

Dangers of Joint Ventures

Despite these advantages, the dangers of failure are many and these must be carefully considered before embarking upon a joint venture strategy. The first major problem is that joint ventures are extremely difficult to integrate into a global strategy that involves substantial cross-border trading. In such circumstances there are almost inevitably problems concerning inward and outward transfer pricing, and the sourcing of exports, in particular, in favour of wholly-owned subsidiaries in other countries. Further, the trend toward an integrated system of treasury management leads to conflict with local partners when the corporate headquarters endeavours to impose limits or even guidelines on cash and working capital usage, foreign exchange management and the amount, and means, of paying remittable profits. As a result of these types of problem many MNCs which operate joint ventures do so outside the strategic objective of global integration, but rather use such operations to service restricted geographic territories or countries where wholly-owned subsidiaries are not permitted.

Unless the agreement establishing the joint venture clearly restricts its geographic market scope, however, a divergence on policy for servicing export markets may well develop if the joint venture decides to compete with its MNC partner in third-country markets. Similarly, unacceptable positions can develop within a local market when the non-joint-venture interests of either partner conflict with the performance of the venture. For example, where the local partner owns a critical raw material source or channel of distribution in which it endeavours to maximise profitability at the expense of the joint venture. This second area of difficulty then tends to materialise when the local company takes a discriminatory line with its MNC partner.

A third area of difficulty arises when the objectives of the partners are, or become, incompatible. For example, the MNC may have quite different attitudes to risk from those of a smaller local partner and be prepared to accept short-term losses in order to accumulate market share, take on higher levels of local debt, or spend more on advertising. Similarly, objectives may change over time with the MNC proving much more interested in growth than its partner, which might be more concerned with personal tax saving for its key executives.

Fourth, problems often occur regarding management structures and staffing of joint ventures. This is especially true in countries where nepotism is common and where jobs for members of the partner's families have to be found. A variation of this problem occurs with patronage when it is considered necessary to find suitable employment for the relatives of politicians or other local worthies. It is, therefore, important to lay down in the founding articles of the joint venture the role of the MNC in management decision-making irrespective of shareholding, and some form of agreement reached on areas where mutual decision-making must prevail or where the MNC can veto decisions it finds unacceptable. An extension of this problem is that in the founding articles some provision should be made concerning the arrangements that come into effect in the case of irreconcilable breakdown. These should permit either party to liquidate under certain circumstances, but give the other party the right of first refusal to purchase the other's equity.

Finally, many joint ventures fail because of a conflict in tax interests between the partners. Many of these could actually be overcome if thought through in advance. One common problem occurs when a loss is expected in the joint venture during its start-up period. Due to fast write-offs, accelerated depreciation and the like it is quite common for capital-intensive investments to show operating losses for the first three or four years. It is therefore probably more attractive for the local partner if these losses can be used to offset against other locally derived profits. However, in order to be allowed to take advantage of such tax losses, a minimum shareholding usually applies. In some countries this may be a bare majority holding, while in others up to 75 per cent of the equity may be required.

This problem can be dealt with in several ways. It may be possible to meet the 'grouping' requirement by creating two classes of shares. The local partner might receive his stake in the form of equity shares while the MNC takes convertible loan stock. The local company thus remains the parent of the joint venture until it comes into profit, after which the MNC may exercise its conversion rights. A similar result might be obtained by granting the MNC the option to purchase at some future time. In order to protect the local partner such schemes would normally incorporate other features such as a loan from the MNC in the case of an option, coupled with a guarantee to the local shareholder or a put option to ensure that the downside risks are equivalent and the MNC cannot get out of its liability in the event of failure. Similarly, when structures do not provide equivalent voting rights then special arrangements can be made during the period when non-equal equity positions are held.[11]

A company may actually not be the most appropriate form of organisation for a joint venture – a partnership or a trading trust often being superior. Under the laws of most countries each partner in a partnership is separately taxed on his share of the profits, so enabling the local partner to obtain tax relief on its share of the losses. This device may also cover the problem of having different distribution policies for the two partners. For the MNC a partnership arrangement should normally not be entered into by the parent company direct, otherwise it will probably be treated as a branch in the country concerned. It is therefore usually preferred to set up a separate subsidiary in the joint venture country to enter into a partnership or do so via a subsidiary located in a third country, usually a low-tax area. Variants on the partnership theme offer additional advantages in several major countries.[12]

Joint ventures may be an especially appropriate mechanism for avoiding the US-controlled foreign corporation legislation and that of other countries which have adopted similar legislation. Under this legislation, US companies are assessable on their proportionate share of certain undistributed income in controlled foreign corporations. It may therefore be possible to set up a joint venture with a genuine commercial purpose in such a way that it is conducted through a tax haven company not controlled by the resident of any one country. If necessary, the odd shares can be given away to third parties in yet another country. The tax-saving advantages from such an arrangement can be substantial and a US company may be better off with a minority holding in a venture with an effective tax shelter than having a substantial majority holding without such a tax shelter.[13]

The Joint Venture Agreement

Because of the potential difficulties that can occur with joint ventures they should be entered into carefully and the articles of association should be drawn up only after consideration of the objectives and strategies of the participants and how these might change in the future. Further, such an agreement should set out in clear language the rights and obligations of the participants, taking care that differences in interpretation due to translation are not introduced when more than one language is used. Such an agreement should then cover the following points:

1. The legal nature of the joint venture and the terms under which it can be dissolved
2. The constitution of the board of directors and the voting power of the partners

3. The managerial rights and responsibilities of the partners
4. Constitution of the management and appointment of the managerial staff
5. The conditions under which the capital can be increased
6. Constraints on the transfer of shares or subscription rights to non-partners
7. The responsibilities of each of the partners in respect of assets, finance, personnel, R & D and so on
8. The financial rights of the partners with respect to dividends and royalties
9. The rights of the partners with respect to the use of licences, knowhow and trademarks in third countries
10. Limitations, if any, on sales of the joint venture products to certain countries or regions
11. An arbitration clause indicating how disputes between partners are to be resolved
12. Conditions under which the articles of the joint venture agreement may be changed.[14]

There are five main forms of joint ventures in practice, with many variations. Firstly, 50:50 ventures with a local company formed from scratch, this pattern being common in Japan. Secondly, the purchase of a share in a local company with the local owners, and sometimes management retaining their identities. Thirdly, the establishment of a new joint venture with a number of local interests, often wealthy individuals. Fourthly, the establishment of a joint venture with a local government or its agency. Fifthly, the case where local ownership is diffused via an equity market, and has no say in the management of the venture.

From the viewpoint of the MNC the final variety is preferred, and many companies have adopted this organisation as a deliberate policy. Thus, Reed International, for example, has made local share placings of its operating subsidiaries in a number of countries. There has been a growing trend, however, towards the development of partnerships with local governments after substantial early resistance to the principle by MNCs. In 1970, for example, US Steel entered into a joint venture with the government of Brazil for a 49 per cent interest in a new iron-ore mining project costing an estimated $300–400m. With a local government partner there is no incentive for controls or harassment and in addition, governments tend to have adequate funds for growth, which for them is a major objective, while being less concerned with day-to-day management.[15]

A number of techniques for controlling joint ventures are commonly used. These include the writing into the articles of the joint venture the allocation of certain key rights to the MNC such as the right to propose the chief executive, and the stipulation that the articles cannot be changed without unanimous agreement of the board. Other techniques include the use of different kinds of stock, involving non-equal voting rights; the use of licensing agreements and management contracts which permit the withdrawal of technology in the event of disagreement; and the arrangement of exclusive marketing contracts with the MNC.[16]

CONCLUSION

The process of capital investment does not fit wholly within the context of the planning system since the timing of many investment opportunities does not coincide neatly with that of the planning cycle. Like the planning system, however, capital investment decisions are seen as very much a behavioural and political process, mainly initiated at local level before ultimately being approved centrally. Only certain classes of decision are usually initiated centrally or involve substantial participation on the part of headquarters executives. These include investments in new overseas locations, licensing strategies and joint venture formation. The factors which should be considered in planning each of these important strategic decisions are discussed in detail, and guidelines for reducing the risk of failure are developed.

8 Planning International Mergers and Acquisitions

In recent years acquisitions and mergers have become an increasingly important route to international expansion. In the decade 1946–57, the leading US multinationals for example made 194 acquisitions in Western Europe. In the next decade to 1967 the number rose to 1193.[1] Most of these moves were, however, acquisitions rather than mergers. In Europe, a report sponsored by the EEC revealed that between 1961 and the first half of 1969 there were 1861 mergers and takeovers within the Community and only 257 between companies from countries in other communities. Non-Community companies made 820 acquisitions of EEC-based companies, while Community-based firms made 215 purchases abroad.[2] While the leading firms have now mainly established themselves in major countries, fill-in acquisitions are still undertaken and newly emerging multinationals, including many of the largest firms in Western Europe and Japan, are also actively engaged in increasing their geographic coverage.

While acquisitions even within a country have relatively high failure rates, cross-border moves tend to be particularly unsuccessful, as shown in Table 8.1. For US multinationals 50 per cent of the acquisitions examined in a recent survey were rated by participating executives as failures or not worth making. German and French multinationals had somewhat higher success rates but the organisations studied were all within continental Europe where local expertise could be expected to be of some assistance. British firms, however, had a relatively poor record for European cross-border acquisitions.

There are many reasons why increased risks occur with cross-border moves but amongst these the following, in particular, have been identified:[3]

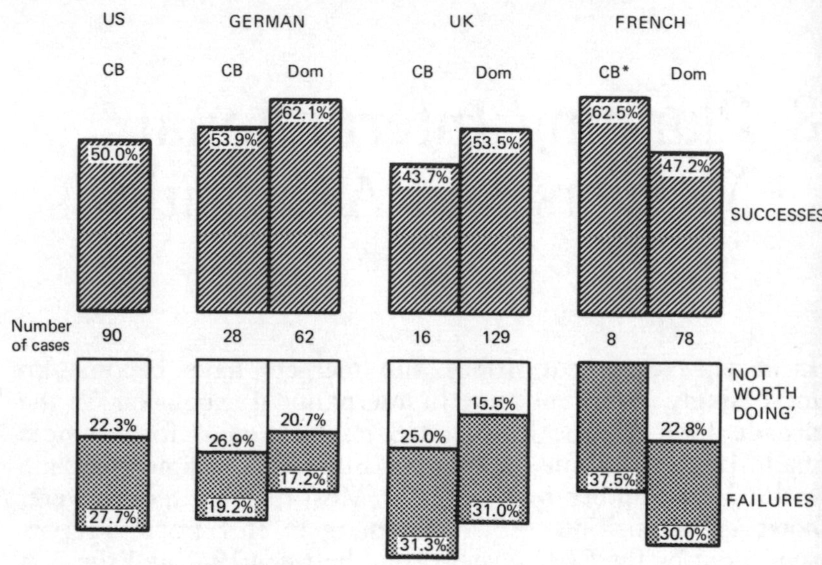

Table 8.1 Success Profiles in Cross-border Acquisitions compared to Domestic Acquisitions

Source: J. Kitching, op. cit., p.88.

1. *Distance* – geographic remoteness makes it more difficult to react when trouble arises.
2. *Culture* – national cultural characteristics can lead to significant differences in attitudes, values, objectives and methods of working.
3. *Communications Problems* – language differences place a serious burden on internal communications.
4. *Information Availability* – commercial data readily available in the USA and UK and some other developed nations is not obtainable elsewhere. Financial data in particular is notoriously unreliable in some countries due to different accounting conventions and standards, local tax patterns and financial market requirements.
5. *Controls* – management information and control systems

vary widely from country to country; and the process of adapting data produced to meet local requirements to those of the parent company can be long and laborious.

KEY FACTORS AFFECTING COUNTRY CHOICE

Despite these problems, however, an increasing number of companies are embarking on a programme of cross-border acquisitions. The main factors found to influence their choice of country are the rate of local economic growth, and the institutional and legal structures affecting acquisitions. These latter include the following:[4]

(a) Exchange control regulations;
(b) National and Supranational (as for example the EEC), anti-trust policies;
(c) Restrictions on foreign ownership;
(d) Regional investment incentives;
(e) Stock market regulations;
(f) Availability of sharcholder information – in many countries this data is not available as equity holdings are in bearer shares. In Europe, banks often provide a proxy service which votes bearer shares, thus the banks may well have data on the true owners of shares.
(g) Requirements to register certain percentage holdings – in most countries publication or notification is required when a shareholding stake is built beyond certain levels. In the UK 5 per cent holdings and above must be notified while in Germany the figure is 25 per cent. It is still sometimes possible to avoid these rules by purchasing in nominee names or warehousing share ownership.
(h) Shareholders' rights – in most countries different shareholding levels confer different rights. While shareholding percentages differ from country to country, the type of rights conferred are typically:

minorité de blocage – rights conferred on minority shareholders holding between 25 per cent and 33 per cent of equity. These can prevent changes in the 'fundamentals' of the business such as its articles of association, nature of business, dividend policy, etc.

management control – 51 per cent of equity typically gives the right to nominate management and control the day-to-day activities of the firm.

outright control – normally this is secured by purchasing between 67 per cent and 75 per cent of the equity. This gives the right to fundamentally change the nature of the business, dispose of assets, etc.

It can be extremely important to understand the rights of minority shareholders at different levels of equity ownership before making an acquisition, in order to ensure that poor acquisition-integration or rationalisation is not severely impeded.

KEY FACTORS FOR SUCCESS IN CROSS-BORDER ACQUISITIONS

In his analysis of European mergers and acquisitions, Kitching has identified a number of key factors necessary for the success or failure of international acquisitions. These include the following:[5]

1. *Choice of Country.* Two main factors have a critical influence on the choice of country in which an acquisition should be made. Firstly, what is the level of business and political risk? Secondly, what is the expected change in the growth rate of GNP? Generally speaking the faster the expected rate of growth, the higher the probability of success. This is further enhanced by the frequent correlation between high growth rate, a good balance of payments position and a low exchange rate risk.

2. *Degree of Diversification.* There is a strong correlation between the degree of diversification represented by an acquisition and the level of risk. This is illustrated in Table 8.2, which shows the success and failure rates for European acquisitions classified according to diversification type, as measured by comparison with the acquiring firm. Success was found to be most common with horizontal acquisitions, where the company purchased was engaged in basically the same product market as the acquirer. Forward or backward vertical integration moves had a somewhat lower success rate, but all

forms of diversification had a higher probability of failure. Marketing-inspired diversifications appeared to offer the lowest risk, but acquisitions to take advantage of a common technology had the highest failure rate of all.

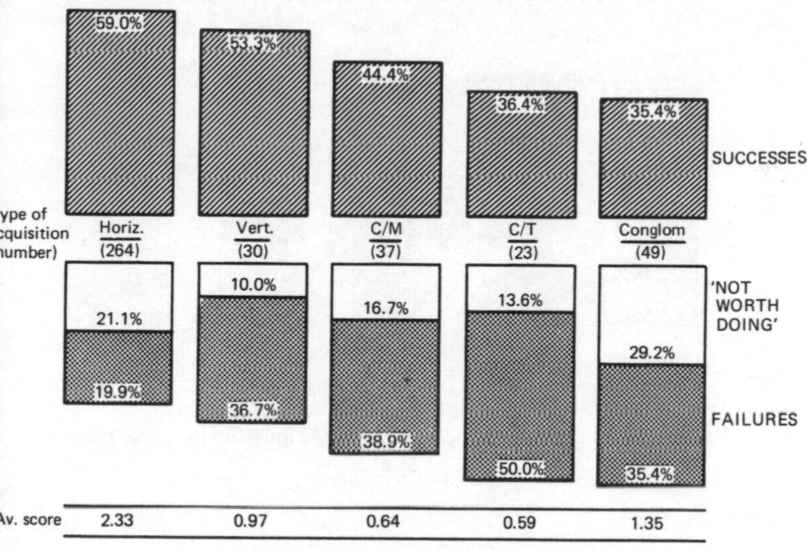

Table 8.2 Acquisition Success and Failure Rates by Diversification Type

Source: Kitching, op. cit., p. 62.

Indeed, pure conglomerate acquisitions, which tend to be in low technology industries, had a lower overall failure rate than all forms of acquisition except horizonal purchases.

3. *Size of Market Share*. Table 8.3 indicates that the probability of acquisition success is almost directly related to the share of market purchased. This is especially true in the case of diversification moves, lower shares being tolerable in horizontal acquisitions where an existing position is being reinforced. Acquisitions with market shares of less than 5 per cent for diversification moves had failure rates of over 50 per cent.

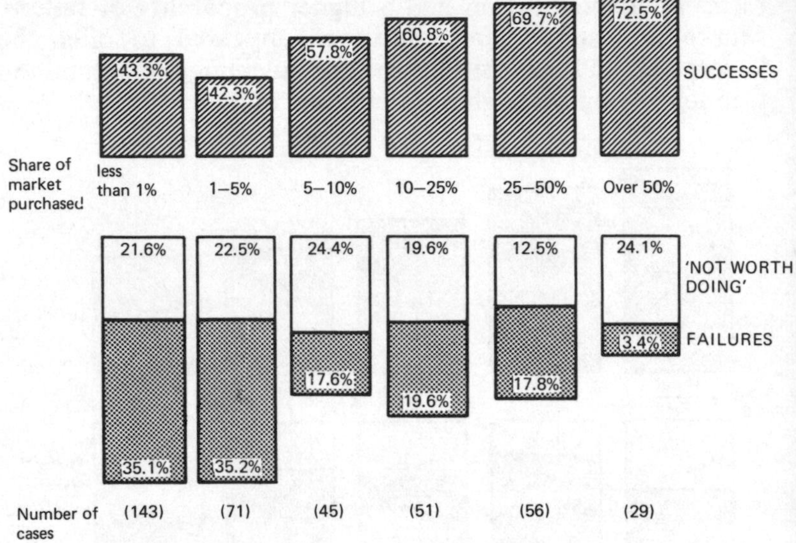

Table 8.3 Impact of Market Share on Acquisition Success Rates

Source: J. Kitching, op. cit., p. 75.

4. *Size of Purchase*. The size of an acquisition relative to that of the acquirer is an important determinant in success. While it may well seem prudent to buy small companies, these usually require a disproportionate commitment of top management time and make little impact on corporate performance. Moreover, for large purchases management makes a determined effort to ensure the new acquisition achieves the results expected of it quickly. This is illustrated in Table 8.4 which indicates that the possibility of success increases sharply as purchase size also increases. Successful small purchases tend to be horizontal acquisitions, which add to existing operations.

5. *Relative Profitability of Acquisitions*. There is a substantial difference between the success rates achieved from high- and low-profit companies as shown in Table 8.5. Turn-round situations require the existence of a skilled management team in the acquiring company, capable of handling such situations. In practice successes in purchasing low-profit

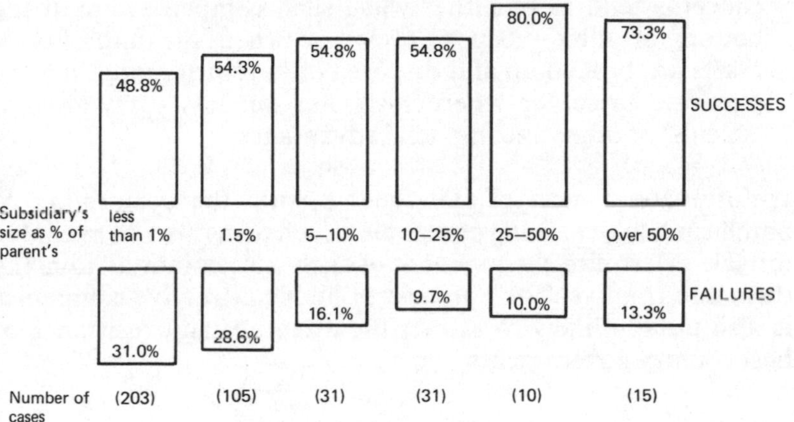

Table 8.4 Impact of Size on Acquisition Success Rates

Source: Kitching, op. cit., p.79.

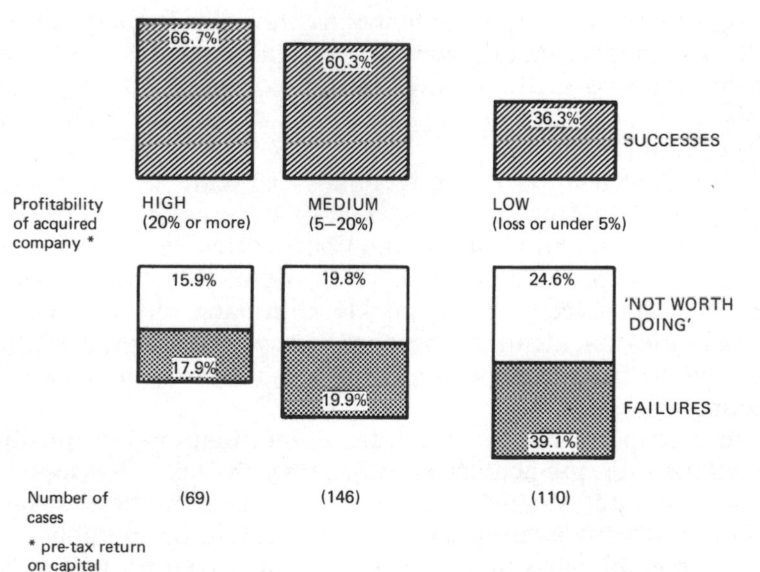

Table 8.5 Impact of Profitability on Acquisition Success Rate

Source: J. Kitching, op. cit.

concerns tend to be either when such companies are at the bottom of their business cycle; or when the unprofitable assets are broken up and disposed of to return more than the purchase price; or where there are tax loss carry-forward 'shields' or other like financial advantages.

Unfortunately, most of the time, despite the desirability of purchasing high earning companies, such firms are not available for sale or require the payment of such a premium as to make them unattractive. The purchase of highly attractive companies is also usually likely to attract the attention and resistance of host country governments.

PRE-ACQUISITION SEARCH PROCEDURES

The first step in planning for acquisition is to develop a suitable set of organisational skills to carry out the necessary screening, negotiation and integration activities. Two main concepts are used, namely the appointment of a business development executive and the establishment of a committee for acquisitions. These organisational devices allow each acquisition candidate to be reviewed in the light of overall corporate strategy while still allowing the maintenance of essential secrecy and confidentiality.

The identification and screening of suitable candidates is a long and laborious task, especially for cross-border moves, when the availability of information is often severely limited. As a first step, therefore, it is often useful to create an initial Go/No Go screen which quickly eliminates the majority of possibilities and identifies those concerns which are probabilities. In a number of developed countries this process can actually be computerised.

In Company S, for example, a multinational acquisitive conglomerate, pre-acquisition screening has been developed to a sophisticated degree. At the central headquarters a small team of security analysts examines the details of all public and, where possible, private companies within a country where data is available from a central source. Detailed data of this type is available for the USA, UK, Holland, Germany and to a lesser extent France, Australia, Canada and certain other developed countries. In some cases proprietary data-bank tapes are available, listing all recent financial information. In Company S these serve as a base and are supplemented by the internal examination of underlying accounts, the make up and distribution of shareholders, valuations of property, details of product lines, backgrounds to key individuals, organisation structure, labour and personnel policy aspects, competitive position and the like. When Company S is interested in making an acquisition the data bank is processed, using a series of financial ratios as surrogates for specific strategic factors, in order to produce a substantially abbreviated list of possible candidates for further consideration. Such financial variables might include market capitalisation, debt equity structure, value added per employee, return on capital, net cash flow and the like, with values being adapted to fit with the particular strategic needs of Company S at a given point in time.

The list of possibilities is then further reduced by supplementing the base data with the other financial and non-financial data collected, to finally produce a short list of candidates for detailed evaluation. In one such case, for example, Company S took some four months to carry out a detailed investigation on three continents of all the assets of one acquisition candidate it subsequently purchased.

NEGOTIATION PROCEDURES

The vast majority of cross-border acquisitions are negotiated rather than contested situations, although contested bids may have a higher success rate. While willing sellers are occasionally found, it is more common that potential candidates must be persuaded to sell. Despite post-acquisition policies which tend to eventually lead to management change, persuasion of local management in the pre-bid stage is important. The most effective persuasion is that a bid will allow the acquired company to realise its growth objectives by linking itself to the superior financial strength of the acquirer. Variations on this theme include:

1. Use of a wider distribution system to provide access to new markets;

2. Supplementing a local product line with new products from the acquirer;
3. Adding new product potential from the larger research and development capacity of the acquirer;
4. Improvement in management techniques from access to computer specialists and the like.

In many countries the shareholdings in companies to be acquired are personally held by individuals or families rather than widely distributed. In such cases negotiation strategy should concentrate on establishing the personal desires and motives of the sellers. Frequently these may involve fiscal considerations, a number of which are dealt with later. For this reason, for example, vendors may request receiving part of the purchase consideration abroad. It is therefore sometimes possible to broke such deals via a third-party tax haven resident. The use of third parties in general who can be trusted by both parties, such as a bank, accountant or other professional can often prove a useful catalyst.

PROSPECT EVALUATION

Since most transnational mergers are agreed, in deciding on whether or not to proceed and what price to pay it is usually possible to obtain relatively complete information regarding a prospective candidate. A systematic approach to such data collection is recommended and a number of checklists are available which help in this respect. Most leading international accountancy firms offer a service which, for a reasonable fee, will provide such a detailed evaluation. A substantially abbreviated version of the checklist used by one such firm is reproduced below:

Pre-acquisition Review

I. History and Nature of Business and Appraisal of Organisation

1. *History of Business*
(*a*) Details of registered office, principal place of business, founder articles, review of past years' books, trade record.
(*b*) Changes made recently concerning product range, fixed assets, sales policy, management strength, capital base.

2. *Ownership*
(*a*) Details of capital structure, and past changes, number, value and type of shares; details of payment and any transfer restrictions; share quotation.
(*b*) Details of shareholders; identity of major shareholders; any nominees and whom they represent; family interests; executive numbers of the company.
(*c*) Recent changes in share ownership and, if possible, when and why these changes were made.
(*d*) Why does the company wish to change ownership now?

3. *Management*
(*a*) Identity of directors and details of their shareholdings, appointments, contracts and fringe benefits.
(*b*) Details of management and committee meetings held and what records are kept.
(*c*) Identities of principal managers, details of responsibilities, salaries, other benefits, ages, qualifications, any contracts.
(*d*) Organisation chart and indications of any weakness in particular skill areas. Any changes needed.
(*e*) Any salary aberrations, profit-sharing schemes.
(*f*) Details of management development systems and identity of any areas not covered.

4. *Labour*
(*a*) Number, sex and age structure of employees by department. Recent history of changes in numbers. Rates of labour turnover. Details of local labour supply.
(*b*) Details of existing union presence. Record on industrial relations. Details of pending union negotiations.
(*c*) Details of fringe benefit schemes, especially pension and bonus schemes, in force.

5. *General Organisation*
(*a*) Are job definitions clear? Formally established? Is there adequate delegation? Is there any duplication?
(*b*) Details of management/workforce communication procedures and committees. Is there an adequate personnel function?
(*c*) Details of working conditions (cleanliness, heating, canteen, etc.). Are these adequate?
(*d*) Location of offices relative to factory. Assessment of

convenience of plant location relative to markets and supplies.
(*e*) Details of insurance policies. Any changes required?

6. *Production and Factory Organisation*
(*a*) Details of location, size, space utilisation. What room for expansion exists?
(*b*) Details of work pattern, number of shifts worked, amount of idle time, critical bottlenecks.
(*c*) Details of volume production by product line.
(*d*) Details of quality control procedures for production in raw materials, production control, inventory management policies, stores procedures.
(*e*) Assessment as to plant management competence.

7. *Purchasing Organisation*
(*a*) Is there a proper purchasing organisation? Is it competent?
(*b*) Details of major suppliers and products supplied by money volume. Any critical dependencies? What alternative sources available?
(*c*) Are prices reasonable? Any evidence of bad buying, too much stock, large stock write-offs, slow-moving stock?

8. *Marketing Organisation*
(*a*) How are sales made, through salesman, agents, etc.?
(*b*) Number and identity of major customers by product line, geography and money volume.
(*c*) Details of recent changes in customer make up or sales volume. Reasons for these.
(*d*) Details of export sales.
(*e*) Are prices determined by free competition, government, cartels, etc.?
(*f*) Details of advertising and promotion.
(*g*) How do company's product quality, prices, promotion, etc. compare with competition?
(*h*) What is the company's market share? What are the shares of major competitors? What recent share changes have occurred and why?
(*i*) Details of sales force, number and organisation, payments and expense systems.

9. *Transport Organisation*
(*a*) Details of vehicle fleet, if any. Details of utilisation and costs.

10. *Accounting Organisation*
(*a*) Details of accounting, control systems, budgetary procedures, costing system, cash flow management, working capital controls, stock records, fixed asset records.
(*b*) Details of filing systems, accounting information, mechanisation, computerisation.
(*c*) Assessment of systems' usefulness. Assessment of accountancy function's competence.
(*d*) Are the 'official' books up to date? Are there any differences between the 'official' books and the general accounting records? Can a letter of indemnity be obtained for the purchaser to cover irregularities?

11. *Contracts with Third Parties*
(*a*) Details of third-party contracts such as leases, royalties, etc. What are the effects of termination?

12. *Patents or Trade Marks*
(*a*) Details of trade marks and patents held. Are these valuable? Are patentable products adequately protected?

13. *Government and Local Government Policy*
(*a*) What is government policy in relation to the company? Any special grants, tax features existing or available?

II. Comments on Financial Statements

14. *Comments on Income Statements*
(*a*) Obtain comparative income statements and explain variations in:

(i) level of sales for each main product line;
(ii) gross profit by product line;
(iii) expense category;
(iv) taxation charge.

(*b*) Details of intra-group business, special items, omitted expenses, excessive expenses, material intangibles.

(*c*) Details of any accounting principle distortions, reallocations, consolidation effects, etc.
(*d*) Details of profitability by product line. Identification of key products, limiting factors on profit improvements.
(*e*) Trends in profitability.
(*f*) Adequacy of provisions for depreciation, bad debts, and stock write-offs.

III. Comments on Balance Sheet

15. *Current Assets*
(*a*) For each category of asset consider:

(i) acceptability of basis at which stated;
(ii) any base variation between years and reasons for change;
(iii) any deadwood in assets;
(iv) normality of asset figures in relation to scale and type of business.

(*b*) Details of cash position and bank arrangements.
(*c*) Details of receivables collection systems and record, aged debtor schedule, is bad debt provision reasonable? Any major debts?
(*d*) What is average credit period given? What is the trend?
(*e*) Details of any large returns, discounts, etc., since last balance sheet.
(*f*) Compute ratios of gross receivables to period sales and explain change.
(*g*) Details of inventory. Basis of evaluation, breakdown by category and product, turnover and ageing, seasonal variations.
(*h*) Details of inventory records, cut-off procedures, identification of slow-moving stock procedures.
(*i*) Basis of inventory pricing, allocation methods for materials, labour and overheads.
(*j*) Details of any intra-group profits in inventory, forward price changes affecting values, third-party inventories.

16. *Investment*
(*a*) Details of any investments showing nominal value, cost, market value (if quoted) and current dividend income.
(*b*) Any contingent liabilities for unpaid accounts on holdings.
(*c*) Details of any management control.

(*d*) Are investments realisable? Pledged? Any advantage to selling?

17. *Fixed Assets and Depreciation*
(*a*) Properties owned and rented with terms of leases, area floor space, use restrictions.
(*b*) Inventory of fixed assets by category showing cost revaluation, depreciation and net, by year of purchase or nearest possible.
(*c*) Check purchases made at arm's length. Check revaluation reliability.
(*d*) When no revaluation how different are book and current market? Is revaluation necessary?
(*e*) Depreciation rates and bases? Are these realistic? Do they agree with the tax guidelines? How have rates changed? Is accumulated depreciation excessive? Deficient?
(*f*) Details of capitalisation policy and treatment of repairs?
(*g*) Details of capital commitments.
(*h*) Arc any interest charges incurred in fixed assets?

18. *Intangibles*
(*a*) Detail intangibles by category showing costs, depreciation, and net amount. Are these of genuine asset value to the acquirer?
(*b*) What is amortisation policy for intangibles? Are balances tax-deductible?
(*c*) Are patents and trade marks important? Should they be investigated by a patent specialist?

19. *Liabilities*
(*a*) Obtain analysis of liabilities and endeavour to find out any material omissions. Are any secret resources included in liabilities?
(*b*) Examine purchases/disbursements register and incoming invoices for first few weeks after balance sheet date for any errors.
(*c*) Comment on size, variability and age of liabilities.
(*d*) Details of creditor schedule. What is average credit period given by suppliers?

20. *Taxation*
(*a*) How is company assessed for income tax? Are provisions adequate? What have been results of recent inspections?

(*b*) What carry-forwards exist and are these agreed? Are there any special exemptions, avoidance procedures, etc.?

21. *Resources*
(*a*) Details of resources. Ease of distribution. Differentiation between declared and hidden resources.
(*b*) Any capitalisation of resources intended or desirable?
(*c*) Any provision in articles regarding disposition of profits, payment of dividends, etc.?

22. *Debentures*
(*a*) Details of nature, amount and period of charge.
(*b*) Details of any conversion rights.

23. *Contingent Liabilities*
(*a*) Details of any litigation in process and financial guarantees.
(*b*) Details of uncalled amounts on shares in subsidiaries or associates.

24. *Future Prospects*
(*a*) Examine operating results since last balance sheet date for any significant changes.
(*b*) What budgeted results for profit/cash flow are made for the future? Do these seem realistic?
(*c*) Any changes expected in product range? New competition? Plant capacity?
(*d*) Any changes expected in capital structure? New loans or debt repayments? Important wage and price negotiations?
(*e*) Will company be affected by any new or projected government legislation.

Apart from the data collected in the checklist such an investigation would also usually show what remedial action is proposed; what economies are feasible; and what targets should be obtained as regards sale and profits. From such an investigation it is fairly easy to establish an acceptable price for the acquiring company to be prepared to pay, although more general financial and fiscal considerations may also influence this. There are many such significant financial and fiscal factors which must be taken into account in transnational acquisitions and a number of these are discussed below.

FINANCE AND FISCAL CONSIDERATIONS

1. Cash Transactions

The majority of transnational acquisitions are made for cash, by comparison with the widespread use of paper in domestic acquisitions. There are several reasons for this. Firstly, while in domestic transactions it is common for roll-over relief from capital gains to be granted to the shareholders of an acquired firm, this is not usually the case when a non-resident acquirer is involved. There may also be exchange control restrictions which inhibit the use of shares. A further and major disincentive, however, is the sheer complexity of using paper for cross-border purchase. Prior government approval is often needed, local stock exchange requirements and securities laws must be met and special consideration usually has to be given to fiscal consequences. In the USA, for example, stock issues would need to be registered with the Securities and Exchange Commission which would usually entail fuller disclosure in corporate reporting and compliance with US financial accounting practices. Other key issues which must be taken into account include the following:

(*a*) *Financial Sourcing Techniques*
Raising finance to make a cash purchase must be carefully thought through. When such cash is raised by borrowing, the loan currency used should be determined with respect to the currency of the earnings to be generated by the acquisition and of its assets. For example, many MNCs which borrowed on the Eurocurrency market to purchase UK companies have found that the declining value of sterling has made such purchases increasingly expensive. In order to reduce exchange risk exposure, therefore, it is usually best to borrow in the currency of the country in which assets are to be acquired, in order to match assets against liabilities. Exchange control rules usually endeavour to prevent this, however, since many European governments woke up to find their residents and financial institutions providing US MNCs with the funds to finance their own ultimate takeover. Such regulations tend to be related to the relative strength of a nation's currency. Thus, those countries with weak currencies will restrict the use of local funds for

acquisitions, while those with strong currencies, such as Germany and the Netherlands, have either restricted the use of external funds or made them considerably more expensive.[8]

(b) Interest Treatments

It is important to ensure that interest payments on borrowed funds can be offset against profits in either the country of the acquisition or against other group profits, the optimum strategy being to offset against the profits with the highest tax rate. Thus, even if a financial holding company is used to raise finance it should lend this out at interest, to enable this to be offset either against local profits or elsewhere in the group. Where a local subsidiary already exists, its profits can usually be used as an offset or where such an activity does not exist a dummy corporation may be established. This concern can then borrow the funds needed for the acquisition directly or via a back-to-back loan or parent guarantee, and endeavour to offset the interest against the profits to be acquired.[9]

(c) Finance Reduction Techniques

There are a number of techniques used for reducing the amount of financing required. The acquired company can often reduce its size by paying substantial dividends to the vendors prior to an acquisition, although this often places an unacceptable tax burden on the vendors unless avoidable. Alternatively, once the acquisition has been made, a dividend can be paid to the parent and used to pay off part of the purchase price. In addition, in many cases it is possible to dispose of part of the assets acquired, such as unprofitable activities or property sale and lease-backs. Complications can arise, however, due to local dividend-stripping restrictions and tax avoidance measures.

(d) Valuation Problems and Risk-reduction Techniques

There can often be serious difficulties in valuing overseas acquisitions. Apart from differences in accounting practices, there are, in many countries, serious problems in obtaining reliable financial data since accounts are often not consolidated and are influenced by tax factors. Accounts may undervalue assets, especially inventories, overstate deductible contingency reserves, omit sales, not reveal true profits, and so on.[10] Unless the acquiring firm is accustomed to evaluating such situations and since most acquisitions are negotiated, the use of professional advisers is recommended to inspect the acquisition as suggested above and in order to provide an independent valuation.

Despite the use of such precautionary measures, however, acquisition agreements should be carefully drafted to take account of unexpected liabilities or contingencies. It is also prudent if possible to place part of the acquisition price in escrow for an appropriate period, to satisfy any unknown tax or undisclosed liabilities which may arise after the acquisition. Earn-out clauses are also widely used. These can aid finance and cash flow, the sums involved only being payable at some future time when certain profit or asset projections are confirmed. Such clauses can cause problems, however. For example, vendors will object to any profit diversion or extraction techniques for reducing tax; capital investment programmes which reduce earnings and the like. As a result most earn-out clauses are linked to restrictions on the purchaser, to prevent the use of profit-reduction policies.

Depreciation policies also cause significant problems, since in most continental countries, unlike the UK and USA, depreciation for accounting and tax purposes must coincide. When 'excess' depreciation is commercially prudent this is usually achieved by changes in hidden reserves. Assets are therefore often deliberately undervalued to avoid taxation. The purchase of assets, as distinct from shares, is therefore less common, since high capital gains might be revealed which could incur a substantial tax liability.[11]

2. Paper Transactions

Transnational mergers, by contrast with acquisitions for cash, specifically involve the use of paper. This creates serious tax and financial problems which have been a significant deterrent to the number of such mergers. Firstly, there is a danger that a merged firm may be deemed to have disposed of its assets, so creating a capital gain, especially in European situations where balance-sheet assets are often substantially less than true worth. Moreover, as discussed above, roll-over relief is not usually available for non-domestic mergers. Accordingly, the tax loss carry-forward of existing losses in an acquired company is also often threatened when a foreign acquirer is involved. Thirdly, vendors may be taxed on a disposal of shares. Fourthly, exchange controls can severely constrain the use of shares by a foreign company in another country by forcing domestic residents to pay a premium. For example, in the purchase of Alloys Unlimited by the British Plessey Company, the US government allowed Alloys' shareholders to acquire a block of dollar-based Plessey stock without paying US interest equalisation tax. The Bank of England also allowed these shares to be issued on condition that they would be separately quoted in New York, so that UK residents would be forced to pay a premium to purchase them.

3. Distribution Tax Avoidance Procedures

The main fiscal problem of cross-border mergers, however, is the existence of two separate profit centres and two separate groups of shareholders located in different countries. As a result, profits earned in Country A may be paid as dividends to a parent or holding company in Country B, only to be redistributed back to the shareholders in Country A. These dividend streams will often be subject both to local tax in Country A, followed by a withholding tax on the payment to Country B. The parent itself then usually bears corporation tax and the net dividend paid back to Country A bears a second withholding tax before the shareholders themselves are finally taxed again. Only the final withholding tax is then usually allowed as relief to the shareholders of Country A. The only satisfactory way to avoid such distribution tax problems in practice is by the formation of a suitable holding company structure or to ensure that dividends do not cross frontiers. A number of approaches have therefore been used to achieve this, notably:[13]

1. *Holding Company Approach.* This solution makes use of an intermediate holding company. Nestlé provides an interesting example of the approach. Although based in Switzerland, which has a low domestic tax rate and a series of bilateral tax treaties, Nestlé would have to pay the 30 per cent Swiss withholding tax on dividends paid to shareholders resident in other countries and not entitled to the benefit of the Swiss tax treaties. This actually makes Switzerland a poor centre for an

independent quoted, dividend-paying, holding company. As a result Nestlé has established a Panama-based holding company, Unilac, and shareholders buying Nestlé's stock receive equivalent shares in this company, the two shares trading as a single entity. A number of the overseas companies are held by Unilac and dividends on these can be paid without a deduction of Swiss withholding tax.

2. *Profit Isolation Approach*. The objective of this method is to ensure that dividends do not cross frontiers, by paying local shareholders out of local profits. The method is most practical when few organisations are involved. Each party might then hold preference shares in the companies to be merged which would entitle them to the income they might expect from the combined merged group.

3. *The Use of Convertibles*. On occasion the use of convertible securities for cross-border purchases can offer advantages for exchange control and fiscal purposes. The rationalisation of the European operations of the South African Rembrandt Group into Rothmans International offers the classic example. This merger involved a combination of British, Dutch, German, Swiss and Belgian interests. The considerations were based on forward income projections from each of the companies involved and a convertible issue by a revamped UK holding company, to acquire the other concerns, was chosen as the optimum solution. This allowed the shareholders of the acquired companies to receive income as interest rather than dividends, this interest being deductible from UK profits and also suffering only a low rate of tax. Eventual equity rights were guaranteed via the conversion possibility. This also solved a UK exchange control problem which treated the bonds as a foreign-based debt until conversion, when the investment premium currency would be needed to purchase them. The only serious problem with this approach has been that although the UK was fiscally the optimum location, this does not necessarily take account of future exchange movements. In the event, the sharp decline of sterling against the deutschmark, in particular, has led to serious paper foreign exchange liabilities accumulating which can affect the holding company's own borrowing capacity.

4. *The Twin Holding Company Approach*. The most notable post-war example of the twin holding company approach has

probably been the Dunlop-Pirelli union. This was complicated by the prior existence of the twin Pirelli holding companies. In principle Dunlop ended up owning 51 per cent of its own operations and Pirelli Ltd in the UK; 60 per cent of its own international operations; 49 per cent of the Pirelli Italian interests and a similar amount of certain European subsidiaries held via the quoted Pirelli SpA; and 40 per cent of the overseas Pirelli subsidiaries held via its Swiss holding company. In return Pirelli held the balancing holdings in each case.

Due to losses incurred by the Italian company, there have been serious practical problems in making the union work. For example, Dunlop was forced to convert its 49 per cent holding in Pirelli SpA into preference shares, in order to remove the Italian concern's losses from the Dunlop accounts. In 1972–3 Dunlop was, however, forced to write its reserves off to make provision for losses on its investment.

Other twin holding companies of significance are the Unilever structure and that of Agfa Gevaert. In the latter case the merger involved the creation of two companies, one in Belgium, the other in Germany, with each partner holding 50 per cent of each. Subsidiary activities were then injected into these new joint subsidiaries by the parents leasing assets to them.[14]

POST-ACQUISITION PROCEDURES

After an acquisition has been made the real task for the management of the acquiring company begins. In successful acquisition situations fast action is usually essential. The first task is to establish communication channels and deal with organisational considerations. These include the decision on whether or not to change the management of the acquired concern. At the very least it is essential to place a member of the parent company into a senior board position in the acquired concern, to act as a liaison link with the parent. Many acquisitive companies prefer to change the top management group of acquired firms, either immediately or soon after the acquisition. This policy is not really recommended in a diversification situation and when done should be accomplished with generous severance terms. It is also important to establish clear reporting relationships and introduce planning and control systems compatible with the parent's control systems at a speed which is suited to the particular situation.

Financial Integration

The first area of integration after the acquisition is usually the finance function. Financial synergy, if present, is relatively easy to achieve, cash and near-cash, for example, can be released and redeployed. Improvements in working capital management can also substantially improve the cash flow and working capital needs of acquired companies and again reduce financing accordingly. In fixed assets, property often offers particularly attractive prospects either for the outright sale of surplus land and buildings or for sale and lease-back arrangements, which may well be a viable method of raising local finance. Other assets which may be saleable might include trademarks and brand names, product groups, plant and machinery and even complete product divisions. Care must be taken, however, to ensure that capital gains and other fiscal disadvantages are not incurred. This type of operation requires a full-time corporate executive group to both conduct evaluations and carry out disposals.

Marketing Integration

The key to achieving marketing synergy is an early examination of all means of achieving combination between the acquired concern and the parent group. A number of such areas have been identified including:[15]

1. Spreading high cost activities over extra volume – perhaps the most common such marketing cost is that of a sales force which can often add an additional product line at little cost.
2. Spreading heavy investments over extra volume – examples of this might include the additional use of high-cost distribution or transport facilities.
3. Improved marketing skills – many European companies have endeavoured to increase their marketing skills by acquiring companies in the USA, which is regarded as being

more competitive and market-orientated than European markets.

4. Product rationalisation – substantial economies can be achieved by the pruning of weak products from either the parent or acquired concern.

5. Price negotiations – these can lead to increased volume by being able to offer lower prices for combinations of products from the acquired or acquiring firms.

Production Integration

Advantages are often difficult to achieve in the area of production and take a long time to materialise. Apart from purchasing overseas assets in order to provide local production facilities and reduce competition, a number of other advantages have been obtained:[16]

1. Plant specialisation – some companies after making acquisitions have specialised their production facilities to produce a narrow product line in each plant and to so achieve economies of scale.
2. Plant rationalisation – the closure of plants is a relatively common phenomenon in post-merger situations. This policy, however, is becoming increasingly difficult in cross-border mergers where local governments frown on any such move unless accompanied by significant positive local economic advantages.
3. Transnational sourcing – a number of cross-border purchases are made to obtain new, more economic production sources than those available to the parent concern.

Significant synergy in other areas is not common. This is especially true of research and development integration, where many companies have reported special difficulties, from professional rivalry and the like.[17] Mergers undertaken for this motive have a high failure rate and very serious consideration should be given to how post-acquisition integration is to be achieved before such purchases are initiated. A more simple and less expensive strategy is usually to endeavour to head-hunt key personnel to add to one's own research function.

A summary of the post-acquisition procedures by Company

T, an acquisitive conglomerate multinational, is set out in Table 8.6. The company divides the timing of its intervention into two stages. The first of these is completed within the first six weeks after the acquisition is finalised. The second, which involves the development of new product lines and the termination of others, can take up to two years to implement fully. In order to carry out its procedures Company T maintains a small team of central office executives, all with wide industrial

Table 8.6 Post-acquisition Procedures

SUMMARY OF POINTS FOR INVESTIGATION AND ACTION

Stage One

(*a*) Visit by parent board member for discussions with management and employees.
(*b*) Details requested of constitution of board, remuneration and pension arrangements. Parent company liaison director appointed.
(*c*) Preparation of accounts as at date of acquisition.
(*d*) Establishment of accounts and budgets for the future.
(*e*) Audit and legal arrangements changed to conform to parent company practice.
(*f*) Banking arrangements revised and surplus cash transferred to central treasury.
(*g*) Insurance arrangements reviewed and amended as necessary.
(*h*) Property details established, walk-round valuations made, surplus requirements identified.
(*i*) Meetings and reports, capital expenditure proposals, procedures installed.
(*j*) Detailed investigation of overhead structure undertaken.
(*k*) Buying arrangements reviewed and integrated with parent company divisions as appropriate.
(*l*) Vehicle fleet and purchasing arrangements reviewed and integrated with parent company divisions as appropriate.
(*m*) Details on analysis of activities, earnings and capital employed conducted. (This procedure is similar to the detailed pre-acquisition checklist provided above.)

Stage Two

(*a*) Termination of unprofitable activities with cash generated being used for (*b*) or returned to parent company.
(*b*) Development of profitable activities.
(*c*) New product development begun or parent company products introduced.
(*d*) Reduction of capital employed by disposal of surplus assets, improved working capital management and the like.
(*e*) Management reorganisation as appropriate.
(*f*) Inter-group commercial and technical cooperation begun by means of linking to global product group committees.

experience and many with financial qualifications, to move into acquired firms. The members of this team provide liaison directors from the acquisition to the parent company and are initially made fully responsible for performance until an

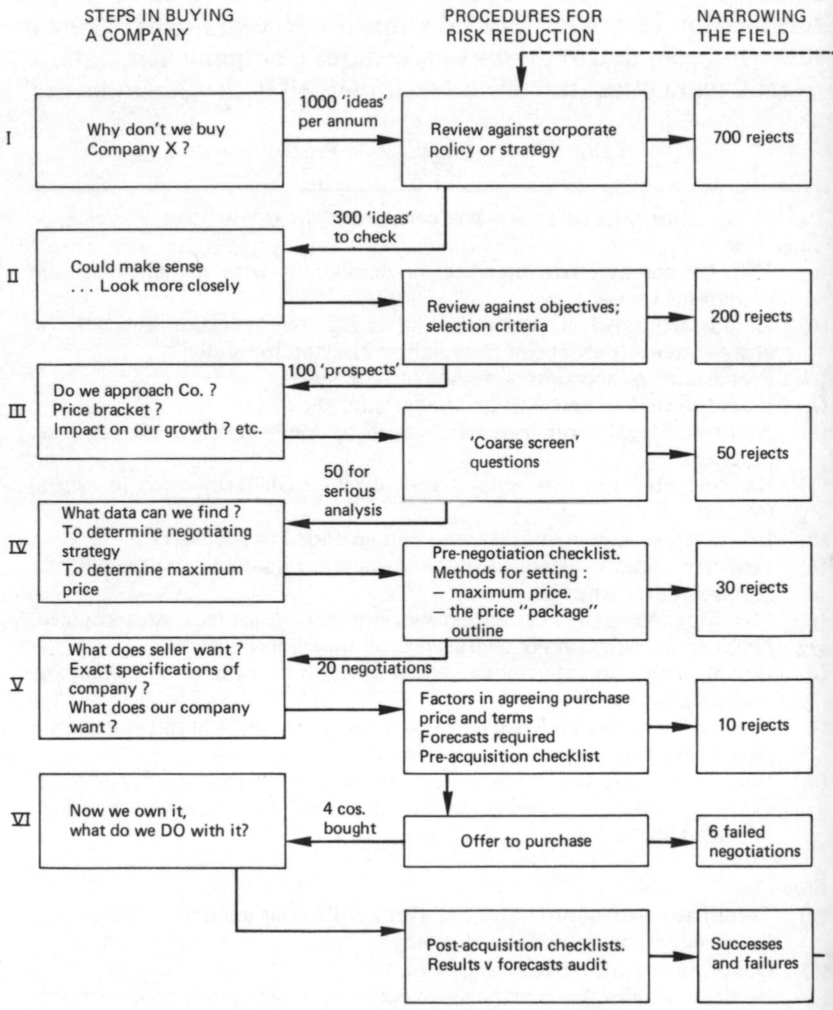

Fig. 8.1 Developing Systematic Procedures for Risk Reduction in Acquisitions

Source: J. Kitching, op. cit., p.154.

organisation for the acquisition is confirmed. Reorganisation does tend to occur in companies acquired by Company T within the first three months, with the former board usually being replaced by executives drawn from the second level of the organisation.

Company T moves swiftly to release whatever financial synergy might be available, all cash, or its equivalent, released, being used to reduce the parent's financing costs. Wide use is made of local high-quality external consultants to evaluate marketing and production operations. Those product areas identified as unprofitable are sold if possible or terminated unless profits can be quickly restored. Successful product areas receive additional financial resources to encourage expansion. All surplus property, or other assets no longer required to manage the business, are disposed of by the small central team also responsible for identifying acquisition prospects.

CONCLUSION

Acquisition as a means of expansion is always risky; when such moves take place across national boundaries the risks are multiplied. It is imperative to take a carefully planned approach if these risks are to be reduced to an acceptable level. This process of risk reduction is summarised in Figure 8.1. This indicates how it is first necessary to review potential acquisition candidates against overall corporate strategy as a preliminary screen to avoid the possible traps from not allowing for those key success factors identified in acquisition situations. Coarse screening techniques allow the population of possible candidates to be reduced to manageable proportions, but the onerous task of detailed data collection on the remaining concerns must be undertaken before serious negotiations can begin.

These negotiations involve personal factors as well as detailed evaluations of the potential partner and careful consideration of the financial and fiscal factors involved. Finally, some purchases may be made and after this the task of management really begins when post-acquisition integration procedures must be implemented, if the objectives originally established for the acquisition are to be achieved.

9 The Management of Political Risk

One distinctive feature of the multinational enterprise is the need for management to adequately balance the political risk exposure of the organisation throughout its global operations. Although managements are becoming increasingly aware of the importance of political factors in determining the outcomes of strategic decisions, systematic attempts to evaluate risk exposure are not common. Indeed there is some evidence to suggest that many multinationals are less sophisticated in their attitude to foreign investment decisions than they are to domestic opportunities.[1] An earlier survey actually revealed that few major US multinationals conducted a systematic evaluation of political risks 'involving their identification, their likely incidence and their specific consequences for company operations'.[2]

The term political risk itself does perhaps require some elaboration. Traditionally, firms operating in international markets have often tended to consider political risk as the possibility of outright sequestration of operating assets resulting from host governmental actions, with the probabilities of such actions taking place being much greater in developing rather than developed countries. In reality the concept is much wider, while geographically, for many organisations, the principal risks probably lie in developed countries and even in their country of origin.

The most common sources of political risk and the major forms it takes are shown in Figure 9.1. In addition to host governments both home country governments and the supranational legislative bodies, such as the EEC, can and do pose political risks for the MNC. Further, the individual requirements of these bodies may often lead to a situation where, to meet the requirements of one, the firm must automatically come into conflict with another. Political intervention, too, takes many forms, from a relatively mild set of standard regulations which apply to all firms, to severe selective sanctions and ultimately expropriation.

Intervention \ Intervention Body	Host Government	Home Government	Supranational Authority
Standard Regulation Intervention	Monopoly Legislation	'Trading with the Enemy'	Right of Establishment
Discriminatory Intervention	Restrictions in Areas of National Defence	Exchange Controls	
Selective Intervention	Contravention of Economic Policy	Extra territoriality	Competition Policy

Fig. 9.1 Political Intervention Sources and Types

Source: Adapted from C. E. Johns, unpublished Master's Dissertation, Manchester Business School, 1975, p. 29.

FORMS OF POLITICAL INTERVENTION

Host Government Intervention

The normal area for consideration of political risk centres on the expected reaction to investments in the host country in which they are made. These considerations might be expected to cover each of the following areas:

Standard Regulations
These may cover specific areas such as:

1. Monopoly and restrictive trade practices legislation.
2. Exchange control regulations.
3. Requirements for the use of local nationals in management positions.
4. Specific image and social benefit regulations.
5. Requirement for a given percentage of local content in assembled products.
6. Regulations regarding taxation of profitability, forms of remittance, without taxes and the like.

Regulations such as these are not specific to the individual firm, but apply in general to all forms of corporation.

Discriminatory Intervention

This form of intervention tends to discriminate against foreign owned corporations to the advantage of domestic operators. Examples of this type of practice might include:

1. Restrictions on foreign firms operating in certain sectors of the economy such as defence or computers.
2. Allowing only joint ventures with local majority shareholdings.
3. Imposition of special operating taxes, fees and other charges not levied on domestic operating firms.

Selective Intervention

This represents the most serious level of intervention. This is an area in which decisions, although perhaps related to a statement of policy, are made in relation to many different pressures and the decision arising may be applicable only to a specific case. Such practices might include:

1. 'Creeping expropriation' as occurred under the Peron regime in Argentina. Profits earned by foreign-owned corporations were not remittable, nor was foreign capital repayable. Instead all such funds had to be reinvested locally where, because of high inflation, they rapidly lost value.[3]
2. The imposition of discriminatory taxation, special levies and similar measures to reduce net profitability to nothing.
3. Changing the rules on concessions agreed between firms and earlier governments so as to claim compensation and new charges. This type of risk in conjunction with the first two above represents perhaps the most common and important form of political risk today. Many host governments carefully calculate the level of 'spoliation' imposed on the profitability of a project at its most vulnerable point so as to stop just short of causing the MNC to abandon the project.
4. Sequestration of the assets of individual corporations such as the takeover by Chile of Kennecott, Anaconda, Cerro, Ford and ITT in 1971, or the nationalisation of the interests of BP in Kuwait Oil Company in 1975.
5. Nationalisation of all foreign assets. This tends to be relatively rare; examples would, however, include the 1960

takeover of all foreign firms in Cuba and the seizure of all British assets in Uganda in 1976.

While there is no comprehensive analysis of the types of intervention discussed above it is possible to observe that risks are far from uniform for different industries. Those industries which can be classified as especially important to the national interest tend to experience significantly greater levels of control and hence likelihood of selective intervention. This is illustrated in Table 9.1 which summarises the expected level of local political concern for different industries based on recent experience. The type of risk faced by particular industries also varies and the results of a recent survey of high-risk MNCs is shown in Table 9.2.

Table 9.1 Political Concern by Industry

	Industry Sector	*Level of Political Concern*	
			Hi
(a)	Defence	Industries producing strategic materials vital to defence	↓
(b)	Infrastructure	Industries providing vital services for the operation of the economy, i.e. communications, transportation, utilities, banking and finance	
(c)	Extractive	Industries which exploit the natural resources of the nation state, i.e. oil, metals, coal extraction	
(d)	Primary Manufacturing	Industries which provide key elements of industrialisation, i.e. iron and steel, heavy engineering	
(e)	Prestige Manufacturing	Industries having particular significance to national pride, i.e. fashion in France	
(f)	Secondary Manufacturing	Productive industries producing goods for local consumption and potentially for export	
(g)	Service	Industries providing services to the community regarded as non-essential	↓
			Lo

Source: Adapted from C. E. Johns, op. cit., pp. 78–9.

Table 9.2 Type of Political Risk by Industry

Mining	*Oil*	*Banking*	LDC *Agricultural & International Trading*	*Chemicals*
Risk of creeping expropriation and increased charges against sunk investment (spoliation risk). Developed countries becoming as bad as developing in demands.	Era of extensive nationalisation ending because: most obvious nationalisation already complete; increasing use of less direct methods; need for high technology in oil extraction makes oil companies necessary. Major risk of legislative & control changes by host governments, e.g. UK North Sea legal changes. Political pricing of oil. Political factors on investment in consuming countries.	Nationalisation still a problem but slowing. Major risk of changes in controls over banking sector e.g. licensing only with participation. Risk of combination of economic and political factors leading to default by the nation state. Emergence of regimes leading to increase of any of the above risks and currency devaluation.	Nationalisation not seen as a major threat. Increased risk of a wide range of controls and restrictions by host governments, often discriminatory and petty in nature. Risk of nationalism especially in extreme left-wing and communist regimes favouring land reform.	Main risk war, revolution and insurgency. Limited risk from government actions since technology inputs regarded as high value to economic development and difficult to duplicate.

Home Country Intervention

While host country political intervention is almost invariably considered in foreign investment decisions, it must be remembered that cross-border transactions have effects in at least two and often more countries. After the host country, the next most significant political risk area is the impact of intervention by the home country of an MNC. Home country interventions can take the following forms:

Standard Interventions

1. Standard regulations covering such areas as exchange control, remittance of profits, the obtaining of domestic or overseas investment capital and the like.
2. Blanket regulations concerning the export of certain areas of knowhow considered strategic, such as the restrictions on the sale of defence equipment to the Middle East.

Discriminatory Interventions

1. Preferential resource allocation regulations which endeavour to prevent overseas investments which might be later used to cause domestic unemployment, balance of payments deficiencies, and the like.
2. Selective ideological restrictions such as US attitudes to trade with Cuba or British restrictions on trade to South Africa.
3. Deterrents arising from the lack of bilateral trade treaties and insurance facilities between home and host governments.

Selective Interventions

The key intervention of this type concerns the issue of extraterritoriality covering areas such as the following:

1. Selective intervention by a home government on firms which affect a subsidiary in a host country. Examples of such action was the intervention of the US government to stop Ford Motor Company's Canadian subsidiary selling trucks to the Chinese, and a similar move by the US government to stop the British selling aircraft to China because they were equipped with US-made navigational aids.
2. Selective intervention by a national government to re-

structure an industry within its own borders which in turn affects the operations of subsidiaries of such firms operating in other countries. Examples include the nationalisation of the steel industry in Britain; the use of anti-trust legislation in the USA against the Gillette Company, in 1968, to try and stop the acquisition of the German Braun AG; and the hold-up to the merger of the two Swiss companies, Ciba and Geigy, by the US on the grounds that this would reduce competition in the US dyestuffs market.

Supranational Intervention

There are a number of international agencies which can effectively intervene in transnational transactions such as the GATT, the IMF and the United Nations Organisation. These bodies are not political in themselves, however, but recently such supranational political agencies as the EEC and LAFTA have begun to emerge. Intervention by such agencies can take a number of forms including the following:

1. The unification of regulations within each member state to remove distortion of market forces throughout the community.
2. The elimination of discrimination between individuals or firms of member states in trading throughout the community and unification of community regulations vis-à-vis the outside world.
3. The establishment of new regulations designed to control operations in the unified market and supersede regulations selectively applied by member states.

FORECASTING POLITICAL INTERVENTION

Many companies are increasingly endeavouring to formalise their assessment procedures for political risk, although as yet most efforts tend to be relatively unsophisticated, despite the fact that one study had found that political instability is the most cited reason for rejecting countries as prospective sites for capital investment.[4] A number of basic approaches have, however, been identified to help resolve the problem:

1. The Go/No-Go Decision

This is the most simple method and accepts or rejects a particular country on the basis of an examination of a limited number of crucial variables such as the feasibility of total ownership. While such an approach is simple, quick and cheap it runs the risk of eliminating countries for only partially rational reasons. It is most applicable to smaller firms which have only limited overseas activity and many prospective investment opportunities for scarce resources.

2. The Premium for Risk

With this system, companies seek to obtain a higher rate of return from their investment in countries considered to exhibit a higher degree of risk compared with investments in countries considered to be politically safe. This method is sometimes used in conjunction with the Go/No-Go approach. The size of the premium sought and the methods of establishing the level vary greatly. In some companies, a consensus of a number of executives is taken to decide on the rate of premium to be attached to specific countries.

Rating scales are useful as part of the screening process for identifying foreign investment sites, but it is difficult to assign weights for each category of the scale. Further, the premium for risk method itself assumes that the degree of risk remains uniform over the life of the project which is extremely unusual. Changes in the future climate of a country therefore tend not to be taken into account in arriving at a single risk premium. Corrections to take account of future changes are so potentially complex and inaccurate as to make such attempts useless. Nevertheless, despite the flaws, in a recent study it was found that 80 per cent of the US-based managers interviewed used the premium for risk technique in some form.[5] A variation of this method makes use of a range of estimates for each factor expected to affect future profitability. This range of estimates is then used for a sensitivity analysis on project cash flow and profitability.

3. Risk Analysis

An even more sophisticated approach makes use of subjective

probabilities in a decision-tree approach as illustrated in Figure 9.2, which examines the risk of nationalisation of North Sea oil. The general questions that need to be asked are: what are the events (variables) that have to be watched? What are the alternative policies that could be generated? What is the expected outcome from these events? And what can be done to minimise the risks?[6] Subjective probabilities can be allocated to each of these questions and the resulting payoffs calculated, with an optimal route being chosen by means of the decision tree. Sensitivity can be tested by varying the probability assessments or by making use of probability distributions.

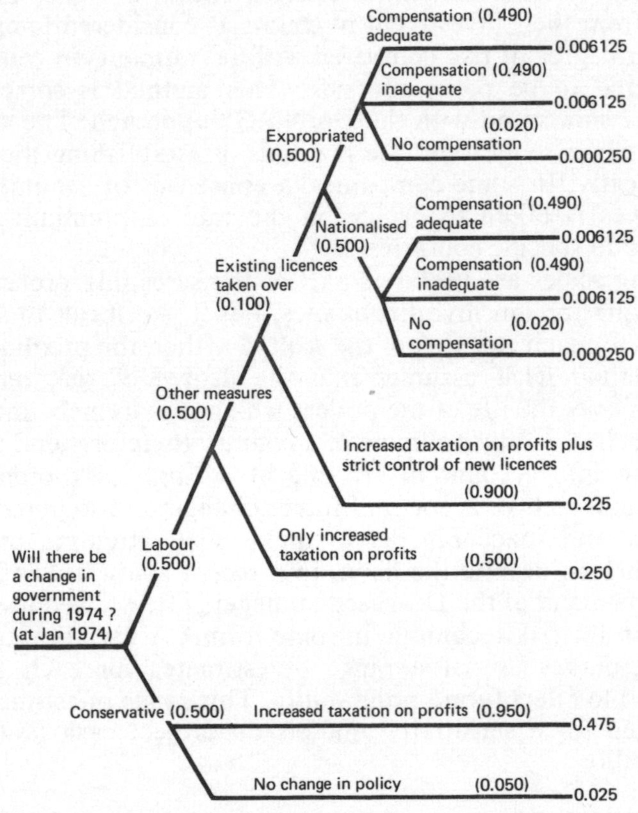

Fig. 9.2 Decision Tree Related to Risk of Nationalisation
Source: B. Lloyd, op. cit., p. 30.

4. Political Acceptability Profile[7]

This method is rather different in concept from those above in that it attempts to allow the investing corporation to evaluate its strategy in comparison to that which the relevant governments are likely to find acceptable. Individual nation states will regard particular investments with more or less favour dependent upon their own goals. These tend to lie in three main areas, namely the economic benefits expected from an investment; the impact on economic sovereignty, ideology, culture and external relations.

These factors can be translated into a series of readily assessable pieces of information such as the following:

(1) *Source of Funds*. Is the investment being funded from outside the host country or is the intention to draw on the local money markets?
(2) *Profit Repatriation*. What percentage of the profits will be reinvested in the host country?
(3) *Export Potential*. What is the overall effect on the terms of trade including import substitution, export promotion and profit remission?
(4) *Type of Investment*. Is the investment of a type which increases the level of production in the host country or is it service-oriented, leading to a higher level of internal consumption? If the investment is of a productive type does it include the depletion of natural resources? Is it labour or capital intensive?
(5) *Importation of New Technology*. Does the investment bring new techniques and require personnel to be trained to a greater degree of skill?
(6) *Value added*. To what extent will the investment add value? Will it create additional demand for local resources?
(7) *Control of the Economy*. What share of the market sector the investment will go into will it take? Will it force local enterprises out of business?
(8) *Local Content*. What percentage of any product produced will be made locally?
(9) *Ownership*. What, if any, percentage of the ownership of the investment will be held locally?

(10) *Control*. How much control will be exercised by the parent vis-à-vis local management?

From questions such as these it is possible to quickly draw up a profile for any country and for investment projects. Comparisons between the two profiles provides indications, from the differences between them, of the level of political risk. The system can be refined to some extent by applying weights to each factor and, by suitably scaling each of these, some quantitative assessment as to the level of risk can be made.

Dissimilar types of countries will be expected to exhibit different profiles as to the type of desirable investment as indicated in Figure 9.3. A less developed country, for example, is likely to place strong emphasis on gaining external investment

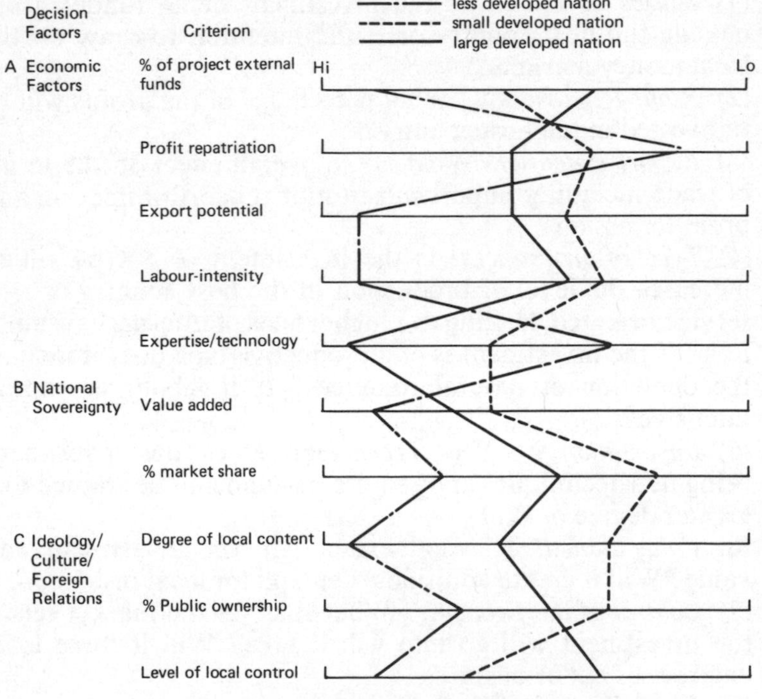

Fig. 9.3 Political Acceptability Profiles

Source: Adapted from C. E. Johns, unpublished Master's dissertation, Manchester Business School, 1975, chapter VII.

funds, on the ability of an investment to save foreign exchange, and to be labour- rather than capital-intensive. Such factors as advanced technology would have less priority.

The LDCs are relatively unattractive to most non-extractive industries due to their lack of purchasing power. Thus to gain investments at all, many LDCs have to provide attractions such as cash grants, tax holidays and the like. Where an LDC such as India seeks to regain control it has led to a net disinvestment. As a result the Indians have introduced a special export zone where companies operate under mandatory export targets in return for 100 per cent ownership and tax exemptions.

By comparison, as an economy develops, it becomes more attractive to the foreign investor. The level of local skills increases and, combined with growing economic activity, leads to the generation of internal industries. At this time the need for foreign investment becomes more selective and government preferences switch to increasing the efficiency of production or introducing new technologies. This situation typically applies to the smaller developed nations. Their attractiveness to foreign investors, however, may often mean local industries are made vulnerable because of their inability to match rates of innovation and economies of scale enjoyed by MNCs. The issue of control thus takes on high importance and is a very sensitive area, as in Canada and Australia, where selective intervention has occurred to restrict the activities of foreign MNCs.

Finally, large developed countries tend to be more open to overseas investment since their own industrial base is relatively secure. Where, however, this is not so, pressure will be brought to bear on the entering MNC. For example in the UK, where Hitachi, Sony and other Japanese electrical appliance manufacturers have attempted to establish new plants, strong pressure against them has come from domestic producers.

POLITICAL RISK ASSESSMENT PRACTICE

A recent research study of 16 high-risk MNCs[8] revealed that while political factors represented a serious and growing problem formal techniques of analysis were relatively underdeveloped. These companies, drawn from the minerals and mining, oil, agricultural commodities and chemical industries, had all experienced a significant amount of political intervention in their international activities. Further, most were operators of very sophisticated strategic planning systems and had extensive international operations on a truly global scale.

A number of the companies had endeavoured to use the more sophisticated techniques outlined above. For example one major oil company had developed an extensive decision-tree analysis for systematising and quantifying the political risks of new investments in a number of Latin American countries. The output of the analysis was a premium for risk based on systematic and 'objective' assessment. In the event, however, these assessments were almost invariably lower than that arrived at subjectively by top management and the latter view prevailed, resulting in the abandonment of the technique.[9]

In the main, qualitative assessments prevailed, resulting in the development of risk premia, although the techniques for collecting such data were usually well established. For example many companies systematically collected information relating to the political environment of overseas territories from commercial and political contacts, overseas employees, top management and staff employees visits (often as part of the planning process), external consultants and published sources. Several of the companies had political intelligence units to monitor and evaluate these data and provide assessments for top management. Such assessments were sometimes clearly converted into economic predictions and their consequences. Predictions as to the forward price of oil were an especially important example of this practice.

The oil and banking corporations were perhaps the most sophisticated in their management methods, with the latter companies being the most active managers of political situations. Most American banks, for example, called for regular quarterly political and economic assessments from all the countries in which they operated. In one case three separate assessments were made based on inputs from local management, outside independent economic forecasters and foreign exchange dealers, with the latter view tending to dominate in the event of any differences of opinion.

Based partly on these assessments the banks developed a portfolio approach in which funds were allocated in a series of interlocking ceilings by industry, country, type of borrower, and currency. The overall exposure of the banks' position was adjusted daily from close of position statements obtained from the global branch network and fed into a central computer installation which provided an output position for each branch to open with the following day.

The establishment of cross-border exposure risks for the overall portfolio was based on a number of factors including in one case:

Domestic economic conditions, outlook and policies

Balance of payments and their management

Trends and prospects for the most important economic sectors

Flow of funds and financial intermediation

Political conditions and outlook

Social conditions

Internal position and relations

Impact of world events – political and economic[10]

RISK REDUCTION MECHANISMS

These techniques of risk assessment are useful for the evaluation of new capital investment decisions in particular host countries. However, the threat of political risk is very real from a variety of sources. Despite efforts to identify and quantify situations it is not usually possible to isolate the risk associated with one particular investment from the effect upon an MNCs position as a whole. Further, capital investment decisions are not once and for all events, but rather MNCs tend to establish a continual presence in any host country. The key element in political risk management is the development of policies for minimising political threats. These can be developed for three key stages, namely:[11]

Preinvestment procedures

Operating tactics for ongoing investments

Tactics for handling expropriation threats

Preinvestment Procedures

(*a*) *Concession Agreements*

These spell out the specific rights and responsibilities of both foreign investors and host country governments. Such agreements were traditionally developed in the colonial era, but have been extended subsequently and are today used in both industrialised and less developed countries. There can be no foreign-owned investments in many countries, including Norway, Japan, India and Mexico, without a formal concession agreement with the host government.

Such agreements have been widely used to cover extractive resources such as oil or minerals. Unfortunately agreements of this type in many LDCs have proved very unreliable, as changes of government have later refused to honour them and have enforced renegotiation. Typical concession agreements do, however, spell out policies on potential sources of conflict such as those listed below:[12]

1. The basis on which funds may be remitted (dividends, management contracts, royalties, patent fees, loan repayments, etc.)
2. The basis for setting transfer prices, if applicable.
3. The right to export to third-country markets.
4. Social and economic overhead required to be built.
5. Method of taxation, including both the rate, base and method of assessing taxable income and property.
6. Access to the host country capital market, particularly for long-term borrowing.
7. Provisions for local equity participation, if any.
8. Price controls, if any, applicable to sales in the host country market.
9. Limitations on securing of raw materials and components.
10. Limitations on nationality of personnel.
11. A clause prohibiting the foreign-owned firm from calling on its home country government to intervene in disputes with the host country government.
12. Provisions for arbitration of disputes.

Although concession agreements establish a contractual obligation on the part of both investor and host government, they tend to be frequently modified in the light of changing circumstances. While it is usual for such renegotiations to be initiated by governments, such as the change in concession agreements granted to oil-operating companies in the British North Sea, on occasion improved terms can be wrung by the MNC such as the renegotiation of the agreement between Chrysler Corporation and the British government regarding the company's UK auto production.

(*b*) *Planned Divestment*

A second technique proposed is that of planned divestment whereby the foreign investor gradually sells majority ownership in its subsidiary over an agreed period of time. The principal argument in favour of this concept is that the main benefits from inward investment accrue to a country in the early years of an investment from the injection of capital, creation of jobs, addition of technology and the like. As an investment matures, however, it may prove a threat to the development of indigenous industry, often in attractive growth areas.

Critics of disinvestment have pointed out a number of disadvantages. Firstly, there is no guarantee that national ownership will be any more productive than foreign. Second, disinvestment may cut a subsidiary off from its markets, its technology or supplies of vital components. Thirdly, it would be illogical for any MNC to build up a serious competitive threat to itself. Finally, there are serious problems of asset valuation in any buoyant situation.[13]

Nevertheless, a number of companies do actively encourage increased local shareholdings. Indeed, the London and Rhodesia Mining Company (Lonrho), a leading British and Kuwaiti-owned MNC, has made local shareholdings in politically sensitive LDCs an integral component in its strategy. Deals are usually struck direct with local governments, with Lonrho being involved in finding sources of finance for capital projects and taking management contracts for joint ventures in which it is often a minority partner.

(*c*) *Insurance and Guarantee Protection schemes*

Many industrial countries provide the MNC with an opportunity to insure against political risk of expropriation, war and the like.

Such schemes operate in Australia, Canada, France, Germany, Japan, the UK and the USA. The United States government offers two programmes which are administered by the Overseas Private Investment corporation, which insures about a third of all new overseas investments by US firms. Two major programmes are offered. The first of these provides investment insurance covering the original capital investment against loss due to expropriation, nationalisation or confiscation by a foreign government, and cover can also be offered for losses due to war, revolution and insurrection. The US system also offers the unique feature of providing extended risk coverage of up to 50 per cent of the loan or equity investment for all the above causes and, in addition, commercial losses except when the cause of loss is fraud or misrepresentation, or it arises because of property which can be covered by normal commercial insurance.

Limitations on this type of scheme are that it is restricted to LDCs which have signed a bilateral tax treaty with the US; coverage is only offered to firms at least 50 per cent US-owned; only new projects can be insured; equity insurance runs for 20 years, loans for the life of the debt; and each specific insured project must be approved by the host government. Fees for coverage are less than 2 per cent for extended all-risk guarantees and less for specific coverage. Further, they are the same for all countries and investments, regardless of the level of risk.[14]

The system in Germany, although similar, is not restricted to countries with a bilateral investment guarantee treaty and commercial risks are not insurable. Maximum cover is up to 95 per cent of the investment, slightly higher than for most schemes, which usually cover about 90 per cent over 15–20 years.[15]

Most of the advanced countries also offer credit insurance for export trade. The British Export Credits Guarantee scheme, for example, covers insolvency or protracted default by a buyer, governmental action to block remittances, new import restrictions, war or civil disturbances in the buyer's country. Insurance may be supplemented by unconditional guarantees of repayment given direct to banks financing an exporter.

Operating Risk Reduction Mechanisms

Once the investment has been made a number of operating

measures can be employed to help reduce the level of risk. These are grouped below under the following headings:

(*a*) Production and logistics
(*b*) Marketing
(*c*) Finance
(*d*) Organisation
(*e*) Political and other

(*a*) *Production and Logistics*

1. *Stimulation of local suppliers*. Where possible the use of local suppliers can help to reduce risk by creating allies. Sears Roebuck de Mexico for example, when faced with a government embargo on a wide range of consumer imports due to a foreign exchange crisis, responded by a massive programme of encouraging new local enterprises as sources of supply. Within six years the company, using some 1300 local firms, was able to buy 80 per cent of its merchandise requirements locally.[16] A variant on this theme is to increase local purchasing and thus reduce the level of local investment and therefore, assets at risk, while retaining control over the marketing and distribution functions.

2. *Specialisation of Production*. A number of companies have specialised their production so that each plant produces some part of a total process. As a result, most subsidiaries will contribute export income to a country of residence. Any insistence by local government on further local production can then be demonstrated as likely to reduce exports. There are dangers with this policy in that overspecialisation leads to possible strikes or disturbances being directed against a vital plant, so affecting other production units located elsewhere. Ford of Europe, which was established to enable various Ford subsidiaries to undertake a regional design and production strategy, initially adopted a policy of total specialisation and concentration of individual component production to specific plants. This strategy was revised after a serious strike in the UK affected the supply of engines for the corporation's German assembly plants, and a policy of at least dual component sourcing was adopted despite the slightly lower economies of scale.

3. *Multiple Sourcing of Production*. One method of resisting

home country pressure for increased local control over subsidiaries is to establish directly competing units within the same organisation, located in different countries. IBM, in a slight variant on this principle, operates a series of production centres which are allowed to bid for the right to manufacture each new range of products. Philips NV operates a similar system of key production centres for particular products.

4. *Location of Facilities*. In extractive industries in particular, production is often located in LDCs while markets are in politically safer countries. Where possible, therefore, the oil companies have located their refineries near to the market thereby reducing political risk and financial exposure. Transport and distribution investments are also located outside the more vulnerable territories. A variation of this technique is to locate the production of key components in politically safe countries, such that expropriation would lead to termination of supply.

5. *Control of Transportation*. In a few cases control of transportation has been an important mechanism for reducing risk. For many years, the United Fruit Company and the Standard Steamship Company had a powerful lever on Latin American banana republics, by owning the refrigerator ships in addition to controlling the market outlets.[17]

6. *Control of Patents and Knowhow*. Control over vital patents and knowhow is an important mechanism for reducing risk. If continual injections of updated research or development inputs are required, expropriation of purely production facilities is useless. Gradual attempts to introduce creeping controls such as cutbacks on profit remittance can be offset by the withdrawal of new developments. It is even possible to partially decentralise R & D effort as IBM does. However, by ensuring that all research information is centralised in a safe (usually home) environment and that key patents are owned by the parent, risk levels can be kept down.

(*b*) *Marketing*

1. *Market Control*. The control of markets outside a country where assets are at risk, such as in the oil and extractive industries, has been historically an important feature in avoiding expropriation. To some extent, however, this has been negated by the formation of producers cartels, OPEC being the most successful, which have combined to nationalise production

sources in many cases and also to operate collectively in world markets. While, as yet, OPEC has not penetrated the refining and distribution stages of the oil industry, collective action has led to a dramatic shift in the economic distribution of returns in favour of the crude producers. In manufactured goods the situation is similar in that much of world trade is within, rather than between, MNCs. Expropriation of a manufacturing unit, therefore, tends to shut off export markets to other subsidiaries of an MNC.

2. *Brand Name and Trademark Control*. This can have a similar effect to the control over patents and knowhow for strongly branded products, such as Coca Cola, where the MNC is able to establish a worldwide monopoly. Expropriation would almost automatically lose the trademark or brand name to a host government since the location of ownership of such items is almost invariable within the MNCs home country.

(*c*) *Financial*

A number of the many financial mechanisms which may be used to reduce risk are discussed elsewhere. Others include:

1. *Maximising Local Debt Finance*. Capitalisation of subsidiaries by means of a thin equity base and utilising high levels of local debt reduces exposure to expropriation or inconvertibility.

2. *Localising Capital Structure*. Differences between industry capital structures in different countries are discussed in Chapter 5, but advantage can be taken of local variations to reduce risk levels.

3. *Utilising Contractual Protection Devices*. The taxation aspects of such devices as back-to-back loans, swaps and the like are discussed in Chapter 6. The use of such devices for risk-reduction centres on the intervention of an international banking intermediary, which a host government is less likely to wish to offend because of possible repercussions for its other international financial relationships.

4. *Internal Money Management Practices*. The possibilities of reducing risk exposure by judicious treasury management are discussed in Chapter 5.

(*d*) *Organisation*

1. *Joint Ventures*. Shared ownership via joint ventures is one of

the most widely used methods of improving host government acceptance. This strategy can be seen as reducing the threat of foreign domination, securing local allies and increasing the role of local business enterprise.[18] In addition, the right choice of partner could contribute equity capital and provide access to local debt, provide local market knowledge and possibly a suitable location and management. Against this, however, the wrong choice of partner can increase political risk if, for example, he has the wrong political connections. Further, it is often the case that the objectives of the MNC and its local partners ultimately diverge, frequently to an irreconcilable degree. Key problem areas which have been identified include the reporting of profitability for tax purposes; dividend policy; capital increases and investment policy generally; rationalisation of production; intercorporate pricing; anti-trust; business ethics with respect to practices on accountancy, bribery and the like.[19]

2. *Multiple Nationality*. In some countries investment by firms of a particular country may be more at risk than that of other countries. One response, therefore, is for firms to adopt a multiple nationality or to undertake projects with firms from other countries. Royal Dutch Shell and Unilever have both exploited their dual nationality to advantage while a number of extractive industry consortium operations, involving firms from several countries, include the Fria bauxite project in Guinea, and the Freeport nickel project in Indonesia.[20]

3. *Management Contracts*. This organisational form permits the generation of some foreign profits without any significant capital investment or exposure. This type of overseas involvement is widely used in the consulting and engineering industries. In recent years, with the growth of massive contract placements by the oil-rich countries, management contracts have become more significant. One list of major international development contracts listed over 200 projects with a capital cost of over $500 million.[21]

A number of MNCs which have had their assets expropriated have ironically later made use of their management skills to take on management contracts to run newly nationalised or new venture investments for a host government. Tate & Lyle has established its own sugar plantation management team, while in 1971, the Cerro Corporation signed a contract with the Chilean government to act as US purchasing agent for mining equipment needed at mines the government had just seized from Anaconda. Perhaps one of the most ambitious operators of management contracts is Lonrho, which in 1973 concluded a contract to handle all imports and exports in the Sudan, and narrowly failed to win a subsequent contract to arrange the supply of oil for all the member states of the Organisation for African Unity.

(*e*) *Political and Other:*

There are a number of direct political moves that can be undertaken to reduce political risk.

1. *Gain Home Country Political Support*. Countries vary in their willingness to bring official support to bear to help their MNCs. Taking home country investment insurance may partially help to generate political support, however. The US government has actively intervened on a number of occasions to support its enterprises. In 1963 it threatened to cut off economic assistance to Indonesia in order to gain better terms for the nationalisation of US-owned oil interests. The US Export-Import bank refused loans to Chile after the Allende regime nationalised US-owned copper interests, and the US has used its influence with international agencies, such as the World Bank, to deny finance to countries taking undesirable action against US firms.[22]

The US government is far from alone in supporting its MNCs, and many other governments have taken retaliatory measures against the expropriation of locally owned assets. Such actions have taken various forms, but most frequently used have been the withdrawal of aid programmes, the termination of international loans, threatened withdrawal of military support, assistance with international legal actions and the use of influence with third party agencies such as the World Bank.

2. *Political Patronage*. A number of companies attempt to gain political support by means of undertaking projects of particular interest to particular politicians or pressure groups. Others seek to appoint influential politicians or their relations and protégés to local boards or senior management positions. Such individuals can provide valuable insights into how local governments are thinking, how particular ministries work and the like. In many LDCs where patronage systems flourish this type of policy is

commonplace and without it doing business is difficult. The key disadvantage is ensuring the selection of the right politicians, since risk can actually be enhanced if the individuals or groups that an MNC works with fall into political disfavour.

3. *Active External Relations Strategy*. Traditionally many MNCs have adopted a low profile within host countries, but this has not prevented them becoming targets for criticism. An increasing number are now beginning to develop a more aggressive stance on external relations by publicising the positive contributions they make to the local society and economy, running education programmes for workers, and becoming actively involved in sensitive political, social and environmental issues. In addition, some MNCs either individually or more likely in conjunction with local companies are active in political lobbying in host countries, in providing financial support for particular parties and even in some cases sponsoring individual candidates. In some cases this can be involuntary and comes close to the next section. An example would be the payments elicited for party funds from international oil companies by the Christian Democrat Party in Italy during the early 1970s. The management of the external relations function is discussed in detail in Chapter 11.

4. *Bribery and Illicit Methods*. In order to do business in many countries it is necessary to bribe or, more importantly, to pay out protection money. Outright bribes are relatively rare, but most firms are expected to make side-payments in the form of political contributions, agents fees or 'consultancy' fees in many countries. Irrespective of ethics it is clearly almost impossible for firms in a competitive situation to resist demands for payoffs when an essential service or function would otherwise be withdrawn or if payments owing would be stopped. An example is the inability of customs officials in certain West African countries to clear goods for several months unless quicker procedures are made worth while.

Companies, therefore, generally pay, at least in LDCs, although there is greater resistance in developed countries. Not all LDCs tolerate bribery, however, especially where left-wing regimes tend to exist. Most firms use agents or consultants, or work through a local joint venture partner in arranging payments.

One serious problem with side-payments may occur in the MNCs home country. In the USA, where the Securities Exchange

Commission scrutinises accounts carefully, undisclosed payments which are wrongly accounted for have led to a number of prosecutions. United Brands was accused by the SEC of bribery of officials of foreign governments, Ashland Oil was charged with failure to disclose large sums of money handled 'without proper accounting procedures or controls', and Phillips Petroleum was charged with diverting funds to Switzerland by means of false book entries. More recently a series of scandals have emerged affecting many major MNCs. The Lockheed Corporation has revealed major bribes paid to secure aircraft orders, and many other major oil companies have disclosed illicit payments. Moreover the US revenue authorities are much more demanding than, in general, their European counterparts.[23] While 'bribery' tends to be relatively common, corruption – which perhaps is bribery, but on a grander scale – appears to be less so. Nevertheless the disclosures of the US Congressional Committee led by Senator Church have led to attempts to introduce legislation in the USA which would make a number of side-payments illegal. There is some evidence that a few firms have adopted corrupt methods for making side payments and even in one reported case endeavoured to support the overthrow of an unfavourable regime. Such tactics are not the norm and cannot be recommended. However until a common ethical standard becomes universally accepted it would be naive to assume that firms wishing to operate in many world markets will be able to do so without making some form of side-payments on occasion.

Tactics for Handling Expropriation Threats

Expropriation seldom occurs without warning. It is, therefore, possible for the firm to take some actions which will reduce the impact of seizure. These might include:

1. The termination, coordination or at least monitoring of all supplies of goods, money and people to the threatened operation.
2. The termination of any parent company guarantees on behalf of the operation. In addition, checking any guarantees held on the threatened investment and seeing if external arbitration is possible.

3. Repatriating whatever portion of capital and remittable funds is possible. Seeing what tangible and intangible assets can be removed from the country, ensuring that trademark and patent licence agreements end if nationalisation occurs. Checking that the affiliate itself owns no trademarks or patents.
4. Attempting to remove vital elements in the manufacturing operation such as a key or secret process, an essential component, knowhow and the like. This can provide a bargaining counter in compensation negotiations.
5. Evaluating the chances of compensation. Trying to establish a 'discounted compensation flow' of what might be obtained under what conditions and in the face of what costs and risks. Determining what losses are tax-deductible.
6. Identifying key people, including local nationals and knowing where they are at all times. Being prepared to evacuate them at immediate notice if necessary.
7. Determining whether (and/or to what degree) to cooperate with the government. Considering opening negotiations rather than waiting for the government to make the first move.
8. Making a detailed physical audit of assets likely to be seized, including date of purchase, current value and so on. Following nationalisation, obtaining a signed receipt for the property seized. Considering granting power of attorney within limits to a trusted local national.
9. After the takeover, following the situation and keeping any claim alive by following the necessary bureaucratic procedures.
10. Looking hard at the possibilities of later re-entering the market. Some countries such as Ghana, Indonesia and Mexico have later handed back seized property. In the shorter term it may be desirable to maintain the corporate image so as to continue exporting after nationalisation.

10 Multinational Marketing Management

Corporate marketing management has become an increasingly important task in the international enterprise as the era of global competition has approached. Today the maintenance of competitive advantage requires new corporate skills. Experience in a local market is no longer a guarantee of continued success, as marketing expertise tested and proven in many national settings is applied by competitors for whom market differences are a minor hindrance rather than a major obstacle. The removal of trade barriers, the growing mobility of consumers, the internationalisation of communication media and the emergence of the multinational customer have all contributed to the transferability of marketing ideas across national frontiers. In the mature multinational, marketing knowledge and skills are transferred globally to buttress existing products and exploit new market opportunities.

One result of the move towards the development of a global marketing strategy is a tendency for the autonomy allowed to local subsidiaries in marketing decision-making to be reduced. The main determinant of the level of local autonomy usually is the relative emphasis placed on developing standardised global products and marketing strategies versus the desire to concentrate on products specially adapted to local markets. Industrial products in general tend to the more standardised approach and with it greater central involvement, while consumer products are more variable, although where standard brand names are used decision-making is usually more centralised. Companies that permit high levels of autonomy tend to be those which market products subject to local adaptation or who have expanded overseas by a process of acquisition. In this latter case, established local brand names may well have been acquired and in these situations the management of such brands is usually left to the local company. In practice, it is not uncommon for firms to actually operate a combination of local and international product lines or brands.

GLOBAL MARKETING AND ORGANISATION STRUCTURE

Each of the major organisation structures found in multinational corporations has its particular strengths and weaknesses. To achieve the potential advantages of a global marketing perspective, therefore, each structure must adjust to meet the particular tasks required. This means in practice that a series of integrative organisational roles or mechanisms tend to be introduced in the form of central or regional staff groups, special product managers and the like. The precise nature of how these roles and mechanisms work varies according to the particular organisation structure, the stage of international development reached by the corporation and the characteristics of its products.

Marketing in the International Division Structure

In the early stages of international development, overseas operations tend to predominantly service the needs of local markets and interdependence is low. As the volume of overseas sales increases, the number of countries with operations is expanded, and knowledge and understanding of overseas trading is built up, the potential benefits of greater international coordination in marketing efforts are recognised. This phase typically culminates in the reorganisation of overseas operations and the creation of a marketing group at headquarters with the aim of stimulating the two-way flow of technology and marketing expertise across countries and between domestic and overseas operations. Greater stress is placed on marketing in the development of plans for overseas business and the new marketing unit becomes responsible for assisting subsidiaries in the development of marketing strategies.

An example of restructuring to improve the effectiveness of international marketing operations is provided by American Can Company. This leading US manufacturer of containers and packaging products and systems and of consumer products reorganised its foreign operations in Canada, Latin American and Europe into a single business unit, American Can International (ACI). Within ACI a new department, marketing and business development (MBD), was created, headed by a managing director. The department was to be responsible for licensing operations, exports, marketing development and business development, with marketing directors for three product areas: flexible packaging, rigid packaging and consumer products. While technically staff executives, these three had considerable influence over the foreign operations with which they were concerned. They were supported by a new European regional office in Brussels which had, in addition to other staff, a business development director. A key task for MBD was to assist subsidiaries in the development of five-year strategic plans by the selective development of a market information base for certain markets and by helping to identify marketing opportunities.

A second mechanism for coordination was provided by the creation of intracompany task forces. One of the marketing directors at MBD headed up a task force of regional and local managers with the brief to redirect marketing programmes for his product line towards the fastest-growing and most profitable segments of the market. The marketing directors also had the specific role of coordinating marketing communications among affiliates and between them and headquarters, particularly relating to new product information from domestic and European sources.[1]

The MBD unit created in ACI thus performs a mainly coordinating role helping in the development of local subsidiary plans, the collection of marketing data and an internal consultancy role in helping local managers redirect their market policies. This type of unit, therefore, performs an integrating role, which by its presence reduces the probability of local managers deviating significantly from corporate headquarters' views, and ensuring a degree of conformity between the policies adopted by different subsidiaries. As such, a central staff unit tends to reduce local subsidiary company autonomy. In addition, the establishment of marketing staff positions and the introduction of coordinating devices such as product committees rapidly accelerates the rate of corporate learning about international operations. The corporate marketing specialists thus perform three basic roles:

1. Data collection, maintenance and dissemination – by providing resources to investigate product-market opportunities which individual subsidiaries could not afford.
2. Quality improvement in marketing decision-making – by helping subsidiaries to identify opportunities.
3. Marketing idea dissemination – by transferring ideas and products generated in one part of the company to meet existing and anticipated subsidiary needs.

The differences in centralisation caused by product market differences is illustrated by Pfizer Incorporated, which also organises its overseas operations into an international division. Pfizer also demonstrates why, in many businesses, a global marketing approach is almost obligatory. Pfizer International, the company's separate subsidiary company, operates a series of local subsidiary companies grouped into regional units. The regional management centres are directly responsible for local country operations across the corporation's major product ranges in pharmaceuticals, chemicals and agricultural products. At the international division headquarters, however, Pfizer has three product development groups charged with ensuring worldwide product coordination.

These groups, each headed by a vice-president, vary in size and involvement in overseas operations. The largest group is concerned with pharmaceuticals development, which is planned centrally on a global scale. This is largely due to changes in legislation which have made the USA one of the last markets for introducing new drugs, due to the obligatory long and rigorous test programmes. The major drug companies have therefore been forced to test the market potential for new materials in international markets around the world. Since research and development is located primarily in the USA, however, new product planning and development are coordinated from the corporate headquarters by the product development groups.

For new products, special task force teams are created, led by the central product managers and made up of marketing and medical directors from several management centres. A central information base is created on drug registrations, disease characteristics and the like around the world, and the task force endeavours to identify a series of typical test markets for a new drug. These must be areas where the drug can be launched relatively quickly, and where the market will be representative of other possible areas with longer test programmes. The team produces a comprehensive schedule of market research and establishes the kind of clinical programmes necessary for each territory.

Once these decisions are made, the headquarters product manager responsible visits each test market, together with a counterpart from the regional management centre. Plans are then laid at local level and adjusted in the light of information generated from the market research and clinical programmes. From the data generated a 'summary report and launch plan' is produced and approved by the task force and the corporate product development staff before reviews by the chairman of Pfizer International and his senior staff. Final approval is given by overall corporate management, and following this the local subsidiaries in the test markets are required to produce a detailed launch plan. This is a separate exercise from the planning system and includes sales forecasts, expenses and profit objectives for a five-year period with the first year forming a detailed operating budget. The plan is reviewed first at the regional headquarters and then at the corporate centre before implementation. A detailed post-launch audit is finally conducted to evaluate the success or failure of the product in the market place.[2]

The special legal characteristics which have become increasingly important in pharmaceutical products have led to a high level of headquarters involvement in the introduction of new products in Pfizer. This has resulted in the creation of a strong central team of marketing executives to carry out the headquarters role. Other international division companies are not always as strongly developed as Pfizer in their central marketing staff, but some functional specialists for coordination purposes are becoming a common phenomenon.

Marketing in Product and Geographic Based Organisations

Other forms of organisation tend to have coordination along an area or a product dimension at the corporate headquarters which is in the opposite direction to the principal line dimension. Thus a worldwide product divisional system will tend to have regional or area coordination at the corporate centre while area-based corporations will have central product coordinators.

Rockwell International for example is organised into five worldwide product 'operations' responsible for aerospace, automotive, consumer, electronics and utility and industry. Each operation is further subdivided internally into groups and/or divisions. The operations vary in their degree of international activity and are staffed accordingly. To coordinate the international activities of all its operations, Rockwell has created a corporate staff unit, 'Corporate International', to work closely with the product operations management to help in the penetration of overseas markets. This unit, led by a vice-president who reports direct to the company president, contains a group of international presidents, including regional business development managers, who perform a wide range of marketing tasks for the product groups and divisions. Although International does not have formal line responsibility for the international activities of the operations, the international executives within these do report on a dotted-line basis to the corporate vice-president International, whose group also participates in the selection, promotion and dismissal of international personnel within the operations. Further, the central unit reviews all foreign investment proposals, appropriation requests and salary changes above certain levels and approves the overseas licensing of corporate technology.[3]

Rockwell therefore represents an example of imposed geographic coordination on product operations. By contrast, Unilever has moved to ensure product coordination on geographic operations. Traditionally the European MNC has evolved granting its local subsidiaries a high level of autonomy, since historically they tended to sell mainly to local markets from production controlled at the local level. As interpenetration of markets, especially in Western Europe, has taken place, however, the need to ensure a common image for global brand names has led to a desire to ensure product coordination. At one time, for example, it was possible to buy a brand of margarine in Holland which was positioned as a low-price product, while across the border in Germany the same brand would be used for the German subsidiary's premium-grade margarine.

Unilever has therefore adopted a structure still based largely on geographic units, but including central office product coordinators. There are four basic management units, namely a profit centre, usually a country subsidiary or an operating division of such a subsidiary; an industry group combining various operating companies in various countries; a country umbrella subsidiary under which are a number of operating companies; and a geographic area including various countries in one managerial group. The central office product coordinators are responsible for ensuring that on products and brands which are developed internationally a common image and approach to the market is established and implemented at local level. In order to facilitate coordination between the geographic operating units and the need for product coordination, therefore, Unilever has introduced two organisational devices. Firstly, at the national level a conference is held at regular intervals in which the chairmen of subsidiaries operating in the country participate, together with national finance and personal staff, and led by the national company chairman. Secondly, at the corporate level for Europe a European liaison committee has been established in which all the product coordinators and the two regional directors for Europe sit. This committee, although not a decision-making body, is a useful device for developing policies that affect several or all the coordinators and which take account of particular local country needs.[4]

Headquarters Marketing Staff Roles

The companies described illustrate the development of two particular headquarters staff marketing roles – the international product or brand manager and the area business development or marketing manager. The first of these roles may have a varying degree of decision-making authority, ranging from high in the case of Pfizer, where the product manager was responsible for all phases of new product introduction, to relatively low in the case of Unilever, where the role was more one of coordination and advice. In practice, the more standardised the product line, the more likely it is that the international product manager will be responsible for certain decision-making, but it is rare that he will be line-responsible for the field personnel with whom he works.

International product managers also do not alone usually have the power to decide what product should be manufactured where, and when it should be introduced, how it should be modified, promoted or sold. Further, they do not usually possess detailed knowledge of the national markets in which the product is marketed, but rather they monitor and coordinate marketing progress in many countries and under different competitive conditions. Their responsibilities might include a knowledge of the product's profitability by geographic area, the position it has reached in the life-cycle in each of its markets and the collection and dissemination of information on local marketing conditions and approaches which might be useful to furthering penetration in other areas.

Area business development or marketing managers operate across product boundaries and focus on an area of geographic expertise. Such a function may be concerned with marketing activities alone, such as researching the potential for a particular product in an area and aiding the development of marketing plans within a region, or more broadly to include searching out licensee, joint venture or acquisition candidates.

Other Integrative Marketing Devices

Apart from the creation of new integrative roles there are a variety of other mechanisms used by MNCs to achieve coordination of marketing on an international basis. Three of the most common are the use of specialist marketing meetings, standing committees and *ad hoc* committees or task forces. There are pros and cons to each of these, but each can be a useful integrative device when used effectively.

In a recent survey, 20 of 25 MNCs used marketing meetings as an integrative device. Half of these merely held meetings at the regional level, where it was considered that markets and operating problems were sufficiently similar to make an exchange of experience and a combined planning perspective useful. The remaining companies tended to make use of both regional and worldwide meetings.[5]

Standing committees are usually established to deal with an ongoing activity or for overall management and control purposes. Because they meet regularly they are often geographically confined to a region or to the corporate headquarters. The regional headquarters of General Foods in Europe, for example, has three such standing committees, two of which are concerned with the major product lines of coffee and confectionery, whilst the third is concerned with new product development. The first two of these committees meet regularly in Europe. They are made up of the general managers of each of the countries with significant business in either coffee or confectionery, and they review marketing and other aspects of operational strategy. The New Product Development Committee, composed of the European product development managers, meets twice a year in the USA for meetings on new products by the US domestic divisions.

Task forces are set up to handle specific problems, after which they may be dissolved. The most common reason for creating them tends to be for planning and implementing new product introductions. Uniroyal, for example, uses such a task force approach for major moves such as entering a new market or launching a major new product. These task forces are called SPD (sales, production and development) Boards and each is made up of the necessary executives drawn from these and other relevant functions required to develop any necessary strategy. The plans produced by such boards are then implemented by regional and local subsidiary sales management, acting under the direction of the corporate vice-president for marketing.[6]

The Growth of Central Support Services

Apart from the creation of integrating mechanisms in order to facilitate global marketing, there is a strong tendency for the growth of a centralised system of marketing support services covering such areas as market research, advertising, promotion, pack design and sales training. The location of such services varies with the overall organisation structure. Thus, in international division structures such services tend to be located at the corporate headquarters, while in product-organised systems they may be at the corporate or international headquarters or at the product division level provided this is justified by the degree of overseas activity. The allocation of such services where regional headquarters organisations exist tends to vary according to whether the regional units are profit-responsible or not. When profit responsibility resides at the regional level a full range of marketing support services tends to be found.

The type of services offered by a central marketing support unit is illustrated below in the case of one international consumer goods company:[7]

1. *Market Research.* The department is responsible for product tests, consumer surveys, advertising communication surveys, etc., conducted by overseas subsidiaries, except for Europe where a regional staff function exists. The goal is to make regional and/or field units self-sufficient in market research, but where necessary the centre designs surveys and either conducts them or supervises outside agencies.
2. *Advertising.* The central unit is responsible for a $1 million umbrella print media campaign in support of exports of its major brands. It also informally monitors creative work for local subsidiaries for major brands.
3. *Market and Sales Statistics and Analysis.* The company has developed a computerised graphic presentation of each country's total markets and sales subdivided by brand, price and other factors. This segmentation analysis, produced monthly, covers both the company's own products and those of major competitors. The introduction of this service was made to provide headquarters and regional management with a consistent, comparable overview of all markets. As such it is additional to the normal control system.
4. *Packaging Design Service.* Headquarters takes particular care over the use and presentation of trademarks and overall design.
5. *Sales Promotion.* Marketing services assembled a catalogue each year offering subsidiaries a number of premium offer items for use in their marketing campaigns.
6. *Trademark Administration.* The central office has now begun to coordinate and act as liaison on the company's wide collection of trademarks between operating subsidiaries, the corporate legal department and outside counsel.

KEY ELEMENTS IN GLOBAL MARKETING POLICY

Product Standardisation or Differentiation

The key decision that must be taken in international product planning is whether to produce standardised products suitable for all markets or to differentiate products to meet the particular needs of local markets. This decision not only affects the nature of the product itself, but also largely determines other elements of the marketing mix and is a critical variable in fixing the locus of marketing decision-making within the organisation. The advantages of standardisation include the following:

1. It allows a common approach to a number of markets, helps create a uniform worldwide corporate image and reduces confusion, especially in consumer markets as increased market interpenetration takes place
2. It facilitates the development of a global marketing mix, in particular with respect to brand name, advertising message, after-sales service, sales training and sales promotion. This may lead to lower costs but also facilitates ease of management.
3. It permits economies of scale in production and stock control and opens up opportunities for tax saving, international production sourcing and transfer pricing.
4. It increases the prospect of rapid investment recovery since the risk of product failure is spread over a much wider geographic area.

The policy of standardisation is not without disadvantages, however, amongst which are the following:

1. There is a failure to match products to detailed local needs, hence some market opportunities may be lost.
2. Standardisation reduces the autonomy of local subsidiary units and hence may deter creativity, and reduce motivation and innovation amongst local personnel.
3. Good-calibre marketing executives in local subsidiaries may be frustrated at not being able to manage the full marketing mix and may leave to join competitors.

The decision whether or not to standardise depends largely upon the particular market needs and the characteristics of the

Fig. 10.1 Assessing International Product Market Needs

External/Uncontrollable Elements	*Controllable Ingredients*			
	The Product – functional Aspects	Aesthetic Design	Branding	Packaging
Environment	–Local ergonomics requirements –Special needs for size, dimensions, standards –Attitudinal constraints –Climatic effect –Available supportive services	–Attitude of local consumers to colours, shapes, general appearance? –Consistency with local taste and traditions	–Is the proposed name acceptable in the market? –Is it pronounceable? –Does it convey the correct message? –Is it easily recallable?	–Available packaging materials in selected manufacturing countries
Competition	–Competitive products and their relative effectiveness (if any) –Unique selling points of competitive products –Product Life Cycle Expectations	–Any design weaknesses identified in competitive products? –Any identifiable aesthetic strengths?	–Competitive practices re names of products –Brand image of competitive products	–Quality of packaging, sizes and special features of competitive products –Can we improve or depart from these standards?

Institutions	–Bodies controlling standards –'Which?' type body testing and comparing qualities –Other institutions that can support and recommend use of product	–Design 'award' possibilities? –Any other body monitoring design quality?	–Are there any institutions that can help us to choose an appropriate brand?	–Are there any packaging testing centres? –Any quasi-legal packaging standards? –Any standards laid down by trade associations?
Legal System	–Laws affecting use of product (e.g. prohibition laws) –Safety rules –Anti-pollution laws –Patent protection	–Can design be registered? –Any constraints on specific shapes?	–Can the trademark be registered and protected? –Any legal constraints on name selected?	–Special regulations re weights, measures, contents to appear on packaging –Rules re prohibited materials –Trade description rules

Source: S. Majaro, op. cit., p. 88.

product itself. In making such decisions it is first useful to draw up the relevant information concerning the product and its market, subdivided into the major components of functional attributes, design, packaging and branding. Each of these factors can be considered in terms of the important dimensions of the external environment, competition strategies, the formal institutions operating in the particular product market and the relevant legal constraints. Together these two sets of factors form a matrix such as that shown in Figure 10.1, which illustrates relevant questions that can be asked in each cell.

One company which notably failed to conduct even an elementary analysis before embarking upon an international strategy was Radio Shack Corporation, which has developed to be the leading US merchandiser of amateur electronic gear and discount hi-fi equipment. The company exported its successful US formula lock, stock and barrel to Western Europe without attempting to modify it to suit local requirements. As a result Radio Shack experienced serious losses from silly marketing mistakes. In Belgium, for example, the company overlooked a law requiring a government tax stamp on all window signs; in Germany, the company promoted its stores with give-away flashlights and was promptly hit with injunctions for violating German sales laws; in Holland the company geared its first Christmas promotion to 25 December, unaware that the Dutch celebrate St Nicholas Day on 6 December; European laws have stopped Radio Shack from selling citizen's-band radios, the company's biggest-selling single-product line in the USA; and finally, the company did not discriminate in its choice of store sites, hence many of the hundreds of the stores opened were in loss-making locations.[8]

Having collected the basic data relevant to assessing the international market needs for the product, a number of key questions can help in the decision whether or not to standardise:[9]

(1) *Is the life of the product likely to be short?*
Short-life-cycle products tend to favour a standardised approach in order to reduce the risk of not recovering the investment outlay.

(2) *Does the product have universal appeal?*
Products that do not need to be differentiated, such as many

industrial and commodity products, clearly can be standardised. However, even products that may require some minor local modification, such as TV sets and other electric equipment, can be designed to ensure the maximum degree of standardisation. The Japanese have been notably successful in achieving a high degree of international uniformity in their electrical products by comparison with US manufacturers, whose products must usually be specially adapted for many export markets.

(3) *What level of service is required with the product?*
Products requiring high levels of after-sales service usually tend to be standardised. This is especially true of high-value industrial equipment such as computers or machine tools which are products for international markets.

(4) *Does the product have a universal brand?*
Where a universal brand policy is adopted this is a strong motive for standardisation. Common global brands of this kind include Coca Cola, Shell and Kodak.

(5) *Are there major production economies of scale?*
When there are substantial economies of scale in production there is a strong tendency for standardisation as in petrochemicals, automobiles and aircraft. On the other hand, products with simple low-investment production processes tend to be able to afford to differentiate on a local basis. Food products are the most common example but others include detergents and adhesives.

(6) *What legal constraints govern the product?*
Legal systems can have a major impact on product design, packaging, pricing and promotion. For example in Canada it is obligatory to provide instructions in both French and English, in the USA many products must clearly show their physical make-up, in the UK automobile steering wheels are mounted on the right, while as seen above there are significant national differences in regulations concerning the introduction of new drugs.

The overall trend observable in international marketing is clearly toward increased standardisation. One recent survey of

27 major multinationals involved in the food, soft drink, soap-detergents-toiletries and cosmetics industries revealed an extremely high degree of standardisation in product brand names, physical characteristics and packaging, as illustrated in Figure 10.2. The same survey also showed a high degree of standardisation for the total marketing programme in some 63 per cent of cases.[10]

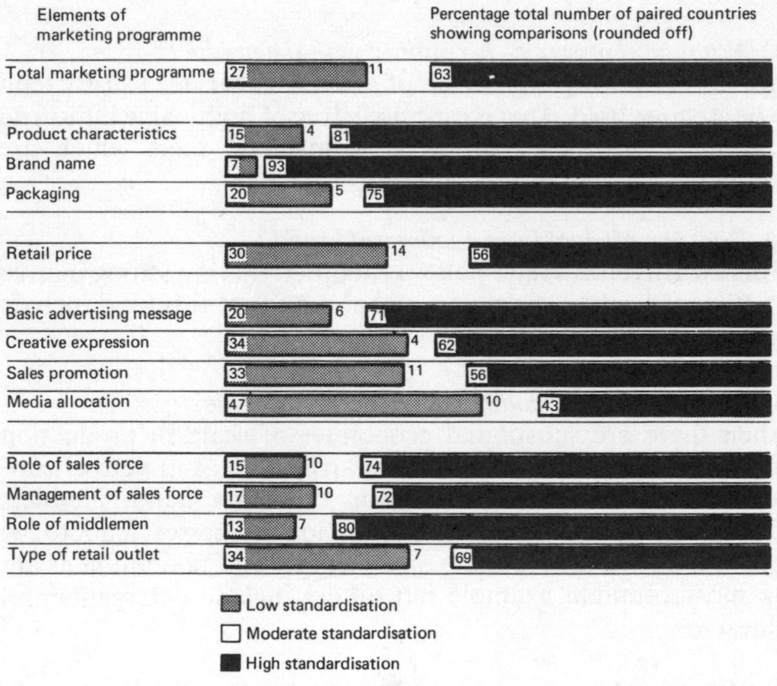

Fig. 10.2 Index of Standardisation of Marketing Decisions among European Subsidiaries of selected Multinational Enterprises

Source: Sorenson and Wiechman, op. cit.

As a result of this trend toward greater standardisation, decision-making autonomy in the local subsidiary company has been sharply reduced. Apart from the development of corporate marketing staff functions already discussed, local subsidiary autonomy may be reduced in several ways. Firstly, decision-making in local companies is usually restricted to mainly routine operating decisions. Although subsidiaries may be involved in strategic issues, often by initiating them, these may well require approval at the corporate level before implementation. Despite an involvement in non-operating decisions, therefore, responsibility does not rest solely at local levels.

Secondly, although some areas of market decision-making nominally reside with the local subsidiary – such as distribution policy – this is only true provided no significant change from existing policies takes place. Any decision to make such a major change, for example a move from selling via specialist retailers to the use of discount mail order, would convert an operating decision into a strategic issue and require a headquarters approval before implementation.

Thirdly, autonomy may be restricted by the way in which marketing support services are provided. Many companies offer their central marketing services functions, such as advertising, design, market research and the like, free or at a nominal price. While subsidiaries are not restricted to purchase these services, any alternatives used have to be paid for at the full market price by the subsidiary, so reducing its profitability – against which management is measured.

The restrictions on local subsidiary autonomy are therefore not often clearly visible, but rather operate in more subtle ways. The end result, however, is clearly that operating managers in local companies learn the boundaries within which they have freedom of decision and these boundaries are usually quite tightly constrained.

International Marketing Planning

Marketing planning forms an integral element in the overall planning process. In particular, international marketing planning is concerned with both old and new geographic markets and old and new product markets. In practice the majority of planning is concerned with three mixes of these elements, namely:

(1) *Existing products – existing markets.* Planning is usually performed mostly at the local operating company level as part of its standard planning contribution.

(2) *Existing products to new markets.* Planning activity may also involve a substantial involvement on the part of local

and especially regional organisations with some involvement by headquarters marketing.

(3) *New products to existing markets.* Planning activity usually involves a substantial involvement on the part of the central headquarters and very limited autonomy on the part of local subsidiaries.

The fourth possibility – launching new products in new markets – is relatively uncommon due to the high risks potentially involved.

Planning for New Geographic Markets

Planning for new overseas markets tends to originate at the level of the local subsidiary. New markets are usually opened either by such local companies as are given leave to seek out new export opportunities or as a result of regional sourcing policies. Many MNCs for example initially sourced supplies of products to the Middle East from their European operations who were given responsibility for both planning and developing these markets. As a result the task of planning for new geographic markets tends to go to whichever part of the organisation takes the initiative, be it local subsidiary, regional headquarters or corporate office.

When no significant capital expenditure is involved such plans initiated at local levels are usually routinely accepted. Indeed, in many MNCs local or regional initiation is actively encouraged since it is argued that it is only at this level that the relevant local information exists. Further, leaving such initiatives at the local level improves motivation. In Alcoa, for example, new market planning is done at local level with little headquarters involvement. For new geographic territories such as Africa and the Middle East, the European regional office would probably investigate market opportunities following initial reports on potential generated from periodic sales visits. Should such opportunities prove worth while, regional management would generate marketing plans to exploit them.[11]

By comparison with Western practice, Japanese companies adopt a much more centralised approach to new markets. In part this is due to the fact that the Japanese trading houses do not operate the same blend of overseas manufacturing units as yet. Ishikawajima-Harima Heavy Industries (IHI), a manufacturing company producing a wide range of ships, marine engines, boilers and industrial machinery, illustrates the approach. When the chief executive for international operations judges that a market opportunity exists, a multi-functional task force is formed from the international division. This group collects data on past and present trends from IHI's overseas offices, trading companies, banks and other sources. From this data a basic marketing plan is developed and a full-scale survey mission dispatched to investigate on the spot. Following the survey mission's report, the company reviews the position and determines whether or not to make a market entry.[12]

The assessment of the potential within a particular geographic market is the first prerequisite in developing a marketing plan. Often the precise data required to arrive at a reasonable forecast of demand is not available and macro-economic surrogates may have to be substituted. This can be crudely done by relating sales to a meaningful variable, such as electricity consumption per capita in the case of an electrical appliance manufacturer. Coupled with a similar knowledge of a developed market an estimate of sales in the unknown market can be arrived at as follows:

$$S_X = S_A \times \frac{E_X}{E_A}$$

where S_X = estimated sales level in country X
S_A = sales level in country A
E_X = electricity usage per capita country X
E_A = electricity usage per capita country A

The precise macroeconomic characteristics most meaningful for particular businesses are usually known from experience. Further, several estimates can be made in order to arrive at a crude consensus. There are a variety of sources of potentially useful macroeconomic data with one of the most comprehensive being produced regularly for over 70 countries by *Business International* and covering some 134 key indicators. These include a number of statistics not commonly available from most collections of economic statistics, such as telephone ownership patterns, per capita consumption rates of various materials and so on. Where adequate market research *is* available the potential of a particular country can be assessed from answers to the type of questions shown in Figure 10.3.

Who are the customers? How many are there? How are they concentrated?
What usage pattern can be expected and at what price?
How sensitive is demand to pricing?
Is product usage the same as in established markets? If not, is there an alternative usage and what is its demand?
How does the market segment by socio-demographics? Usage pattern? Other?
Are there any particular customer information/usage needs that must be satisfied?
Are there any other products or materials used in conjunction with the product and are these available at a reasonable price?
How and where would the product be purchased? Are these channels same/different from those with which company is experienced?
Is the product unique? If not, how does it compare with competitors on price/quality?
Who are competitors? What size? Market shares? Strengths and weaknesses?
Are there any special seasonal buying patterns?
Who is the purchase initiator? Who actually buys?
What methods are most appropriate for reaching purchase initiators? Buyers?
What media are available for advertising and promotion and how important is each for reaching potential users?
How fast will the product become obsolescent? Need a facelift?
Will the market change in the near future in a way which will significantly alter the demand pattern?
Are there any special legal, government measures which affect the packaging? Branding? Contents? Pricing? Distribution? Advertising of the product?

Fig. 10.3 Checklist for Assessing Overseas Market Potential

New Product Planning

New product development is usually closely controlled by corporate headquarters. Most US MNCs maintain their major development facilities in the USA. In addition, although some have established research units overseas, the US usually acts as the centre for collecting information and coordinating research plans. Moreover, such overseas research units are usually more concerned with technical support for existing products than with new product development. An exception to this practice occurs when companies have developed by acquisition and have purchased overseas subsidiaries with well-established research facilities. Apart from products designed for local needs, however, even in these cases criteria for international new product development are normally generated at the corporate headquarters. For example, the guidelines for new products issued to its overseas research facilities by one US specialist engineering products manufacturer included the following criteria:

They should be technologically and market related to existing products

They should have a wide range of applications

They should require low marketing investment

They should be compatible with company philosophy (the company believed itself to be a good developer of ideas rather than a research-based innovator)

They should not be in markets with price leadership

They should not be in a market dominated by governments

Products should be expandable worldwide

They should have a high value added[13]

Although product development is usually centralised, new product introductions, while usually formally the responsibility of the corporate headquarters, also involves local subsidiary and regional units in the planning process. This involvement has several features. Firstly, a number of companies do not insist that new products are adopted at local level if the subsidiary wished to decline them. Such a move may come after the headquarters, having provided background data, has received a negative market evaluation from the local operating unit. Secondly, some modification to the original domestic marketing strategy is usually permitted to meet local conditions. Although there may be similarities between domestic and overseas markets there may also be important differences which require the involvement of local management to identify and correct for.

In the Swiss MNC Sandoz, for example, new dyestuffs are developed by central research and application units. These are screened with major overseas subsidiaries receiving samples of the new products. These subsidiaries report back to Basle on the market volume for the new product, possible price competition and other factors particular to the individual countries. From this data a promotion letter is prepared at the corporate headquarters, advising overseas companies of product availability, delivery dates, technical applications and prices. A post-launch audit is conducted about a year after product introduction when a further exchange of information between the headquarters and overseas operating units takes place, itemising product progress, market approaches adopted and the like.[14]

Overall, US MNCs tend to operate with more headquarters involvement in new product launches than their European counterparts. For example, Company U, a major US producer of office equipment, has a highly centralised approach. For new product introductions the corporate headquarters staff conducts its own evaluation of overseas market potentials in conjunction with local outside agencies. It then provides its local operating subsidiaries with full details of product strategies to be adopted, including product positioning, key selling points to be used in promotions and sales campaigns, prices, credit terms, supply sources and the like. Each local subsidiary then generates its own sales forecasts, and on the basis of known productivity ratios, its pattern of sales and servicing expenses. These plans are submitted to the centre for review and strict scrutiny before acceptance as the subsidiary company target.[15]

Traditionally it was the case that new products were first developed in the domestic market and only launched internationally after they had become established. Internationally, markets could be classified as being at different stages of the life-cycle for particular products. As a result companies could adopt the policy of progressively entering new markets as countries reached an appropriate stage in the life-cycle.

This policy is becoming progressively more difficult to apply for new product introduction, as the gap between the time a home market reaches maturity and overseas markets develop has become progressively shorter. The rate of innovation transfer is today extremely rapid due to much greater ease of travel and communication. As a result it is becoming increasingly necessary for companies to launch their new products on a much wider geographic basis since failure to do so may well result in copies of the product appearing in overseas markets long before the original innovator is ready to tackle them. When ultimately an entry is made the innovator may find he is now competing against an established competitor who has already pre-empted the market.

An example of this problem is provided by the worldwide struggle raging between Gillette and the French Bic Company. In 1975, Bic entered the shaving market with the launch in Europe of a range of disposable razors, widely distributed and at a low price. This attack bit significantly into Gillette's traditional strength in Europe as worldwide brand leader of razor blades. Thus, when Bic turned its attention to North America and launched disposable razors in Canada in 1976, Gillette reacted. It rushed into production with its own brand of disposable razor for the United States market and went national with the product early in 1976. Bic was not able to get its own disposable product into the US market until later that year and was not scheduled to have any local manufacturing capability until 1978, as a result of which Gillette were already dominating the disposable segment when Bic endeavoured to enter the market.[16]

International Pricing

The exchange risk and tax aspects of intracompany product transactions were considered in earlier chapters. As a result of these financial considerations, intracorporate and all forms of cross-border pricing, including exports from overseas subsidiaries, are usually strictly a central office decision area. In addition to the financial considerations this centralisation of decisions also ensures relative uniformity in global pricing structure and discourages customers from switching sources of supply or overseas subsidiaries becoming engaged in dysfunctional competitive pricing by pursuing the same export markets.

This policy is not true within national boundaries, however, where, as seen in Figure 10.2, local subsidiaries tended to enjoy a relatively high level of discretion. There are many reasons for local involvement in national market product pricing including differences in manufacturing costs, competitive prices, promotional expenditure levels, distribution system practices, local tax structures and import tariffs. In practice, the actual level of pricing autonomy granted at local level is therefore limited both by external factors and by the budgetary process, when price levels are scrutinised at the corporate headquarters.

Industrial products tend to be more likely to have standardised prices than consumer products. This is especially true of commodity products such as industrial chemicals, basic metals and the like, where prices are more or less uniform over wide geographic areas. These products are less subject to price variation due to production, marketing and tax differences, although occasional distortions can occur as a result of such factors as government price controls. As a result of price controls, for example, the price of many bulk industrial chemicals in the UK became substantially lower than those prevailing in Western Europe for a time during the mid-1970s. This led to a number of local shortages as domestic producers preferred to export their production at higher returns than those obtainable in the home market.

In adjusting prices to suit local market needs the following factors should be taken into account:[17]

1. Are there any social or cultural taboos on the consumer that may affect the amount of money he is prepared to spend on the product?
2. Is it customary to build 'special reductions' into the price structure to allow for traditional haggling?
3. Are there any psychological Do's and Dont's pertaining to consumer attitudes to price?
4. Who are the 'brand' competitors and also 'functional' competitors? Obtain a summary of their attitudes to pricing decisions.
5. How do competitors behave in the face of pressure on prices?
6. Can competitors' prices be linked with specific market segments?
7. Are there bodies which must be consulted prior to determining the price?
8. Is there a consumers' body which compares the cost/benefit of products, thus influencing prices?
9. Are there any limitations on the freedom to determine a price?

10. Any legal constraints on price changes?
11. Resale price maintenance?
12. Legislation against restrictive trade practices?
13. Legal limitations on margins?
14. Need to print price details on product and/or packaging?

International Channel Management

Distribution policy tends to be a relatively decentralised area of marketing decision-making, provided that the policies advocated at local level do not deviate seriously from established patterns. Further, many industrial products are sold direct rather than through a distribution channel, while for many capital goods bidding and negotiation are largely conducted by the corporate headquarters. The degree of local autonomy is also restricted by trade custom and practice within the particular territory. As a result, changes from domestic distribution patterns may be inevitable when such channels do not exist in overseas markets.

Channel decisions are an important feature of international marketing, however, and they often involve the corporation in long-term legal commitments which can be difficult and expensive to modify if it is decided to change the initial distribution arrangements. The initial choice of channel is therefore vital and a careful analysis of the distribution needs, both for the present and the future, should be undertaken. A number of factors should be borne in mind including:

1. *Product characteristics.* These may have a major influence on channel design. For example, high ticket items requiring significant after-sales service and sold to industrial users would normally be sold direct. Perishable products require more direct marketing because of delays caused by frequent handling. Low-value bulky items such as cement, soft drinks and some packaging products usually require local production and the minimum of transportation.
2. *Customer characteristics.* This is a key element in channel design. The number, geographic distribution, shopping habits, usage pattern and distribution preferences of customer groups must be considered. In this area many multinationals refuse to recognise substantial differences between countries and major errors often occur.

3. *Channel availability*. The availability of a channel may not be the same as in a domestic market in that it may not exist, for example large department stores in rural economies; it may belong to a competitor; it is fully committed and does not wish to take on another product. Where similar channels are available to those used previously it is common for MNCs to adopt them, often without consideration as to whether they are the most appropriate to service the needs of a different market.

4. *Cost considerations*. The cost of various distribution methods is an important consideration. This is especially true in the early stages of market entry when the level of sales may not justify the establishment of a direct sales force or warehousing operation. At this early stage there is a strong tendency to use agents, commission salesmen, manufacturers' agents and other classes of middleman. While this is usually a cheap initial solution it can prove expensive in the long term if the system needs to be replaced with a direct sales presence, when compensation legally due to middleman can be substantial. Other financial factors include margin differentials that need to be given to gain distribution, promotion costs to support channels, warehousing and physical distribution costs and the costs of local staff and administration.

5. *Legal considerations*. There are sales laws in operation in most countries and these can differ significantly from one to another. For example, in some countries resale price maintenance is legal while in others manufacturers cannot set resale prices. Other areas which need to be considered include unfair channel-pricing laws, consumer protection and product liability legislation, exclusive franchise laws, legislation affecting middleman and dealer rights, and compensation terms for termination, territorial restrictions, cartel practices, and reciprocal selling.

6. *Competitive situation*. The channels used by competitive products will also clearly influence channel choice. While it is normal that most companies will use the same type of distribution channel as their competitors, a number of multinationals have successfully developed new channels which they can dominate or have exclusive use of, such as Tuppaware and Avon Cosmetics.

International Advertising and Promotion

International advertising and promotion is one of the key functions in global marketing. It requires both a headquarters and a local subsidiary perspective in view of the large commitment of financial resources often involved, the careful use of valuable brand names and trademarks while at the local level a detailed knowledge of consumer preferences, custom and practice is a vital ingredient in successful communications. In order to reconcile the potential conflicts between a move toward global standardisation of communications strategy and the need to tailor spending programmes to local market needs, media availability and the like it is usually necessary to involve both the corporate headquarters staff and local management in the design of most advertising programmes. This is not always the case, however, and the relative balance of decision-making power varies according to the type of advertising involved. Four basic types of international programmes can be identified:

(1) *International Corporate Advertising*. This type of campaign endeavours to create awareness about the corporate name, image or philosophy. Such campaigns are usually the sole responsibility of the corporate advertising function and the cost is usually not allocated directly to overseas subsidiaries.

A checklist which takes into account many of these factors is shown in Figure 10.4.

	Channels of distribution	Physical distribution (logistics)
ENVIRONMENT	details of GNP, growth rate and their possible impact on demand financial/capital climate consumer buying habits and preferred location local attitudes to foreign firms setting up own subsidiaries as against using local agents/distributors	details of geography, distances to main consuming conurbations; distances to main rural areas details of ports, aircraft, rail system and other logistics infrastructures frequency and quantities likely to be expected by channels of distribution/other middlemen

	Channels of distribution	Physical distribution (logistics)
COMPETITION	do competitors use sales subsidiaries or local distributors? Appraise their respective performance evaluate the relative effectiveness and productivity of agents versus 'own' subsidiaries of various competitors	identify the physical distribution practices of competitors including: mode of transport used; inventory levels warehousing/depot facilities. Appraise their respective costs. Consider cheaper methods
INSTITUTIONS	identify available channels for specific products is there a suitable distributor that one can buy? are there any government controlled channels (like monopoly channels e.g. in the USSR) are there any cartel arrangements? appraise financial reliability of available institutions	study available logistics institutions and compare costs of using each one of them or combinations thereof investigate reputation of each institution available for reliability, punctuality of service and geographical coverage
LEGAL	identify legal 'red tape' in relation to channels, their selection and dismissal government regulations on foreign-owned subsidiaries corporate/legal structures and their respective advantages and disadvantages	list special rules pertaining to safety, packaging markings, size of vehicles, etc. other legal constraints on transporting procedures legal formalities and their cost

Fig. 10.4 Assessing Overseas Distribution Channels

Source: S. Majaro, op. cit., p. 145.

Such campaigns make heavy use of international print media such as *Time, Newsweek* and their regional editions, *The Economist* and *Vision*.

(2) *Global Multiproduct Advertising*. This type of advertising is mainly conducted by diversified industrial product companies and is usually intended to create awareness amongst

specialist audiences such as contracting engineers and the like. Such campaigns are also usually run from the corporate centre especially when the products featured cross divisional boundaries. When individual divisions or product groups are involved, however, this type of campaign may be run by the product division provided it has its own professional staff and subject to the approval of the corporate headquarters. These campaigns are mainly placed in specialised print media, many of which have a worldwide distribution, or in international journals like those used for corporate campaigns. Advertisements are normally developed by the domestic agency and any overseas placements are coordinated with overseas agencies used by subsidiaries, which in many cases are the branch offices of the domestic agency.

(3) *Global Product Line and Brand Advertising*. The corporate headquarters is usually heavily involved in the preparation of advertisements which emphasise a particular product line or brand name on a global or regional basis. In particular the corporate advertising department ensures the message and theme are consistent and often arranges the placing of advertisements even within individual subsidiary territories. Such campaigns are most widely used by consumer goods and service industry companies and they tend to support product advertising done in specific markets as local campaigns. International print media are again the most common channel. Costs are usually drawn from the product division or allocated across overseas operations.

(4) *National Product Campaigns*. It is this type of advertising which is normally thought of as 'international advertising'. It consists of the special campaigns run in individual overseas territories in support of local sales. These campaigns may refer either to internationally standardised or branded products or to products produced purely for local markets. Such campaigns are the major item of advertising expenditure outside the domestic market. It is in this area that local managements play an important role in advertising decision-making and where costs are allocated almost entirely to the overseas subsidiary.

There are a number of particular areas where the question of central or local control is at issue. The first of these concerns who makes the choice of advertising agent. The international advertiser has three basic choices when considering the appointment of an advertising agency:

(*a*) *Domestic agencies with overseas branches*. An agency familiar with the parent business, international in outlook and with well-coordinated overseas offices is likely to appeal strongly to companies equipped to handle marketing globally.
(*b*) *Local agencies*. Where specialist contacts and local knowledge are particularly important and the company has local marketing expertise in its subsidiaries, agents or distributors, then the advantages of localisation may outweigh the problems of poor coordination.
(*c*) *Specialist international agencies*. Where many small markets are involved it may be desirable to employ a specialist agency to create overseas campaigns or to develop the many different modifications from a successful existing domestic campaign. This helps to achieve economies of scale in production, particularly in the case of less developed countries.

The growth of international agencies which provide a coordinated network of creative services and a consistency of interpretation of basic campaign themes has been a significant aid to increased central control. Many companies, therefore, direct their overseas subsidiaries to use the local branches of a centrally chosen international agency. Local autonomy in the appointment of an agency remains common, however, especially where the subsidiary can argue that it can get better and cheaper services than those provided by the international agency.

Secondly, the control of creative content is usually the subject of conflict. In practice, control over creative content is usually highly centralised for basic themes and the use of brand names and trademarks. Some local variation is, however, commonly permitted, subject to headquarters approval, in order to allow local management to adjust its campaigns to particular cultural and market segment needs. In order to attain a high degree of standardisation some companies produce prototype campaigns at the centre, which are then sent to subsidiaries. Such basic campaign themes can be incorporated into local advertisements with modifications to suit local needs.

Amongst the most centralised organisations with regard to creative content are the US multinational cosmetics companies. These usually decide centrally the general advertising theme, its creative expression, the copy layout and text. Subsidiaries are provided with sample advertising copy for each product, together with detailed instructions on how this should be reproduced for local campaigns. By contrast in multinational food companies, creative content is largely a matter for local control.[18]

Language is often one area where adaptation of creative material must be made to meet local requirements. Important precautions must be taken to ensure the avoidance of serious blunders due to translation mistakes. Useful guidelines include:[19]

1. Avoid the use of idioms and jargon.
2. Layout and artwork should be designed with enough free area to expand the text where necessary since foreign languages often use more words than English.
3. Legal requirements or recognised codes of conduct that control advertising content must be carefully checked.
4. Translation must be carried out by competent professional translators.
5. Translators must be thoroughly briefed and the translation checked by competent linguists or the local management.
6. Typesetting and printing must be undertaken by specialist foreign-language printers.

Advertising budgets are indirectly subject to headquarters control via the annual budgetary process. The plans of the individual subsidiaries are usually reviewed both at regional and corporate levels annually and contain both the aggregate amount of projected spending and in most cases a detailed breakdown of where the expenditure will be made. The corporate headquarters thus has the opportunity to review spending programmes and to influence both their size and direction.

The area where local subsidiaries enjoy the greatest degree of autonomy is in media selection. There are several reasons for this. Firstly, it is common that the choice of media available will be different from country to country – for example, commercial television is not available in many countries while

	The Promotional Mix			
	Advertising	*Sales Promotion*	*Publicity*	*Personal selling*
ENVIRONMENT	Language details; literacy levels; readership details; response to symbolism; general attitude to advertising; details of buyer, decider, influencer patterns, various segments; demography	Same language, culture, demographic details as in the case of advertising Consumer's attitude to 'below-the-line' type activities	Details of consumer response to publicity. Readership details broken down to socio-economic, demographic segments Kind of stories sought	General attitude in the market-place to salesmen and salesmanship Expectations of the channels of distribution as to salesmanship
COMPETITION	Identify competitive advertising practices; their expenditure and ratio to sales over a period Research strengths and weaknesses of competitors' advertising policies	Competitive practices and expenditure; identify quantitative relationship between expenditure on advertising and sales promotion Observe for creative ideas	Details of publicity 'mentions' gained by competitors How were they achieved?	Obtain full details of the kind, size and effectiveness of competitors' sales forces Identify areas of weakness in competitive practices; also areas of creativity
INSTITUTIONS	Total advertising expenditure in country; media available and growth in expenditure patterns; technical facilities (e.g. colour) Media details—circulation, readership and segments, media costs, frequency. Any special media; research	Institutional facilities available to help in performing promotional activities Barbour Index type organisation (calling on specific professions such as architects)	Public relations facilities available in market; appraise cost and effectiveness. Bodies controlling code of practice and message	Bodies controlling the quality and professionalism of salesmen Organisations available to help in performing the selling task 'Sales force to Hire' systems

	bodies; code of advertising; various organisations			
LEGAL SYSTEM	Trade description legislation Special rules pertaining to various products (e.g. cigarettes, drugs, fertilisers) Laws limiting expenditure Use of languages	As with advertising	As with advertising	Laws against selling practices Laws against inertia selling Legislation on 'cooling off' periods (e.g. insurance or hire purchase deals)

Fig. 10.5 Evaluating International Communications Strategies

Source: S. Majaro, op. cit., p. 169.

others do not have commercial radio. Trade journals are usually often national and may not exist in many sectors. Cinema advertising may be popular in some countries while cinema-going may be declining rapidly in countries with extensive television coverage. As a result, strict centralised media decisions are uncommon and the choice of media and allocation of expenditure between these is largely a matter for local choice.

International Communications Strategy

The precise design of a successful international communications strategy is a skilled task. Significant variations do exist between countries as to the most appropriate methods of communicating. There are, in fact, a number of mechanisms for communications, including advertising but also embracing sales promotion activities, public relations and publicity and personal selling. The precise balance of these channels that is most appropriate will tend to vary according to the basic characteristics of the product, the availability of media and local legal and institutional conditions. In general, industrial products rely much more heavily on personal selling as their primary channel of communications, while consumer products make much greater use of advertising and sales promotion. A checklist which aids the decision as to the most appropriate choice of message, contents and channels for communication is shown in Figure 10.5.

CONCLUSIONS

Global marketing planning involves few new principles to operating within a single market. However, it requires a number of significant variations in the organisation of the marketing function, and in particular necessitates the development of new integrative mechanisms to ensure a consistent global strategy is adopted. The precise nature of these mechanisms will vary from company to company according to its overall strategy and structure. In general, however, the adoption of a global marketing approach can be expected to result in an increased degree of central control over local subsidiary activities. This reduction in autonomy will not always be uniform and will vary according to the nature of the product and the element of the marketing mix concerned. A move toward standardised products, for example, will lead to greater centralisation, while cross-border pricing decisions become the responsibility of the corporate headquarters. Distribution and communications strategies involve local subsidiary companies more, but even here there are either central checks on changes in established corporate policies or a growing tendency for headquarters involvement in decision-making.

11 External Affairs and the International Corporation

In the 1970s major multinational companies are being forced to reassess their relationships both with stakeholders such as employees, shareholders and suppliers, and with society at large, represented by governments, pressure groups and international institutions. Education, affluence, mass communications and many other locally significant factors have combined to make the various publics with which a corporation interacts more aware of the ways in which it influences their lives. The increasing significance of the operations of multinational enterprises for many national economies has made such firms a natural focus for those interested in the economic social and ecological future of their country. Advocates of a New International Economic Order see international firms as key mechanisms for the redistribution of global wealth. The domination of important industries such as electronics, chemicals, oil and motor vehicles by relatively few major international companies has resulted in internationally coordinated surveillance of company operations. The growing awareness of the scale of ecological problems, and of the limits to natural resources, have contributed to pressures on large resource-transforming companies for anti-pollution measures, environment protection and conservation. The increasing acceptability of concepts such as industrial democracy and corporate accountability are also changing the traditional roles of management and ownership and creating new interest groups. In the face of these trends corporate management is being forced to devote more and more time to issues which are not directly concerned with profitability, in the short term, but which may in time have a profound effect on the survival of the corporation. Political and social management skills in addition to the traditional economic decision-making skills have become essential not only at local but also at regional and corporate levels of the multinational company.

THE MANAGEMENT OF EXTERNAL AFFAIRS

For the multinational company the management of external affairs can involve many types of issue, ranging from international affairs to the treatment of minority groups. Local offices or

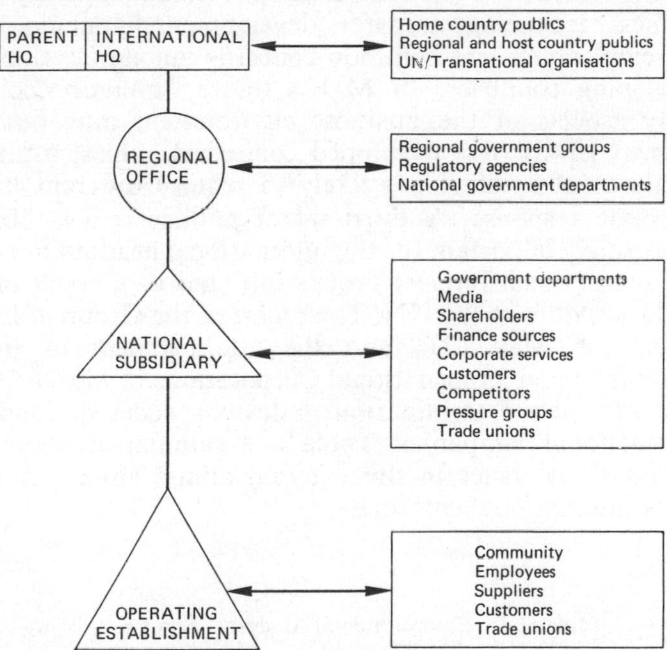

Fig. 11.1 The Multinational Enterprise and its Publics

plants, national subsidiary headquarters and international headquarters each handle different sets of relationships with the company's publics and stakeholders, although many issues recur across the organisation as indicated in Figure 11.1. Community relations, employee welfare and environment protection issues, for example, arise at many company establishments and require special local knowledge and skill to deal with them. The national subsidiary headquarters office has in addition to these establishment problems a further set of responsibilities for external affairs which result from its coordinating role. Such corporate responsibilities may include relationships with suppliers, merchant banks and advertising agencies, in addition to trade associations, government departments and consumer groups.

For the international headquarters office normally located in the home country of its parent company the external affairs problem expands dramatically. In addition to relationships with home country institutions, a variety of different host country issues need to be handled. Government participation in business, technology transfer, development financing, exports and employment are common concerns among developed and developing countries. In MDCs (more developed countries) many aspects of the business environment may be similar whereas LDCs (less developed countries) values, aspirations, standards of conduct are likely to require different kinds of corporate response. A third set of publics is also becoming increasingly important for the international headquarters office: the international interest groups initiated as a result of third-world activities in the UN. The report of the Group of Eminent Persons in May 1974 and the establishment of the UN Commission on Transnational Corporations in March 1975 are signs of a new determination to develop codes of conduct for multinational companies. Table 11.1 summarises some of the potential key issues in the external affairs environment of a major international enterprise.

Table 11.1 Environmental Analysis – Some Key Issues

Main issue	*Sub issues*
1. Multinationalism (pressure on multinational companies)	Economic nationalism; transfer pricing; technological transfer; mergers, monopolies; threat of bloc action; manufacturing; developing countries; international trade unions; legislation, regulations (national, continental international).

Main issue	*Sub issues*
2. Employee Participation	General industrial relations climate; theory and practice of participation; participation through works councils, trade unions, staff associations, etc.; codetermination; cooperatives; attitudes of employers, employees; fears: redundancy, unemployment; motivation; automation; international developments and comparisons; legislation, regulations.
3. Environmental Pollution	Air, water; noise; resource conservation; resource allocation; recycling; new technologies; legislation, regulations local, national (EEC, UN, etc.).
4. Individual and Organisation	Alienation; pressure groups; power groups; role of trade unions; civil rights; women; immigrants; participation in planning; consumer protection; legislation, regulations.
5. Consumer Affairs	Pressure groups; fair trading; customer service; advertising; responsibility of manufacturer, retailer; subsidies; shortages; substitutes; legislation, regulations.
6. Business and Society	Ownership; profit; disclosure; big v. small business; entrepreneurship; qualifications; training and retraining; philosophy of work; marketing concept; government intervention; capitalism v. socialism; mergers, monopolies; social responsibility; social audit; centralised control; move to service economy; inflation; prices and incomes; investment and jobs; company legislation, regulations; exports.
7. Government	State of politics, political parties; democracy; nationalisation; responsibility; devolution; EEC; internationalisation; defence; direct intervention; civil service practices; legislature v. executive; participation; inflation.

Main issue	*Sub issues*
8. Technological Change	New technologies; technological impact; mass communications; rate of change; investment in research; responsibilities of technologist, scientists; spin-off; technology transfer; scientific entrepreneurs; developing countries; social impact/technology assessment; intermediate technology; education for a world of change.
9. Changing Values/Social Trends	Materialism v. quality of life; growth v. no growth v. balanced/reasoned growth; desire for participation; leisure; crime, security; health (physical, mental); drugs; sex; alienation; elitism; invasion of privacy; morals, ethics, religion; attitudes to business, government; role of youth; home, family; education; demand for information; racism; minorities.
10. Urban Affairs	Inner city slums; infrastructure; decision-making, participation; transport; education; housing; social services; local government finance; minorities.
11. The Third World	North and South; power blocs; East v. West; role of private enterprise; role of EEC, UN, OECD etc.; aid; population; natural disasters; education; training; pollution; technology; use of power by resource rich LDCs (oil, tin, cobalt, etc.).
12. Resources	Energy; raw materials; basic foodstuffs; fresh water; conservation; recycling; new sources; oceans; man-made substitutes; legislation, regulation (national, continental, international).
13. International Affairs	EEC; East-West relations; Europe-US relations; Far East; Middle East; trends in nation states; GATT, trade bodies; OECD; UN and agencies; Commonwealth; monetary situation; global inflation; expropriation; war; security.

Source: J. Hargreaves and J. Dauman, 'Business Survival and Social Change' (Associated Business Programmes, London, 1975).

EXTERNAL AFFAIRS – THE NEW PRESCRIPTIONS

The management of external affairs has traditionally been associated with public relations: maintaining an acceptable corporate image among the various publics and stakeholders who have and are likely to have a significant impact on company policies. Many companies have long-established departments with responsibilities for dealing with government relations, industry liaison and media contacts.[1] Initially these tasks were often assigned to the parent company secretary or government relations executive who interpreted and disseminated information on business related legislation. Their activities were likely to be concerned primarily with domestic developments and contacts. As the scope of parent company external affairs activities widened, to deal with consumer affairs or a new set of government departments for example, outside advisers were also used to provide additional legal, public relations or lobbying expertise.[2] External affairs issues abroad tended to remain the responsibility of local subsidiary management. However, successive reorganisations to cope with the problems of growth and diversity abroad had the effect of adding regional and sometimes national levels of management. Responsibility for relationships with governments, regional institutions and other significant interest groups were then divided among the various levels of management according to the needs of particular businesses. For example, as EEC legislation increased greater emphasis was placed on the role of the European regional headquarters office in representing the corporation to the Community.

The public relations view of external affairs management has been superseded in the 1970s by several broader approaches to the relations between an enterprise and its publics which introduce concepts of responsibility and ethics and stress the need for improved sensitivity to environmental change.

Three general themes or prescriptions recur currently in discussions of external relations management:

1. strategic responsiveness;
2. corporate social responsibility or corporate citizenship;
3. corporate conduct.

1. Strategic Responsiveness

This – the ability to respond effectively to environmental change – has become a measure of managerial effectiveness.[3] In an era of change and discontinuities, contingency planning, environment monitoring departments and flexible project teams are among those methods proposed for organisations which wish to improve their reaction time to threats and opportunities and to help anticipate developments in the environment as far ahead as possible. The range of trends, topics, events and relationships scanned for should not be confined to market or industry conditions but should include social trends, political relationships and technological and ecological developments. Techniques such as delphi, scenario writing, and matrix analysis are recommended for planning staffs and line management as part of a set of tools for environmental analysis. Sensitivity to external affairs is necessary as part of the management philosophy of the organisation, with different parts of the organisation responsible for diagnosis and for implementation, linked by corporate plans and policies intended to translate strategy into action. The change of emphasis in external affairs management should also be reflected in modifications to corporate objectives. Some organisations consider social and political factors in planning but treat them as constraints to the achievement of economic goals. For the responsive organisation the management of relationships with corporate constituencies becomes an end in itself, as managements recognise the need for business to assume new responsibilities to society.

2. Corporate Social Responsibility

Whereas strategic responsiveness has been widely accepted as a concept – if not widely implemented – by many organisations, corporate social responsibility has remained a controversial subject. Social responsibility is a term frequently used by critics of business but is interpreted as covering a considerable variety of issues by managers, depending on their particular circumstances. It has been defined as 'an obligation which business assumes or has placed on it to take account of the interests of society independently of considerations of profit'.[4] Questions of resource allocation are still involved, however. A management which wishes to engage in socially responsible behaviour has several potentially difficult decisions to make:

1. Choosing the section of society which is to benefit from its actions – in a situation of limited resources or surpluses one section's (or country's) gain is another's loss.
2. Deciding what constitutes advantage or disadvantage for given sections of society and estimating equivalent values so that trade-offs can be made. Maintaining polluting industrial processes may have to be balanced against the consequences of a shut-down for employment.
3. Making judgements about the time-frame of costs and benefits. Socially responsible action to improve community amenities will reduce profits in the short term, but can be expected to bring long-term advantages.

A summary of the advantages and disadvantages for business of assuming social responsibilities is set out in Table 11.2. Critics of the concept argue that in a free-enterprise economy, business is socially responsible when it makes profits since this is its unique contribution to society: some go further and argue

Table 11.2 Assuming Social Responsibilities – the Case For and Against

For	*Against*
1. *Long-run Self-interest* A better society produces a better environment for business	1. *Profit Maximisation* Businessmen are responsible for making profits. Socially responsible actions impose costs or 'taxes'
2. *Public Image* A socially responsible public image corresponds to public expectations	2. *Costs of Social Involvement* Investment in social projects result in low returns and diminish corporate resources, forcing marginal firms out of business
3. *Viability of Business* Business must assume responsibility to justify its powerful position in society	3. *Lack of Social Skills* Businessmen are economists – and technically-oriented people who lack the perceptions and skills for social affairs

For	Against
4. *Avoidance of government regulation* Responsible private decision-making avoids costly government intervention and regulation	4. *Dilution of Business's Primary Purpose* Involvement in social goals diverts business from its economic role
5. *Socio-cultural Norms* Society's norms are guiding businessmen to include the satisfaction of social goals in decision-making	5. *Weakened International Balance of Payments* Social costs increase export prices and lower international competitiveness, affecting the balance of payments and jobs
6. *Stockholder Interest* Stockholder with diversified portfolios benefit from improvements to the corporate sector, e.g. training	6. *Business Power* Business already has enough social power – more would endanger a free pluralistic society
7. *Business Capabilities and Resources* The management talent, functional expertise, capital resources, innovative ability and productivity orientation of business can result in a unique contribution to solving social problems. In many cases other institutions have failed	7. *Lack of Accountability* Business is not socially accountable to the public and may become paternalistic
8. *Employee Morale* Employees identify with company initiatives since they feel an obligation to society	8. *Lack of Broad Support* Controversy over business involvement in social issues will cause business to fail to achieve a social mission

Adapted freely from K. Davis, 'The Case for and Against Business Assumption for Social Responsibilities', *Academy of Management Journal,* Vol. 16, No. 2, 1973.

that social responsibility, by diverting business from profit-seeking, may endanger a free society.[5] Its defenders see socially responsible behaviour as more akin to other investment projects in spite of the difficulties involved in calculating rates of return, i.e. most investments are not undertaken solely for their tangible economic benefits, but also for a longer-term qualitative contribution to corporate well-being. At the very least socially responsible behaviour is in the long run self-interest of companies since it promotes a better environment for business. A more powerful justification is that the rationale for business is to meet the needs of society. Business loses legitimacy when it fails to match society's expectations.

Social responsibility thus requires more than conformity with the minimum requirements of the law and implies the acceptance of a 'moral imperative' to 'recognise duties and obligations (within the context of the objects for which a company was established) arising from the company's relationship with creditors, suppliers, customers, employees and society at large; and in so doing to exercise their best judgement to strike a balance between the interests of the aforementioned groups and between the interests of those groups and the interests of the proprietors of the company.'[6] Much of the debate about social responsibility turns on this question of balance between groups of interests, both nationally and internationally.

Companies also need to find a balance between initiative and reaction as they consider possible projects and actions. In addition to the potential dangers for the company which ignores societal pressures there are also problems for the company which takes an active approach towards social responsibility. Accusations of paternalism, manipulation or favour-seeking may greet any attempt to lead public opinion. Trade unions may be suspicious of additions to employee benefits such as free medical services or convalescent homes. Security checks to prepare safeguards against kidnapping of executives may be seen as prying into private lives. Communities dominated by one large employer may resent philanthropic projects. Whereas 'balance' is likely to be impossible to achieve, 'social responsiveness' may be more feasible. By anticipating the possible side-effects of its actions on its various publics, taking a stand on public issues, adopting institutional ethical norms and being open in communications a corporation may claim to have changed its behaviour to meet social needs. This may be the most advanced form which socially responsible behaviour can take in an organisation. Three possible approaches to corporate social responsibility are set out in Table 11.3.[7] A company which pursues a policy of keeping within the prescriptions of the law conforms to social obligations. Social responsibility implies bringing corporate behaviour up to a normal level where it is congruent with the prevailing social norms, values and expectations of performance. Socially responsive activities go one stage further and are anticipatory and preventive in nature.

The social responsibility of business is frequently discussed as though the obligation is towards 'society', implying that an organisation's publics in society share common aims, values and standards. The 'stakeholder' or 'constituency' view of organisations recognises that there are many different publics each of which may be concerned with different issues as shown in Figure 11.2. However, in each country the significance of the various constituencies is likely to differ. The company which wishes to set internationally consistent standards of corporate behaviour has to develop skills in diagnosis in addition to generating a responsive climate at the headquarters office. Two management tools in particular are recommended for these tasks: the Social Responsibility Audit and the Corporate Impact Assessment.

The Social Responsibility Audit (which should not be confused with the accountability concept of the Social Audit discussed below) is proposed as a method for examining 'systematically on an organisation-wide basis the existing policies and practices relating to social responsibilities, internal and external to the organisation'.[8] It focuses on issues rather than constituencies and provides a detailed series of questions for an enquiry supervised by a policy team, board member or senior corporate manager. Table 11.4 sets out a checklist covering the principal areas of concern in the external and the internal environments of the company. The questions are designed to expose corporate practice in relation to each of the issues, e.g. in relation to packaging: 'To what extent could your packaging be criticised on environmental grounds?' This inventory-check approach to corporate policies is orientated towards the individual firm and its immediate publics.

However, in addition to auditing the social policies of each of its subsidiaries at home and abroad the socially aware international company is also likely to want to assess the effect of its activities on the economies of the countries in which it operates. Many of the criticisms of multinationals are based on judgements about the contribution which overseas companies should make to national economic objectives. It is therefore important for each company to undertake its own assessment of its role in the economies in which its presence is significant. Such an assessment

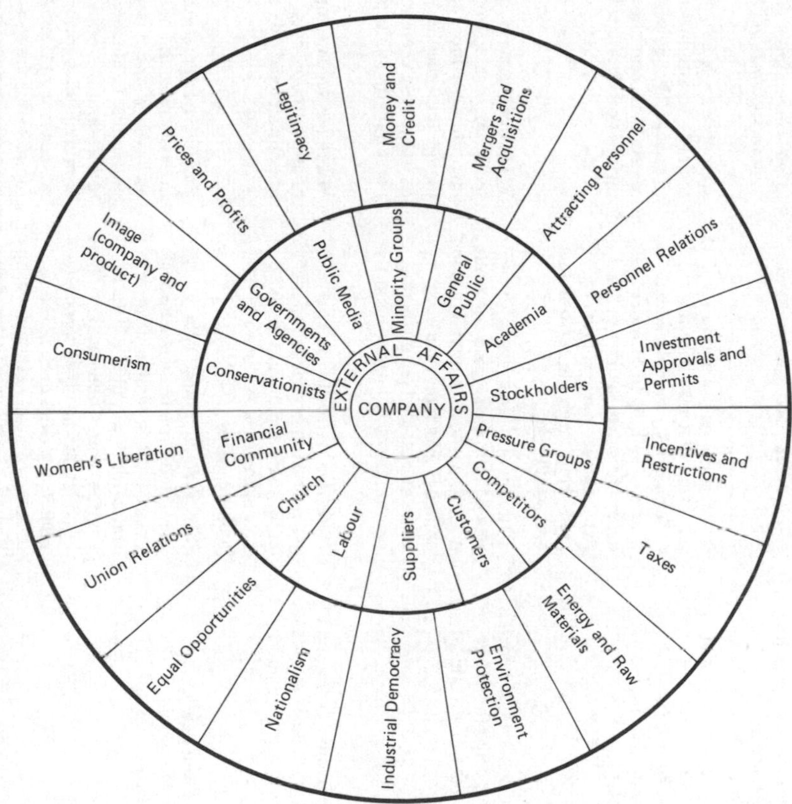

Fig. 11.2 The MNC's 'Constituencies'

Source: Business International Dec. 1975.

can take the form of a corporate impact assessment[9] carried out by local regional or international management. Four steps are involved.

(*a*) *A Social and Economic Impact Statement*

This is designed to evaluate the beneficial and harmful effects

Table 11.3 A Three-State Schema for Classifying Corporate Behaviour

Dimensions of Behaviour	*State One: Social Obligation Proscriptive*	*State Two: Social Responsibility Prescriptive*	*State Three: Social Responsiveness Anticipatory and Preventive*
Search for legitimacy	Confines legitimacy to legal and economic criteria only; does not violate laws; equates profitable operations with fulfilling social expectations.	Accepts the reality of limited relevance of legal and market criteria of legitimacy in actual practice. Willing to consider and accept broader – extra-legal and extra-market – criteria for measuring corporate performance and social role.	Accepts its role as defined by the social system and therefore subject to change; recognises importance of profitable operations but includes other criteria.
Ethical norms	Consider business value-neutral; managers expected to behave according to their own ethical standards.	Defines norms in community related terms, i.e., good corporate citizen. Avoids taking moral stand on issues which may harm its economic interests or go against prevailing social norms (majority views).	Takes definite stand on issues of public concern; advocates institutional ethical norms even though they may be detrimental to its immediate economic interest or prevailing social norms.
Social accountability for corporate actions	Construes narrowly as limited to stockholders; jealously guards its prerogatives against outsiders.	Construes narrowly for legal purposes, but broadened to include groups affected by its actions; management more outward looking.	Willing to account for its actions to other groups, even those not directly affected by its actions.
Operating strategy	Exploitative and defensive adaptation. Maximum externalisation of costs.	Reactive adaptation. Where identifiable internalise previously external costs. Maintain current standards of physical and social environment. Compensate victims of pollution and other corporate-related activities even in the absence of clearly established legal grounds. Develop industry-wide standards.	Pro-active adaptation. Takes lead in developing and adapting new technology for environmental protectors. Evaluates side-effects of corporate actions and eliminates them prior to the actions being taken. Anticipates future social changes and develops internal structures to cope with them.

Response to social pressures	Maintains low public profile, but if attacked, uses PR methods to upgrade its public image; denies any deficiencies; blames public dissatisfaction on ignorance or failure to understand corporate functions; discloses information only where legally required.	Accepts responsibility for solving current problems; will admit deficiencies in former practices and attempt to persuade public that its current practices meet social norms; attitude toward critics conciliatory; freer information disclosures than State One.	Willingly discusses activity with outside groups; makes information freely available to public; accepts formal and informal inputs from outside groups in decision making. Is willing to be publicly evaluated for its various activities.
Activities pertaining to governmental actions	Strongly resists any regulation of its activities except when it needs help to protect its market position; avoids contact; resists any demands for information beyond that legally required.	Preserves management discretion in corporate decisions, but cooperates with government in research to improve industry-wide standards; participates in political processes and encourages employees to do likewise.	Openly communicates with government; assists in enforcing existing laws and developing evaluations of business practices; objects publicly to governmental activities that it feels are detrimental to the public good.
Legislative and political activities	Seeks to maintain *Status quo*; actively opposes laws that would internalise any previously externalised costs; seeks to keep lobbying activities secret.	Willing to work with outside groups for good environmental laws; concedes need for change in some *status quo* laws; less secrecy in lobbying than State One.	Avoids meddling in politics and does not pursue special-interest laws; assists legislative bodies in developing better laws where relevant; promotes honesty and openness in government and in its own lobbying activities.
Philanthropy	Contributes only when direct benefit to it clearly shown; otherwise, views contributions as responsibility of individual employees.	Contributes to non-controversial and established causes; matches employee contributions.	Activities of State Two, *plus* support and contributions to new, controversial groups whose needs it sees as unfulfilled and increasingly important.

Source: S. Prakash Sethi, 'Dimensions of Corporate Social Performance: An Analytical Framework, *California Management Review*, spring 1975, Vol. XVII, no. 3.

Table 11.4 Social Responsibility Audit – Checklist of Headings

External Environment
1. Social responsibilities in new (business) opportunities
2. Community relations
3. Consumer relations
4. Pollution
5. Packaging
6. Investment relations
7. Shareholder relations

Internal Environment
1. Physical environment
2. Working conditions
3. Minority groups
4. Organisation structure and management style
5. Communications
6. Industrial relations
7. Education and training

Source: J. Humble, op. cit.

of company operations on a national economy. It can include the following areas;

(i) Balance of payments effect (outflow of funds, inflow of funds, savings of foreign exchange attributed to MNC).
(ii) Expenditures by MNC in host country (labour costs, local purchases, taxes, other costs of doing business).
(iii) Costs incurred by host country as a result of MNC activity (government subsidies and incentives, industrial and social infrastructure costs, damage to environment, opportunity costs).
(iv) Technology transfer (kinds, value, costs to host country, local research and development).
(v) Manpower effects (number employed, comparative wage figures, nature and cost of fringe benefits not mandated by government, percentage of indigenous workers, promotion of local workers, stability of employment, nature value and extent of training, industrial relations issues, safety concerns).
(vi) Secondary effects (provision of industrial and social infrastructure, indirect employment generated, development of and aid to local suppliers and industry, impact on government revenues and community life).

(vii) Effect on industry (concentration, capacity of industry, prices).
(viii) Use of national resources.
(ix) Assessment of corporate policies towards government – plans, laws, customs (local community, employees, restrictive business practices reducing local benefit and growth).

Much of the data is likely to be in qualitative form. Whenever possible it is important to indicate standards against which performance can be evaluated, e.g. usage rates at equivalent plants in the country.

(*b*) *A Social Programme Inventory*
This is a review of corporate social activities not required or suggested by government and which are not directly linked to enhancing the efficient operations of the firm, e.g. increasing the health and nutrition practices of employee families, maintaining roads and budgets, subsidising teachers' salaries in local schools, etc. There are likely to be substantial country-by-country differences in what is regarded as normal company practice and careful evaluation is necessary.

(*c*) *A Corporate Social Profile*
Surveys of the significant policy makers and interest groups are undertaken by a subsidiary in order to examine local, regional and national attitudes to the company. Candidate groups at the various levels could include: workers, indigenous managers, union officials, suppliers, customers, government officials, politicians, community leaders, business leaders, media people, academics, clergy, etc.

In addition to increasing the awareness of the company about the impact of current activities, indications of possible future areas of conflict may also emerge.

(*d*) *Management Evaluation*
The purpose of this exercise is to examine internal company practices and procedures including the management of the external or public affairs function, the development of public affairs objectives, management accountability and rewards for social programmes, training in public affairs skills and orientations, internal communications and subsidiary feedback to

headquarters on external affairs. It is likely to be a corporate rather than a subsidiary project in preparation for a review of external affairs strategies throughout the company.

In this way the international firm can supplement local 'social responsibility' with 'good corporate citizenship' in the countries in which it operates. Concern with the national economy and development goals, openness to local publics, training of local workers and management, obedience to local laws, practices and traditions are thus key characteristics of good corporate behaviour, in addition to any social programmes directed at the immediate constituencies of operating units.

3. Corporate Conduct

A new dimension has been added to external affairs management as a result of the publication of codes of conduct for international enterprises. The OECD code published in June 1976 sets out guidelines for the behaviour of multinational companies.[10] These guidelines are voluntary but the 24 members, who together cover most of the developed world and 80 per cent of all multinational operations, plan to review the system in three years. Mandatory action would replace voluntary recommendations if they proved inadequate. The code is the first successful attempt to establish international standards against which the performance of multinational enterprises can be judged. Corporate citizenship has become an international corporate obligation, albeit voluntary at this stage.

The UN Commission on Transnational Corporations has also been given the task of preparing a code, motivated by third-world beliefs that international businesses need to be controlled. They argue that multinationals have the flexibility to move investments, technology, cash and profits round the world and are in a position to discriminate against countries at will. By subversion or by threatening to withdraw from a country, for example, they can also use their power to overcome opposition to their plans. A code would impose restrictions on them, require higher standards of business practice and compel disclosure of information on their activities. These international obligations would be legally enforced. A preparatory review of relevant material proposes three main areas for the code.[11]

1. General Principles of Behaviour – observance of laws,

adherence to economic goals, social cultural and development objectives. Respect for human rights.

2. Transnational company behaviour – political issues, corrupt practices, economic and commercial issues, information.

3. Principles of government policy – jurisdiction over MNCs, treatment of MNCs.

Although covering many of the same economic and commercial topics as the OECD code the UN list as seen in Table 11.5 places greater emphasis on 'interference' issues, particularly alignment with national development objectives and corrupt practices.

Potentially the most significant element in these and other codes[12] on related topics is the emphasis on information disclosure.

The OECD code requires companies to give geographical breakdowns of sales, production, investment and profits, and to declare accounting policies on consolidation and transfer pricing. The ICFTU Charter[13] goes further and asks for specific legislation to compel multinational companies to disclose detailed financial information on branch operations including investment intentions in the form of annual reports to workers. In addition the UN, the EEC and the International Accounting Standards Committee are each developing accounting standards on consolidation and disclosure designed to provide governments and other interested parties, such as trade unions, with the basic information necessary to assess the economic behaviour of transnationals.

The development of codes of conduct is part of a wider 'North-South' debate between the developed and developing countries about the distribution of global resources. A political consensus about the approval and enforcement of guidelines for business behaviour will be influenced by the results of bargaining over such issues as development banks, commodity prices and international loans. Although widespread internationally co-ordinated action to enforce a binding code is unlikely, some guidelines will emerge from the UN Commission.

In the short term the behaviour of multinational companies in OECD countries will indicate how the guidelines have been interpreted by companies. How OECD governments use their own code against multinationals will also be a useful test of the ability of states to influence company behaviour. Whereas

Table 11.5 Key Topics in a Code of Conduct for Transnational Enterprises

1. General Principles of Behaviour of Transnational Corporations
   - A Observance of local laws
   - B Adherence to economic goals and development objectives
   - C Adherence to socio-cultural objectives and values
   - D Respect for human rights and fundamental freedoms
2. Issues related to policies and practices of Transnational Corporations
   - A Political issues
     1. Interference in national political affairs
     2. Interference in intergovernmental relations
   - B Corrupt practices, particularly illicit payments
   - C Economic and commercial issues
     1. Ownership and control
        - (*a*) permanent sovereignty
        - (*b*) terms of admission and operations
        - (*c*) forms of ownership and phased changes in ownership
     2. Balance of payments and financing
     3. Transfer pricing
     4. Taxation
     5. Competition and restrictive business practices
     6. Transfer of technology
     7. Employment and labour
        - (*a*) Information
        - (*b*) Industrial relations including consultation and participation in decision-making
        - (*c*) Protection of rights of employees and conditions of employment
        - (*d*) Employment
     8. Consumer protection
     9. Environmental protection
   - D Information
3. Principles of Government Policy and Issues of Jurisdiction
   - A Treatment of Transitional Corporations
   - B Allocation of Jurisdiction
   - C Nationalisation and compensation

Source: 'Material Relevant to the Formulation of a Code of Conduct' (New York: UN, January 1977); submitted to the Intergovernmental working group of the Commission on Transnational Corporations on the Code of Conduct.

companies have moved to deal with bribery and illegal payments by issuing new guidelines,[14] they may be more reluctant to conform to outside expectations in relation to transfer payments and tax policies for example. Moreover, for these codes to be effective there is also a need for governments to maintain stable policies in their treatment of MNCs rather than the constant changes in treatment currently commonplace.

EXTERNAL AFFAIRS STRATEGIES AND PROGRAMMES

Company attitudes to the concepts of strategic responsiveness, corporate citizenship and corporate conduct vary considerably.[15] Although the ideas have been widely discussed for some time, the number of companies who could be classified as 'socially responsive' is small, and is dominated by a few opinion-leaders. However, many companies support socially-oriented programmes which they have inherited from earlier days or which have resulted from local custom. An increasing number of firms are also experimenting with a limited number of activities without necessarily embracing a new 'philosophy' of management. There are several recurring themes in the programmes or strategies through which corporate citizenship is expressed. They fall into two major categories: those concerned with the social aspects of citizenship such as education and community affairs and those related to the economic aspects of citizenship, including standards of employment, transfer of knowhow, etc.

1. Social Citizenship Strategies

(*a*) *Philanthropy*
Most firms make small donations to charities or worthy causes. A few companies are associated with independent charitable or public service trusts established by the founder of the business. The three Rowntree Trusts established in 1904 include a social service trust which is non-charitable and enjoys no tax exemptions, and which has been able to support political parties, pressure groups and community action in what its trustees perceive as the public interest.[16] New funds are also being established, however. An international bank has set up a development fund which receives 1 per cent of bank profits each year.[17] Funds are used to support projects anywhere in the world, which would not succeed on commercial terms in the bank's judgement, but which are a valuable contribution to

development in the country or area. 'Pump-priming' projects are particularly favoured. Proposals are submitted by local banks, international charities, etc., and are reviewed by a committee headed by the deputy chairman of the bank. Assistance may take the form of grants, interest-free loans, equity participation or normal commercial loans.

The advantages of setting up a social fund are that it channels funds directly to projects which the company thinks are worth while and that it signals a long-term commitment to social action which is not subject to the ebb and flow of budget allocation. The creation of a panel or trust with a high proportion of independent members protects the project against public suspicions of commercial interest. The potential disadvantage of such a trust is the size of the financial commitment required before any worthwhile results can be seen. It may also be regarded by shareholders as a wasteful or even damaging use of corporate funds, especially when controversial projects are supported.

(*b*) *Sponsorship*

Sponsorship activities are growing in popularity among companies since they provide a means of simultaneously furthering business interests and providing benefits to the community. The arts and sports are the main recipients, although sporting events are frequently directly associated with marketing and public relations programmes. The sponsorship tradition is stronger in the United States, but the role of British business in patronage of the arts, particularly music, is increasing. In addition to funds, company assistance can take the form of product or material donations, loan of company facilities, management advice, scholarships and commissions. Many such unpublished activities take place at establishments throughout companies. The major advantage of sponsorship is its flexibility both in terms of level and length of commitment.

Overseas, sponsorship programmes are more likely to be directed at local development needs, especially education and training. For example, General Motors in South Africa grants high school scholarships to children of African and coloured employees, runs a bursary plan which covers the cost of prescribed books and school fees for children in addition to making contributions to coloured and African educational organisations.[18] It is also possible to use such funds in a way that is not only philanthropic but also helps to generate new business opportunities for the corporation. For example, over the past ten years Control Data has extracted many business opportunities from a variety of social problem areas including inner city ghettos and habitual offenders who keep returning to gaol. Its most recent success is a community health care programme which has dramatically reduced the level of disabling diseases amongst the 10,000 Indians on a reservation in South Dakota. The company expects the systems of computerised health care developed to deal with the reservation problems to ultimately provide a large and profitable market in developing countries.

Social responsibility at Control Data is therefore, not purely philanthropic and the company ultimately expects products and services born of social responsibility to become a major source of income. To decide upon what areas of social need the company should tackle Control Data has a corporate social responsibility committee, made up of fifteen people from all levels of the company. The committee meets several times a year and has to present a budget to the corporate board of management. At present this consists of some $3 million. Further, as business opportunities emerge from a social responsibility project part of the finance is drawn from normal R & D funds. Eventually the business unit supplying manpower and expertise to a project takes it over completely and includes it in its own annual budget or potentially spins it off as a separate company.[19]

(*c*) *Community Involvement*

Company involvement locally can range from providing infrastructures for the community to the widespread practice of allowing employees time off with pay for volunteer activities. One major British company which bases the major part of its activities in one town in the UK owns and subsidises the town theatre and makes grants for civic projects. Their involvement now also extends to helping the local authorities to attract new kinds of employment as technological change forces them to make employees redundant.[20] Another company which dominates a small region lent one of its specialists to help reorganise the local education system and has helped the local transport

Fig. 11.3 Clark Equipment Co. – Foreign Investment Balance Sheet (*financial figures in US$ m*)

	1972		1973		1974	
	EXIMIA[1]	ECSA[2]	EXIMIA	ECSA	EXIMIA	ECSA
A. EMPLOYMENT BENEFITS						
Total employees	332	3,310	331	4,934	381	4,890
Salaried						
Transferred from foreign operation	—	6	—	6	—	4
Local residents	151	1,081	180	1,1516	213	1,647
Hourly						
Transferred from foreign operation	—	—	—	—	—	—
Local residents	181	2,223	151	3,412	168	3,239
Expenditure for training personnel	$ —	$ 97	$ —	$ 147	$ —	$ 203
Number of personnel trained	—	188	—	264	—	318
B. CONTRIBUTION TO LOCAL ECONOMY						
Total salaries and wages (including fringes)	$ 932	$ 9,830	$1,350	$16,062	$2,187	$23,020
Total taxes	$ 519	$ 9,514	$ 854	$13,251	$1,391	$16,141
Total import duties	$ 589	$ 1,298	$ 579	$ 2,364	$ 846	$ 3,301
Total value of local purchases (including fixed assets)	$2,457	$21,355	$3,418	$39,029	$5,678	$48,569
Number of local suppliers	1,206	974	1,441	1,143	1,656	1,125
Credit granted to local customers	$3,265	$28,387	$3,722	$45,173	$6,536	$68,340
C. BALANCE OF PAYMENTS CONTRIBUTION						
Exports (fob)	$ 107	$ 598	$1,262	$ 1,328	$ 3,970	$ 4,953
Imports (fob – including fixed assets)	$1,887	$ 8,750	$1,662	$11,546	$ 1,535	$19,390
Dividends, interest and fees remitted to foreign entities	$ 660	$ 273	$ 209	$ 546	$ 261	$ 5,647[4]
Import substitution value of local production[3]	$4,214	$24,147	$6,169	$37,113	$10,811	$49,328
Capital increase from foreign sources	$ —	$ —	$(139)	$ —	$ 647	$ —
Loans from foreign sources	$1,650	$ 6,055	$1,650	$ 3,000	$ 950	$23,115
Total BOP contribution	$3,424	$21,777	$7,071	$29,349	$14,582	$52,359

[1] EXIMIA – Eximia Industrias Clark Argentina SA; [2] ECSA – Equipamentos Clark SA (Brazil); [3] Estimated at 66% of sales; [4] Includes payment of loans.

Source: *Business International*, 20 June 1975.

undertaking to remodel their bus routes and timetables using their computing capacity and experience. The economic dominance of a company town established during a previous era brings many problems, however, as social values and economic rationales change. Such involvement is unavoidable in development situations as the creation of company houses, schools, roads and shops by international firms in many countries testifies, but leaves the company open to later accusations of welfare paternalism.

In the UK, in contrast to the United States, there is little evidence of extensive company involvement with urban problems and minority groups. A US survey published in 1975 lists 1500 programmes in areas such as job training, minority enterprise education, environment, housing and such like.[21]

(*d*) *Publication*

Communication strategies are under review in many firms as the pressures for 'participation' and disclosure mount. Internal company newspapers and journals, 'popular' versions of the annual accounts and presentations to employee councils have been widely introduced.

In addition to information about company performance, social programmes are also given extensive coverage. Many of these communication policies are being extended internationally, supplemented by special efforts to provide information on the contribution of the company to the local economy. The Argentine and Brazilian subsidiaries of Clark International, for example, have for several years drawn up balance sheets which describe employee benefits, contribution to the local economy and balance of payments contributions (see Figure 11.3). The summarised information has helped management in presentations to obtain import licences, expansion permits and other government approvals.[22] This kind of presentation goes some way towards providing the information which many LDC governments want to see in the UN code.

Additional stimulus for greater public disclosure of corporate activities has been provided by the increasing number of external social audits carried out by public pressure groups, institutional investors, consumerists, churches and universities. Companies are frequently selected for their social 'irresponsibility' and the quality of the analysis varies considerably. They are part of an increasing trend towards public accountability,[23] however, and legislation is being considered in several countries, although the problems of quantification and measurement in social auditing remain intractable. Internal social audits had been undertaken by at least half the top 500 US companies in 1974, it has been estimated (mainly in growth sectors of the economy, e.g. consulting, banking, chemicals), but few European companies had attempted comprehensive reviews by 1977.[24]

2. Economic Citizenship Strategies

Although the social citizenship strategies of international companies make substantial contributions to local and national development in many countries, it is the economic aspects of citizenship which particularly interest national governments. The headings in the UN document on material relevant to a code reflect their concerns: economic goals and development objectives, employment, taxation, investments, balance of payments, technology transfer, etc. These are the substantive issues to which the multinational enterprise is expected to address itself. The concept of external affairs management as public relations or programme development for corporate constituents is changing in the international context to the challenging one of managing corporate economic citizenship. Companies in strategically important industries are having to take a view on the nature of their future involvement with a particular country and the contribution which they intend to make to its development.

Some industries like oil and mining have long experience of handling such issues and companies in them have developed top-level skills in analysis and negotiation. Other less exposed companies are now beginning to issue policy statements on economic citizenship addressed to both internal and external publics. Caterpillar Tractor has issued a 'Worldwide Code of Business Conduct' which sets out the company's beliefs regarding the reciprocal responsibilities of host countries and their governments.[25] The code covers ownership and investment, corporate facilities, relationships with employees, inter-company pricing, differing business practices, competitive conduct, observance of local laws, business ethics, public responsibility and international business. It specifically mentions transfer prices: prices for goods and services are to be set on the basis of arm's-length transactions. Foreign exchange dealings will only be carried out in order to cover requirements for business operations. Technology transfer will be achieved by exchanging design and specification data from facility to facility and by developing technical expertise of employees and suppliers in host countries. Implementation of the code is the responsibility of local management.

3. Technology Transfer

Technology transfer is emerging as one of the key issues in economic citizenship. An UNCTAD Code of Conduct for Technology Transfer is in preparation and corporate technology strategies are coming under critical scrutiny. In the case of Caterpillar Tractor the transfer of technology is assisted by the worldwide coordination of engineering specifications by central design control departments in the US. Design improvements and manufacturing techniques are communicated throughout the organisation and an extensive training programme for suppliers, employees and distributors is operated to build and maintain technical expertise.

Similar technological strategies are operated by many manufacturers with worldwide product-markets. IBM coordinates its international procurement policies through centres in New York, Essones and Tokyo. Ford operates an extensive network of product planning, plant design and manufacturing and marketing assistance centred on its regional offices, and with extensive back-up units in the headquarters office in Dearborn.[20] Affiliate companies can call on 'foreign service officers' from other parts of the organisation to deal with local problems, for example in the case of plant start-ups. For the new transmission plant at Bordeaux, Ford Dearborn carried out the product design, Ford Europe conducted the manufacturing feasibility study, Ford Cologne drew up the plant design and US engineers contributed the latest in processing and tooling technology. Ongoing technical assistance comes through a worldwide technical communications network: engine standards, specifications and test procedures are disseminated to all affiliates, for example. A by-product of Ford procedures is the development of higher standards for affiliates' suppliers as the expertise of US suppliers is transmitted abroad and vice versa.

The major criticisms of the current state of technology transfer internationally are directed at the allegedly protectionist licensing and patent policies of multinational companies. The technologies transferred have not been modified to suit developing countries, it is claimed, and many of the products marketed are too sophisticated to appeal to more than a limited elite. Royalties have required excessive foreign exchange payments and the terms of licences have been too restrictive, e.g. the benefits of patents have not been widely available to other producers in the country and restrictions have been placed on exports. Companies on the other hand, see these licences or joint venture packages as based on normal commercial transactions and market delimitation agreements, and expect participating governments to honour signed contracts. Royalty payments are in their view payment for R & D investment. They argue that governments for their part can help the technology flow process by creating a favourable investment climate, by assisting in the practical problems of transferring people and equipment, and by adopting consistent long-term policies on prices, patents and ownership which are not arbitrarily revoked.

The issue of R & D strategy and national development policies must remain a continuing source of fundamental conflict between governments and international companies for some time. R & D in the majority of major multinationals is situated in or tightly controlled from the home country, and research into simpler labour-intensive technologies can only be one of many projects. Although the establishment of local support laboratories is increasing, the major thrust of corporate effort is toward multimarket rather than locally adapted products and applications.

ORGANISATIONAL RESPONSES

The organisational responses of international companies to the new challenge of external affairs management have been limited in scope. In the majority of companies, restructuring has yet to follow strategic adaptation: local management is expected to cope with the new pressures for social and economic responsibility without special training, and by relying negotiations on 'judgement' and 'feel' for the local situation. Many companies still feel that a polycentric approach to the variety and complexity of problems facing the company around the world is the only possible response. In the case of South Africa this has led to several difficult situations for some UK firms when, for example, corporate headquarters offices are being urged by shareholders and the government to increase the levels of African wages while the local subsidiary boards regard their employment policies as relatively enlightened.

Codes of conduct have found favour with some companies, stimulated partly by the publicity over bribery disclosures, and many others are considering them. They are also seen to have the advantage of communicating a general set of corporate standards or a corporate ethic. Several major multinationals have followed North American practice and set up public affairs departments either as information or public liaison units. These are staff departments, however, with no line authority, and remain outside the mainstreams of corporate decision-making.

Consideration of social issues is starting to become incorporated in the domestic planning process for several UK companies. A survey of social responsibility in 28 firms in 1974[31] reported that employee relations, employee working conditions and product safety were the areas where companies had most fully developed policies, objectives, operational plans, financial budgets and social impact monitoring. Twenty of the firms had made organisational changes in the last three years in response to new social pressures and expectations and half the companies had one man or department with central responsibility for coordinating and controlling social public affairs, mostly reporting direct to the managing director. Typical tasks involved information research and policy studies as an input to the planning process. Research at the Manchester Business School has shown, however, that planning practice abroad lags behind domestic developments in many European multinationals. Sophisticated social analysis abroad is thus rare.

A recent survey highlighted the coordination problems for US companies in handling public affairs abroad.[29] Although some advanced companies had incorporated special departments in their regional offices, many still relied on informal contacts between headquarters departments, primarily orientated towards domestic affairs, and subsidiary managing directors. External affairs analysis was given low status and priority as a result and despite the widespread existence of regular internal briefings through bulletins and newsletters, management was reluctant to spend much time on it.

EXTERNAL AFFAIRS ANALYSIS

Formal techniques for external affairs analysis have not been widely adopted by multinational companies, partly because social responsiveness has not been incorporated into decision processes. However, a move towards the integration of external affairs management and decision-making has been made by the head office planning department (rather than the public affairs department) of the Royal Dutch Shell Group. As a result of work on project planning they have developed a technique to evaluate social responses which are likely to result from specific major company actions.

The Societal Response Matrix has two dimensions: issues which are of concern to the company and interested parties or constituents. The concerns can be of several types:

(*a*) general public concerns which are likely to be affected by actions which the company undertakes nationally or internationally, e.g. balance of payments, transfer of technology.
(*b*) specific concerns which are likely to affect several important constituencies of the firm, e.g. safety hazards, information disclosure, consumer relations.
(*c*) issues directly connected with a particular project under consideration, e.g. food supply security, cost reduction of protein concentrates.

These concerns are plotted against the constituencies seen as potentially important influences on the success of a particular project or plan, as illustrated in Figure 11.4.

The concerns are then assessed from the point of view of each constituency and their expected reaction is ranked as one of three categories, namely supportive, neutral but interested, or hostile. These reactions are usually colour-coded so as to provide a visual guide to management action. Hostile expected reactions are usually highlighted in red and policies are considered which could be introduced into the project so as to divert potential hostility into support or, at worst, neutrality. In the event that a significant number of expected hostile reactions cannot be eliminated by changes in the project proposal, the proposal itself

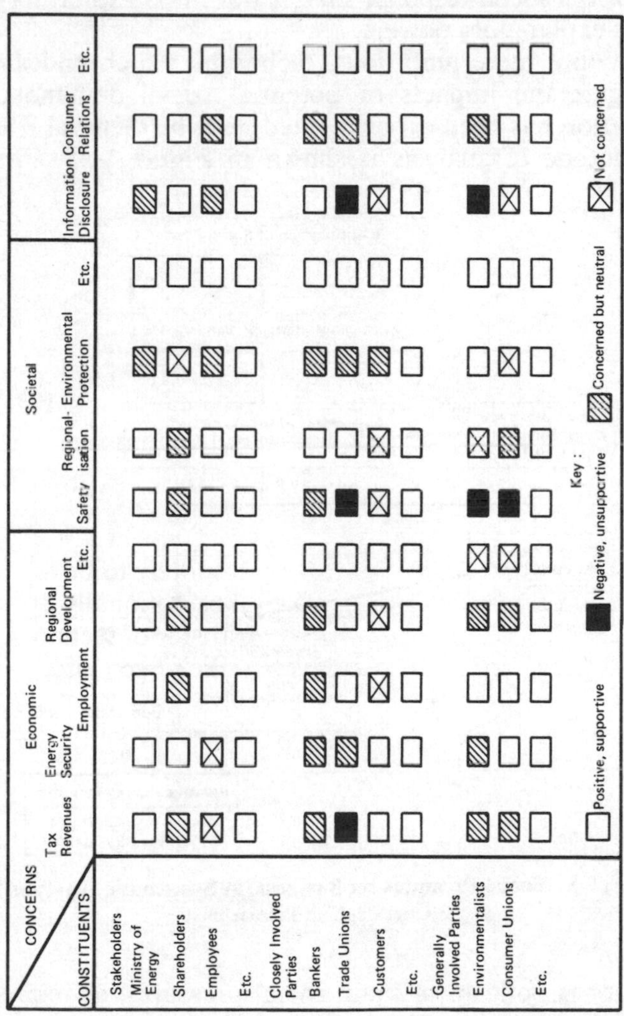

Fig. 11.4 Societal Response Profile Assessment Matrix

Source: Royal Dutch Shell Group.

will be dropped. The company now employs the social response matrix as one of the tools used to evaluate all major capital projects. By examining the full range of issues and the likely public reaction, a better appreciation of the social implications of a project is obtained. As with many planning tools, the major value of the social response matrix lies in its exploratory rather than its explanatory powers.

A second, more ambitious, technique which endeavours to investigate the impacts of potential social demands on the corporation has been experimented with by General Electric.[30] This method of analysis is shown in Figure 11.5. Firstly, an

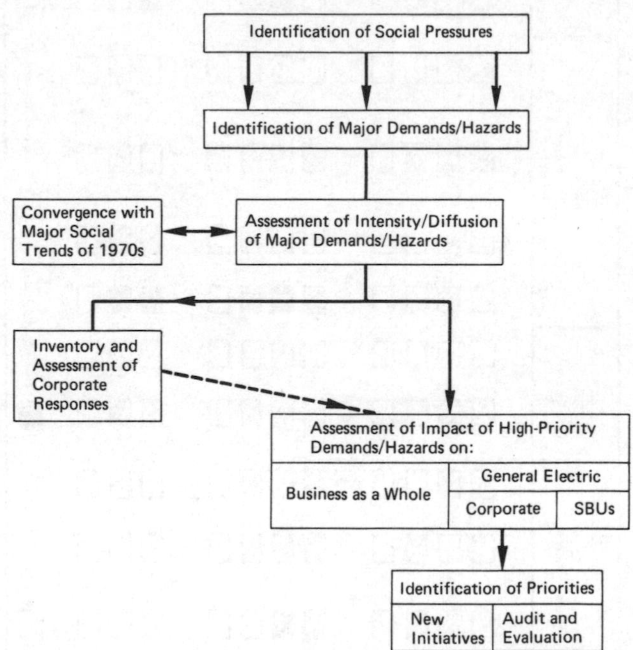

Fig. 11.5 Social Pressures on Business: A Systematic Analysis for Corporation Priorities

inventory is built up of main social pressures, as expressed in the major complaints frequently made about corporate performance. These are grouped into eight principal categories: Marketing/Financial, Production Operations, Employee Relations/Working Conditions, Governance, Communications,

Community and Government Relations, Defence Production, and International Operations.

Secondly, the major demands and hazards associated with these complaints are identified. These are then screened by a two-phase process in order to assess their relative societal validity and importance. These factors are assessed by comparing the demands and hazards against a series of major societal trends with the impact of each demand on each trend being assigned a numerical score from 1–10 either positive or negative, and the total aggregated to provide an overall convergence score. The relative pressure for each demand is assessed by ranking each one from 1–4 according to which quartile the demand might be assigned to by each of fourteen constituencies/pressure groups in terms of their pressure for it. An aggregate intensity/diffusion score is then computed for each demand.

As a result of this assessment each demand can be plotted on a matrix of convergance and intensity/diffusion. The objective of this is to identify the demands which fall in the high/high quadrant which are the demands most likely to be experienced by the corporation.

The remaining two steps of the procedure are then performed on these high-priority demands. Firstly the impact of each on the business community as a whole is evaluated, together with the effect on General Electric at both the corporate and SBU level. Finally, an inventory and evaluation of corporate responses to these demands is developed.

ORGANISING FOR EXTERNAL AFFAIRS MANAGEMENT – SOME ALTERNATIVES

The responsibility for external affairs rests largely with the top manager on the spot in a national subsidiary or operating establishment. In some regional offices regular formal surveillance of public affairs issues takes place, but more frequently it is handled on an *ad hoc* basis by international headquarters managers.

While social responsibility may remain the individual responsibility of national managers it is difficult to see how international companies can avoid developing a more coordinated view of corporate citizenship worldwide and in particular in relation to economic responsibilities. Currently corporate attitudes depend on the perspectives of senior executives and board members who bring to the task a functional specialism and experience in a variety of postings at home and abroad. For the international enterprise which wishes to develop its external affairs capabilities there are several possible approaches:

1. *Codes, information and training*. Without changing the existing network of responsibilities, a greater awareness of corporate citizenship can be disseminated through widely distributed codes of conduct and special internal and external courses on the new international world order. A regular briefing service on issues affecting multinational firms for senior management worldwide contributes to the development of a corporate ethic.
2. *Individual or departmental appointments*. For many firms the significance of the issues warrants a senior managerial appointment in the area of external affairs who acts as external negotiator and internal consultant (and missionary) to operating units. He may be supported by a staff which develops special expertise and analytical techniques for handling corporate citizenship issues.
3. *Plans and procedures*. The inclusion of assessments of social issues in plan formats and capital expenditure requests is increasing. There may be scope for the development of a corporate 'citizenship plan' which draws together the strands from the many different business plans.
4. *Organisation restructuring*. Partly as a result of legislation and other pressures on top management there is a trend towards the appointment of outside advisers or external directors at headquarters, regional and national levels of companies. Whether in the form of audit or advisory committee, the role of these outsiders demands particular skills in trading off involvement with objectivity. As mechanisms for 'participation' become established their influence on corporate decision-making will increase.
5. *Recruitment*. The widespread practice of promoting locally recruited management in subsidiaries abroad helps to extend the corporate perspective on local issues. Special programmes

are then required to establish consistent international policies and practices on citizenship.

IN CONCLUSION

Discussions of external affairs management currently oscillate between economics and business ethics. For the operating manager, translating the concepts of corporate citizenship into the practice of planning and negotiation presents many problems. As the strength of the corporate office of multinational companies in policy-making grows, corporate guidelines on citizenship will become more prevalent. Only through a process of widespread debate can the conflicting interests of the constituencies of the multinational be reconciled to the point where citizenship has some consistent meaning and standards of conduct can start to develop.

References

CHAPTER 1

1. J. Dunning, 'The Future of the Multinational Enterprise', *Lloyds Bank Review*, Mar 1974.
2. J. W. Vaupel and J. P. Curhan, *The World's Multinational Enterprises*, (Harvard Business School, Division of Research, 1973).
3. Economist Intelligence Unit, 'The Growing Multinationality of Japanese Industry, *Multinational Business*, No. 2, 1974, p. 11.
4. See for example Y. Aharoni, *The Foreign Investment Decision*, Harvard Business School, Division of Research, 1966).
5. S. Robock and K. Simmonds, *International Business and Multinational Enterprises* (Irwin, 1973), p. 403.
6. U.S. Department of Commerce, *Survey of Current Business*, Nov 1954 and Oct 1971.
7. D. F. Channon, *The Strategy and Structure of British Enterprise* (Harvard Business School, Division of Research, 1973), p. 78.
8. L. Franko, *The European Multinationals* (New York: Harper & Row, 1976).
9. H. E. Ekblom, European Direct Investments in the United States, *Harvard Business Review*, July/Aug 1973, p. 18.
10. K. A. Ringbakk, 'Strategic Planning in a Turbulent International Environment', *Long Range Planning*, June 1976, pp. 2–11.
11. 'Piercing Future Fog in the Executive Suite', *Business Week*, 28 Apr 1975, p. 48.
12. Ibid., pp. 48–54.

CHAPTER 2

1. Business International, 'Managing Global Marketing', *Business International*, 1977, p. 3.
2. The Conference Board, *The Changing Role of the International Executive* (New York, 1966), pp. 182–4.
3. 'Can Alcan Fabricate a Healthier Future?' *International Management*, Feb 1972, pp. 40–2.
4. 'Reviewing Worldwide Organisations: How RCA is Set Up', *Business International*, 13 Sept 1974, pp. 292–3.
5. 'Decision Making in International Operations', *Business International*, 1974, pp. 20–22.
6. James Ensor and D. F. Channon, 'Ford of Europe', MBS/BP/12, Manchester Business School, 1973.

7. 'Corning Glass Reshapes its International Operations', *International Management*, Oct 1974, pp. 32–37.
8. D. F. Channon, *Strategy and Structure of British Enterprise*, op. cit., pp. 140–1.
9. 'Managing Global Marketing', op. cit., p. 8.
10. T. Lester, 'Pechiney's Polytechnic Challenge', *Management Today*, Nov 1974, pp. 68–73.
11. 'Bringing Mitsui Together Again', *International Management*, Feb 1974, pp. 28–31.
12. D. F. Channon, *The Strategy and Structure of British Enterprise*, op. cit., pp. 78–85.
13. J. Stopford and L. T. Wells, *Management and the Multinational Enterprise* (Longmans, 1972), pp. 21–8.

CHAPTER 3

1. C. K. Prahalad, 'Strategic Choices in Diversified MNCs', *Harvard Business Review*, Sep–Oct 1976, p. 76.
2. M. Leontiades, 'What Kind of Corporate Planner Do You Need?', *Long Range Planning*, Apr 1977, pp. 56–64.
3. 'The Opposites: GE Grows While Westinghouse Shrinks', *Business Week*, 31 Jan 1977, pp. 60–6.
4. D. F. Channon, 'Prediction and Practice in Multinational Strategic Planning', *Long Range Planning*, June 1975.
5. *Business International*, 6 Feb 1976, pp. 44–5.
6. Channon, *Prediction and Practice*, op. cit.
7. Ibid.
8. G. A. Steiner and H. Schollhammer, 'Pitfalls in Multinational Long Range Planning, Apr 1975, pp. 2–12.
9. H. Buckner, *Business Planning for the Board* (Gower Press, 1971), pp. 13–17.
10. H. Jones, *Preparing Company Plans* (Gower Press, 1974), p. 109.
11. G. Tavernier, 'Planning for the Unusual', *International Management*, May 1977, pp. 19–23.
12. *Business Week*, 28 Apr 1975, p. 48.
13. Ibid., p. 48.
14. I. H. Wilson, 'Reforming the Strategic Planning Process: Integration of Social Responsibility and Business Needs', *Long Range Planning*, Oct 1974, pp. 2–4.

CHAPTER 4

1. Boston Consulting Group, *Perspective on Experience* (1970).
2. B. D. Hedley, 'Strategy and the "Business Portfolio"', *Long Range Planning*, Feb 1977.
3. S. Moose and A. Zakon, 'Frontier Curve Analysis as a Resource Allocation Guide, *Journal of Business Policy*, spring 1972.
4. See for example *Business Week*, 28 Apr 1975, p. 49.

5. Royal Dutch Shell Group, *The Directional Policy Matrix*, 1976.
6. Details of PIMS findings are available from a number of papers including S. Schoeffler, R. Buzzell and D. Heany, 'Impact of Strategic Planning on Profit Performance', *Harvard Business Review,* Mar/Apr 1974; R. Buzzell, B. Gale, R. Sultan, 'Market Share – a Key to Profitability', *Harvard Business Review*, Jan/Feb 1975.
7. William E. Rothschild, *Putting it all Together* (AMACOM, New York, 1976), p. 159.
8. Adapted from D. F. Channon, 'Use and Abuse of Analytical Techniques for Strategic Decisions', paper presented at TIMS XXIII International Meeting, Athens, July 1977.

CHAPTER 5

1. Observation by J. C. S. Kimber from his research notes. Within the context of this chapter we will not always clearly differentiate between the controllership function and the treasury function. J. C. S. Kimber, 'Financial Planning in Multinational Corporations: The Impact of Strategy on Structure', unpublished MBA dissertation, Manchester Business School, 1976.
2. S. M. Robbins and R. B. Stobaugh, *Money in the Multinational Enterprise* (Basic Books 1973), chapter 3, identified three phases. The details set out below are developed from Robbins and Stobaugh but significantly adapted especially for the advanced phase as a result of further research conducted at the Manchester Business School under the direction of the present authors.
3. Ibid., chapter 3.
4. Ibid.
5. The Conference Board, *Managing the International Finance Function*, Studies in Business Policy, No 133, 1970.
6. Conference Board, ibid., pp. 65–6.
7. A. Morris, 'How BP Manages its Money', *Euromoney*, June 1973, p. 34.
8. Karl-Ludwig Hermann, 'How BASF Runs Its Treasury', *Euromoney*, May 1974, pp. 88–91.
9. E. G. Collado, 'How Exxon Handles Its Finances', *Euromoney*, Oct 1973, pp. 108–13.
10. T. Green, 'Capital Investment Decisions in the MNC', unpublished MBA dissertation, Manchester Business School, 1977, p. 75.
11. Ibid., p. 84.
12. Ibid., p. 91.
13. A. Stonehill and T. Stitzel, 'Financial Structure and Multinational Corporations', *California Management Review*, fall 1969, pp. 92–5.
14. J. Kimber, op. cit., p. 101.
15. J. T. Wooster and G. R. Thoman, 'New Financial Priorities for MNCs' *Harvard Business Review*, May–June 1974.

CHAPTER 6

1. H. Schollhammer, *Locational Strategies of Multinational Corporations* (1972).
2. 'Information Guide for U.S. Corporations Doing Business Abroad' New York, Price Waterhouse and Co.), included in Stonehill and Stitzel, op. cit., pp. 169–77.
3. 'Summary Study of International Cases Involving S482 of the IRC', US Treasury Department, 1973.
4. See D. F. Channon, 'Hoffman la Roche', MBS/IB/10, Manchester Business School, 1975.
5. M. Edwardes Ker, *International Tax Strategy* (In Depth Publishing Ltd. 1975), chapter 5, p. 3.
6. Ibid., chapter 7, p. 13.
7. Ibid., chapter 7, pp. 22–3.
8. John F. Chown, *Taxation and Multinational Enterprise* (Longmans, 1974), p. 86.
9. Edwardes Ker, op. cit., chapter 9, pp. 7–10.
10. J. C. S. Kimber, op. cit.
11. Chown, op. cit., pp. 139–40.
12. Ibid., pp. 144–6.
13. Edwardes Ker, op. cit., chapter 32, p. 8.
14. Ibid., chapter 32, p. 13.
15. Chown, op. cit., p. 123.
16. Ibid., pp. 128–9.

CHAPTER 7

1. T. E. Green, op. cit., p. 77.
2. Ibid., pp. 81–7.
3. D. J. North, 'The Process of Locational Change in Different Manufacturing Organisations', in F. E. Hamilton, *Perspectives on Industrial Organisation and Decision Making* (Wiley, 1974).
4. J. Leontiades, 'Plant Location – The International Perspective', *Long Range Planning*, Feb 1974, pp. 10–14.
5. Edwardes Ker, op. cit., chapter 15, p. 4.
6. Ibid., chapter 15, p. 24.
7. E. B. Lovell, *Foreign Licensing Agreements: Evaluation and Planning*, Studies in Business Policy No. 86, National Industrial Conference Board (New York, 1958), p. 15.
8. Ibid., p. 52.
9. T. Collier, 'Do's and Dont's of Foreign Licensing Arrangements', *Business Abroad*, Vol. 96, 17 Feb 1971, p. 17.
10. C. H. Lee, 'How to Reach the Overseas Market by Licensing', *Harvard Business Review*, Jan-Feb 1958, pp. 78–81.
11. J. Chown, op. cit., pp. 70–1.
12. Ibid., pp. 71–3.
13. Ibid., pp. 75–6.

14. A. V. Phatak, *Managing Multinational Corporations* (Praeger, 1974), p. 304.
15. Robock and Simmonds, op. cit., p. 225.
16. 'Decision Making in International Operations', *Business International*, 1974, p. 52.

CHAPTER 8

1. J. Vaupel and J. P. Curhan, *The Making of Multinational Enterprise*, (Harvard Business School, Division of Research, 1969), introduction.
2. J. Kitching, 'Acquisitions in Europe: Causes of Corporate Successes and Failures; *Business International*, Geneva 1973, pp. 59–60.
3. Adapted from points raised by Kitching, ibid., pp. 87–9.
4. Ibid., pp. 94–7.
5. Ibid., pp. 56–86.
6. Ibid., p. 116.
7. Adapted from 'Business Man's Review', Price Waterhouse and Company, 1972.
8. Edwardes Ker, op. cit., chapter 13.
9. Ibid., chapter 13.
10. J. Chown, op. cit., p. 196.
11. Ibid., pp. 196–200.
12. Edwardes Ker, op. cit., chapter 13.
13. Mainly adapted from J. Chown, op. cit., pp. 219–31.
14. Edwardes Ker, op. cit., chapter 14.
15. J. Kitching, op. cit., pp. 177–9.
16. Ibid., pp. 179–83.
17. Ibid., p. 183.

CHAPTER 9

1. James R. Piper, Jr., 'How US Firms Evaluate Foreign Investment Opportunities', *MSU Business Topics*, summer 1971, p. 11.
2. Franklin R. Root, US Business Abroad and the Political Risks, *MSU Business Topics*, winter 1968.
3. David K. Eikeman and Arthur I. Stonehill, *Multinational Business* (France, Addison-Wesley Publishing Company, 1973), p. 229.
4. *Obstacles and Incentives to Private Foreign Investments 1967–1968*, Vol. 1 (New York: The Conference Board, 1969).
5. Stobaugh, How to Analyse Foreign Investment Climates, *Harvard Business Review* (Sept–Oct 1969), p. 103.
6. B. Lloyd, 'The Identification and Assessment of Political Risk in the International Environment', *Long Range Planning*, Dec 1974, p. 29.
7. This system was developed by C. E. Johns and the next section is drawn from his unpublished Master's dissertation, Manchester Business School, 1975.
8. J. Grewe, 'The Management of Political Risk by the MNC', unpublished MBA dissertation, Manchester Business School, 1977, chapter 4.

9. Ibid., pp. 66–8.
10. Ibid., pp. 93–4.
11. The scheme for this part of the chapter has been freely adapted from that used by Eikeman and Stonehill, op. cit., chapter 10.
12. Eikeman and Stonehill, op. cit., p. 238.
13. Jack N. Behrman, 'International Divestment: Panacea or Pitfall', *Looking Ahead*, National Planning Association, Nov–Dec 1970.
14. 'Financing Foreign Operations', *Business International*, Apr 1971, pp. 45–56.
15. Ibid., pp. 58–8c.
16. Robock and Simmonds, op. cit., p. 223.
17. Eikeman and Stonehill, op. cit., p. 243.
18. L. G. Franko, 'Joint Venture Divorce in the Multinational Company', *Columbia Journal of World Business*, May–June 1971, pp. 13–22.
19. 'Decision Making in International Operations', op. cit., p. 51.
20. Robock and Simonds, op. cit., p. 226.
21. 'The Fashionable World of Project Finance – Some Major Projects, *The Banker*, Jan 1976, pp. 77–81.
22. Robock and Simmonds, op. cit., p. 223.
23. 'Bribery, Corruption or Necessary Charges?' *Multinational Business*, No. 3, 1975.

CHAPTER 10

1. *Business International*, 26 Mar, 1976, pp. 102–3.
2. 'Managing Global Marketing', op. cit., pp. 9–10, 47–9.
3. *Business International*, 21 Feb, 1975, pp. 62–3.
4. *Business International*, 21 Mar, 1975, pp. 94–5.
5. 'Managing Global Marketing', op. cit., p. 118.
6. Ibid., p. 122.
7. Ibid., p. 126.
8. *Business Week*, 20 May, 1977, p. 55.
9. S. Majaro, *International Marketing* (Allen & Unwin, 1977), pp. 89–91.
10. R. S. Sorenson and U. E. Weichman, 'How Multinationals View Marketing Standardisation', *Harvard Business Review*, May–June 1975, pp. 38–54, 166–7.
11. 'Managing Global Marketing', op. cit., p. 40.
12. Ibid., p. 41.
13. 'Prediction and Practice in Multinational Strategic Planning, op. cit.
14. 'Managing Global Marketing', op. cit., p. 46.
15. 'Prediction and Practice in Multinational Strategic Planning', op. cit.
16. *Business Week*, 28 Feb, 1977, p. 59.
17. Adapted from Majaro, op. cit., p. 111.
18. U. E. Weichman, 'Integrating Multinational Marketing Activities, *Columbia Journal of World Business*, winter 1974, p. 11.
19. S. Majaro, op. cit., p. 178.

CHAPTER 11

1. *Organising for Effective Public Affairs*, National Industrial Conference Board (New York, 1969).
2. C. Aguilar, 'External Affairs at the World Headquarters Level of the US Based Industrial Multinational Enterprise, unpublished PhD dissertation, New York University, 1973.
3. For a discussion of these concepts see 'From Strategic Planning to Strategic Management', H. I. Ansoff, R. P. Declerck and R. L. Hayes (Wiley, 1976).
4. Social Science Research Council, *The Social Responsibilities of Business*, (1976).
5. M. Friedman, *Capitalism and Freedom* (University of Chicago Press, 1962).
6. *The Responsibilities of the British Public Company* (Confederation of British Industry, 1973).
7. Similar three-level models of social reponsibility are proposed by J. Hargreaves and J. Dauman in *Business Survival and Social Change* (Associated Business Programmes, 1975) and T. P. Rogers, *The Social Responsibilities of Business–Policy–Yes, Audit–No*, MBS–CBR Occasional Papers (Manchester Business School, 1974).
8. J. Humble, *Social Responsibility Audit – a Management Tool for Survival* (Foundation for Business Responsibilities, 1973).
9. This section draws on D. H. Blake, 'Measuring the Socio-Economic Impact on a Host Country: Practical Approaches to Identifying Particular Company Issues and Impact, *Public Relations Journal,* May 1976.
10. Published with a covering statement as a British Government White Paper, Cmnd 6525, 1976.
11. A full list of topics is given in Figure 11.6.
12. Other international bodies working on codes include: The International Chamber of Commerce (Paris 1972), the Non-Aligned countries (Group of 77), the Organisation of American States, and the ILO.
13. International Confederation of the Free Trade Unions, Eleventh World Congress, Mexico, 1975.
14. 'Gulf repairs image with no-nonsense code and staff internal controls', *Business International*, 14 May, 1976.
15. J. Smith, 'The Management of Social Responsibility in Multinational Companies and its Effect on Corporate Planning'. Unpublished MBA dissertation, Manchester Business School, 1977.
16. W. McClelland, *And A New Earth* (Friends Home Service Committee, London, 1976).
17. J. Smith, op. cit.
18. E. M. Estes, 'General Motors and South Africa', in R. Jackson (ed.), *The Multinational Corporation and Social Policy* (Praeger, 1974).
19. 'Making Social Responsibility Pay', *International Management*, July 1977, pp. 18–21.
20. J. Smith, op. cit.
21. *The Handbook of Corporate Social Responsibility – Profiles of Involvement, Human Resources Network* (Chilton Book Company, Pennsylvania, 1975).

22. 'A "Balance Sheet" that shows host countries what you do for them', *Business International*, 20 June 1975.
23. See for example *The Corporate Report* (Accounting Standards Steering Committee, Institute of Chartered Accountants in England and Wales, 1975).
24. J. Smith, op. cit.
25. 'Self-Regulating Corporate Behaviour: Caterpillar's New Code of International Conduct', *Business International*, 18 Oct, 1974.
26. J. N. Behrman and H. Wallender, 'Transfer of Manufacturing Technology within Multinational Enterprises' (Ballinger, Cambridge, Mass., 1976).
27. J. Smith, op. cit.
28. F. Harman and J. Humble, *Social Responsibility and British Companies* (Management Centre Europe, Dec 1974).
29. 'External Affairs: Blueprint for Survival', *Business International*, 1976.
30. I. Wilson, op. cit.

Index